# JEWISH MEMORY
## COSMOPOLITAN ORDER

# JEWISH MEMORY AND THE COSMOPOLITAN ORDER

## HANNAH ARENDT AND THE JEWISH CONDITION

Natan Sznaider

polity

First published in 2011 by Polity Press

Polity Press
65 Bridge Street
Cambridge CB2 1UR, UK

Polity Press
350 Main Street
Malden, MA 02148, USA

ISBN-13: 978-0-7456-4795-1
ISBN-13: 978-0-7456-4796-8(pb)

A catalogue record for this book is available from the British Library.

Typeset in 10.5 on 12 pt Sabon
by Toppan Best-set Premedia Limited
Printed and bound in Great Britain by MPG Books Group Limited, Bodmin, Cornwall

For further information on Polity, visit our website: www.politybooks.com

# CONTENTS

# ACKNOWLEDGMENTS

This book owes much to conversation with friends and colleagues. More than anything else, it is the product of an ongoing exchange and research agenda that I started with Ulrich Beck. The book is partly a result of long conversations about the virtues of universalism and particularism. It is also a constant intellectual and emotional engagement with his ideas and thinking about the world.

I thank Daniel Levy for his support and friendship over the years. His engagement with my ideas was a constant challenge. I thank him for his criticism and suggestions. I also would like to thank Michael Pollak for his enthusiasm and support throughout.

I would also like to thank my academic home, the Academic College of Tel-Aviv-Yaffo for granting me the academic freedom and financial support to engage in this research. Many institutions have provided me with access to their collections which made this book possible. These include the Manuscript and Archival Collection of Stanford University – here I would like to thank Zachary Baker for his support; the Center for Jewish History in New York, where I would like to thank Frank Mecklenburg; the Hannah Arendt Center at the New School for Social Research in New York – here my special appreciation goes to Jerome Kohn who was never tired of guiding me through the ideas of Hannah Arendt. Thanks to Dorothy Smith of the American Jewish Archives for providing me with important materials. In addition, I appreciate the support of the Gershom Scholem Archive at the Hebrew University of Jerusalem and the Central Archives for the History of the Jewish People in Jerusalem for providing generous access to their holdings. Writing this book was indeed a journey through the current centers of Jewish life and learning.

# — 1 —

# INTRODUCTION: KÖNIGSBERG, JERUSALEM, PARIS, AND NEW YORK

Auch stünde es schlimm um Europa, wenn die kulturellen Energien der Juden es verließen. [It would be bad for Europe if the cultural energies of the Jews were to leave it.]

Walter Benjamin (1972: 834)

That is what Walter Benjamin wrote to his Zionist friend Ludwig Strauss as a twenty-year old, and it is also the central theme of this book. Is there a Jewish perspective on Europe? And if so, is this perspective religious, ethnic, or political? Is there such a thing as a Jewish Europe, or a Europe of Jews? Can one even speak of Jewish voices or a Jewish epistemology without reducing thought to a matter of origin and birth?

This book addresses a broad set of historical and intellectual developments that attempts to shed light on these questions. It is not a "Jewish book," but it uses "Jewishness" as a metaphor for people on the margins, people who are minorities, whether against their will or by choice. At the same time, it is a book about cosmopolitanism, as theory and praxis that sees Jews not in terms of their victimhood but explores the possibilities of autonomous cosmopolitan social and political action. It also tries to illuminate Jewish voices that self-consciously examine what Europe meant to them before and after the Holocaust.

Some of these voices stress the sanctity of this world and speak of the autonomy of the individual as one of the fundamental principles of modern society. Many Jewish intellectuals were concerned with moral individualism, which is both transcendental and of this world (this was not, of course, only a Jewish agenda). In their view, this was the true expression of modernity. The particular world of devout

1

Jewry was no longer sufficient to cope with the challenges of modernity. Thus, they were looking for universal guidelines, both within and outside the state. This trend was exemplified by the French sociologist Emile Durkheim, who came from a religious Jewish family and described the birth of civil religion at the end of the nineteenth century. Durkheim was a firm believer in the religion of humanity, the worldly belief in salvation through the action of human beings. It is this religion of humanity that also allows Jews to be incorporated into the universality of the rational state. A similar point can be made today about the "secular" religion of cosmopolitan morality: it, too, has transcendental features and places the human being in the foreground. For cosmopolitan theory, this means the tangible human being – not the idea of a human being, the universal man of modern theory.

Hannah Arendt, the Jewish intellectual, is the main protagonist with whose help I will explore those questions. She expressed this sentiment in an early essay of 1945 on guilt and responsibility. We will see how these concepts like guilt and responsibility became central to a cosmopolitan theory of being "my brother's keeper." What does "universal" responsibility mean? Arendt was asking this question at the moment when World War II came to an end. She addressed it in one of her first essays in 1945; it occupied her for the rest of her life.[1] The essay concludes with Arendt's comments about universal responsibility and its relation to the concept of humanity, which she sees as part of the Jewish tradition: "Perhaps those Jews, to whose forefathers we owe the conception of the idea of humanity, knew something about that burden when each year they used to say: 'Our Father and King, we have sinned before you,' taking not only the sins of their own community but all human offenses upon themselves" (Arendt 1994: 131–2). Thus both Durkheim and Arendt tried to push the boundaries of their collective existence from particular premises to universal ones, combining the monotheistic message of the Jews with the universal claims of the Enlightenment. Arendt and many of her Jewish contemporaries serve in this book as personifications of a cosmopolitan ideal, with all its inherent contradictions.

The choice of Arendt is not arbitrary. Perhaps more than that of any other thinker of the twentieth century, the urgency of her writing on totalitarianism, democracy, critical judgment, and evil remains relevant today. Her being born Jewish, her engagement with the fate of the Jews (which caught up with her life in Germany in 1933), her work with Jewish and Zionist organizations, her criticism of Zionism from within, her engagement with Jewish history and politics on a theoretical and on a practical level – all of these things make her a good fit with the subject of this book. But this is not a book about Arendt's political theory.[2] Her political theoretical work of the 1950s and 1960s is well known and established her reputation as one of the most important political thinkers of the twentieth century. Less well known are her writings on Jewish issues and her professional work with Jewish agencies and institutions, which in my view laid the groundwork for her later theoretical work.[3]

But even within this framework, Arendt is usually considered a secular thinker whose relationship to Jewish thought was one of critical distance. She was supposed to be engaged with Jewish politics but not with Jewish thought and philosophy.[4] There are, of course, connections between her earlier work on practical matters of Jewish politics and her theories about politics, democracy, pluralism, and federalism. Her experiences during World War II, and what would later be called the Holocaust, kindled practical concerns about the future of the Jewish people and the future of Europe, and at the same time fed her theoretical interest in the relationship between universalism and particularism. Her life experiences – growing up in Germany as a Jew, escaping from Germany to Paris in 1933, leaving France in 1941 for the United States, working with Jewish organizations, her political observations, her philosophical writings – make her the embodiment of Jewish cosmopolitan existence, and through this analytical prism her life and work can shed light on the possibilities and impossibilities of such an existence.

Arendt studied philosophy in Germany with Martin Heidegger and Karl Jaspers. She studied ancient Greek and Protestant theology and enjoyed the typical classical education of assimilated German Jews.[5] Arendt can be our companion and guide in the search for a Jewish existence on the margins. My purpose in this book is not to essentialize her Jewishness, but just the opposite. I consider Jewishness in this study as a political identity, circumscribed by political events and historical contingencies. I will show how Arendt's Jewish identity changed over the decades, how she tried to combine universal philosophy and cultural Zionism, how she became a politicized Jew through the rise of the Nazis and her exile in Paris, how she turned away from Zionism and closed the circle through philosophy again.[6]

It is my intention to bring Arendt's particular Jewish experience back into the equation of her universal horizons, and in doing so to show how she constantly navigated between universalism and particularism through her understanding of political judgment, the revolutionary tradition, federal republicanism, and other issues she examined through the prism of the Jewish fate. By looking at her theoretical and practical works, I attempt to develop a more historically informed notion of cosmopolitanism. Throughout her work, Arendt was concerned with language and its ability (or inability) to express extreme experiences. What language do we need to speak, and can we speak, when we talk about the destruction of the Jews?[7] On the one hand, the destruction of the Jews challenged concepts of the Enlightenment, became part of the so-called dialectic of the Enlightenment and the debates surrounding the project of modernity. On the other hand, destruction was not only foundational for postwar criticism of the Enlightenment but also for attempts to reconstruct the Enlightenment through institutions that promoted human rights legislation and sought to prevent genocide. The aftermath of the war, that is, witnessed an attempt to rebuild the basic principles of modernity through institutions that went beyond the confines of the nation-state. Thus, for Arendt, one of the crucial questions was whether there can be a universalist minimum that does not involve giving up particular demands at the same time. Language is indeed crucial here, and different texts tried to come to terms with the catastrophic history of the Jews during World War II. One of them, the Universal Declaration of Human Rights, tried to frame the catastrophe in universal terms: "Whereas disregard and contempt for human rights have resulted in barbarous acts which have outraged the conscience of mankind . . . "[8] It was clear to the framers of the Declaration, in December 1948, which barbarous acts were referred to. This language was clear for the framers three years after the war, but at the same time it has since then turned into foundational language, without the clear-cut historical context. The memory of the Holocaust becomes decontextualized and detached from the historical event. It becomes a symbol. Human rights are therefore based not on clear-cut philosophical or religious worldviews but rather on historical experiences and concomitant memories of catastrophe.[9] We will see in the following chapters how this language has been constructed and reconstructed.

At about the same time that the Universal Declaration was being written, the state of Israel was founded. Its declaration of independence frames the Jewish catastrophe differently:

The catastrophe which recently befell the Jewish people – the massacre of millions of Jews in Europe – was another clear demonstration of the urgency of solving the problem of its homelessness by reestablish-

4

ing in Eretz-Israel the Jewish State, which would open the gates of the homeland wide to every Jew and confer upon the Jewish people the status of a fully privileged member of the comity of nations.[10]

The same catastrophe was given two completely different meanings: barbarous acts versus the massacre of millions of Jews in Europe; or "crimes against humanity" versus "crimes against the Jewish people." These poles became crucial for Jewish intellectuals who thought they needed to navigate these apparent contradictions and tensions. As we will see in chapter 5, they also became crucial for Arendt's thinking about the cosmopolitan role that Jews could fulfill in a global world, while at the same time a sovereign Jewish state was coming into existence. This book demonstrates how Arendt, in her controversies with Jews and non-Jews, tried to defend the principles of universalism and particularism at the same time.

I also argue that Arendt's political theory and praxis can be understood as exemplary of Jewish thinking and conduct before and after the catastrophe. It is the intention of this book to locate Arendt's thinking within the context of Jewish history and experience without neglecting the universal claims she consistently worked to develop. Thus, Jewish history and universal history are seen not as two different lenses through which to view the past but as part of one common project.[11] If one excludes the particular memories of Jews, one risks falling back on a Kantian conception of either cosmopolitanism or multiculturalism, which are both rooted in a universalism that has no conceptual or actual place for the persistence of particular attachments. It is my argument that the universalist narrative obliterates the cosmopolitan potential of the Jewish experience, which straddles the interstices of universal identifications and particular attachments.

Cosmopolitanism combines appreciation of difference and diversity with efforts to conceive of new democratic forms of political rule beyond the nation-state. As we will see, this corresponded with Arendt's theory of political federalism. In this view, cosmopolitanism differs fundamentally from all forms of vertical differentiation that seek to place social difference in a hierarchical relation of superiority and subordination, whereas universalism is the dissolution of all difference and represents the countervailing principle to hierarchical subordination. Universalism obliges us to respect others as equals in principle, yet for that very reason it neglects what makes others different. On the contrary, the particularity of others is sacrificed to an assumed universal equality that denies its own origins and interests.

5

Universalism thereby becomes two-faced, involving both respect and hegemony. Cosmopolitanism differs in its recognition of difference as a maxim of thought, social life, and practice, both internally and externally. It neither orders differences hierarchically nor dissolves them, but accepts them as such – indeed, invests them with positive value. It is sensitive to historic cultural particularities, respecting the specific dignity and burden of a group, a people, a culture, a religion. Cosmopolitanism affirms what is excluded both by hierarchical difference and by universal equality – namely, perceiving others as different and at the same time equal.[12]

What I propose in this book is to reinscribe the Jewish voice in a more general narrative. In other words, universal aspirations and particularistic ethnic identification are not merely part of Jewish history but are relevant for, even constitutive of, contemporary debates about minorities and their rights.[13]

My goal is to bring into the open the possibility of a cosmopolitan Jewish Europe, which involves reviving the memory of the systematic breakup of the process that led to the domination of a national perspective on politics and society. The Jews were transnational and had to face a national world. They encountered a clear division between inside and outside, domestic and foreign. In addition, however, in the surrounding of the Jewish world, the nation-state was the principle of order, even though it was not theirs. A cosmopolitan Jewish Europe, or so-called rooted cosmopolitanism, on the other hand, is defined as a composite of the two extremes of being at home everywhere and being at home nowhere. Clearly, the notion of "rooted cosmopolitanism" does not refer only to Jewish concerns. The concept was developed by scholars working from postcolonial perspectives who argued for cosmopolitanism without homogenization.[14] These tendencies demarcate a shift from one universal culture to cultures in the plural.[15] I aim to show in this book that rooted cosmopolitanism produces new forms of localism that are open to the world. By "rooted cosmopolitanism," I refer to universal values that descend from the level of pure abstract philosophy and engage people emotionally in their everyday lives. It is by becoming symbols of people's personal identities that normative cosmopolitan philosophy turns into a social and political force. As Durkheim taught us a century ago, by embodying philosophy in rituals, such identities are created, reinforced, and integrated into communities.[16] A commitment to global or cosmopolitan values does not imply that cosmopolitans are rootless individuals who prefer some abstract "humanity" over concrete human beings. This became historical reality for many Jews

6

when emancipation demanded that they give up their traditional religious ties. Arendt very early considered the central shortcoming, politically and analytically, of a universalism that operates with an ahistorical notion of history, one that seeks to mold and freeze particular memories of the past into universal standards for the future. This kind of universalism fails to recognize the persistence of particularism and exclusion as central features of human life. This kind of universalism sees nationalism as the opposite of cosmopolitanism and as something to be overcome.[17] Rather than treat cosmopolitanism as the antidote to nationalism, I seek to relate it to particular national attachments as potential mediators between the individual and the global horizons against which identifications unfold. The historical analysis in the chapters that follow attempts to contribute not only to a much-needed historical–empirical operationalization of cosmopolitanism; I hope that it will also serve as an important reminder that theories of cosmopolitanism must attend more closely to political culture and the underlying beliefs and ideals that foster shared understandings, identity, and belonging, in national, ethnic, and religious groups. The case study under consideration here is Jewish politics and thought.

How do particular values come to define personal identity and thereby also acquire political significance? Cosmopolitanism diverges from universalism in assuming that there is not one language of cosmopolitanism but many languages, tongues, and grammars. This belief corresponds to the languages in which Jews wrote and spoke. There was no one Jewish language but many. Thus Jewish culture is by definition multilingual, and this has implications for multiple cultural identities as well. Moreover, nationality also means memory. Is there a shared European memory? A glance at textbooks and encyclopedias reveals attempts to construct a shared past and identity, starting with the Greco-Roman heritage and moving through the humanism of the Renaissance, the era of Enlightenment, the dawn of democracy, and the Christian heritage. Even the term "Europe" is part of Western Christianity and Greek mythology.[18] The boundaries of Orthodox Christianity and Islam define Europe as Europe.[19] What role did and do the Jews play in this conception of Europe? Did a Jewish nation exist in Europe, though dispersed and lacking territory and sovereignty? Weren't the Jews of Europe assimilated, emancipated, acculturated, orthodox, socialist, nationalist and even non-Jewish at the same time? Was it not this lack of belonging that stirred the ontological evil of anti-Semitic fantasies and the anti-Semitic state, which tried to destroy the transnational cultures of the Jews in the heart of Europe? After the war, Europe needed to pick up the pieces and to try and forget what had happened to the Jews throughout Europe under the Nazis.[20] Thus, if Europe is indeed "laboring under a national-misunderstanding" (Beck and Grande 2007: 4), perhaps one reason can be found in amnesia about the transnational Jewish presence in what was once Europe. There was a time when Jews tried to become a European people unrestricted by borders or nations. Jews were cosmopolitans before Europe became cosmopolitan. If cosmopolitanism indeed combines an appreciation of difference and alterity, and also attempts to experiment with democratic forms beyond the nation-state, then it must reach back to its own Jewish sources which existed in Europe and were destroyed by the most ruthless project of destruction Europe has ever known. And this was one of the political demands Arendt made when she looked at the Jewish tradition as a source for the future of Europe.

After 1945, it initially seemed for many Jews that only Zionism could make whole for Jews what the German Nazis had shattered. Zionism held out the promise of a Jewish state for a stateless people, the promise of safety and security. Between the wars, Zionism was one of various political alternatives for Jews, but after 1945 it became one of the major viable alternatives, as the language of the Israeli declaration of independence so clearly states. The new state of Israel thus began to employ an ethnic definition of its nationhood, trying to make homogeneous which was by definition heterogeneous. At the same time, many Jews saw the United States as the other viable alternative. Thus American and Israeli definitions of nationhood are closely entwined with the well-known tension between two fundamental definitions of nationhood. The first is territorial and political and has roots in Western Europe; the second is ethnic and is typical of the historical experience of Eastern and Central Europe.[21] Both are conceptualized through the boundaries of the state. One variety is associated with "rational" principles of citizenship and democratic virtues. The other, the dominant one in the Israeli context, is organic and is associated with beliefs that supersede the voluntaristic nature of the first type. "Enlightened" political nationalism has gradually been replaced by organic forms of nationalism that were embraced in Central and Eastern Europe and went on to become the origins of the Jewish nation of Israel. But are these the only alternatives? For Arendt, more was at stake here. She looked at the concrete political makeup of the Middle East and proposed a federal political structure that corresponded to her understanding of politics and judgment which differed from ethnically oriented forms of Zionism.

Jews lived in constant tension between universalism and particularism as part of their history. The respective milieus of seminal Jewish
cosmopolitans shaped their perceptions. But there came a historical
moment when this tension took center stage for Jewish actors, especially in Central Europe. The circumstances of their lives transformed
especially the Jewish elite into cosmopolitan actors. Central Europe
had already been the venue for a struggle between cosmopolitanism
and nationalism in which Jews played a major role. It was the site of
ethno-national tensions, the Holocaust, and the expulsions after
World War II. Cosmopolitanism was one of the refuges of a small
circle of intellectuals who thought they had nothing to gain from the
emerging ethno-politics. A typical example was Karl Popper's *Open
Society and Its Enemies*, a seminal Cold War text that defended the
openly cosmopolitan imperialism of the West. As Malachi Hacohen's
analysis of Popper shows, because of anti-Semitism, this type of
universalism was not able to mediate between nationalism and cosmopolitanism. Its antidote to nationalism was an "enlightened imperialism," whether the Habsburg Empire or, for Popper and others,
the British. This universalism was also the milieu that gave birth to
Zionism's seminal text, Theodor Herzl's *The Jewish State* (1896),
which declared the failure of emancipation and demanded a sovereign
state for the Jews. On the other hand, Popper's hostility to Zionism
(as to any other form of ethno-nationalism) was typical of a dichoto-
mous worldview that conflated cosmopolitanism with universalism
and could not see how cosmopolitanism could be squared with
nationalism. Popper's imagined "open society" became the "assimilated Jewish philosopher's cosmopolitan homeland" (Hacohen 1999:
136). It was an imperial homeland, a kind of westernized modernity
in its global vision that attempted to imitate late Hellenic culture. It
was dominant, progressive, the wave of the future, assimilationist,
admirable, seductive, and beautiful, as it always was and is for
Jewish particularism. Its vision of a democratic cosmopolitan empire
attracted many Jews, like Popper, to Great Britain, whereas Zionists
recognized the need for Jews to secure a common past that was inextricably tied to cultural artifacts and national history. If we take the
long historical view, the fundamental meaning of Jewish cosmopolitanism for both its proponents and its antagonists was a sign of
Jewish civilization.[22] Diaspora for the Jews meant that they were an
ethnic-religious-national community that juggled all of these compo-
nents. For Jews (and others) who wanted to regard themselves as
different, this is a crucial point. Paul Gilroy (1993) made this
point clear in *The Black Atlantic*, which opens with this statement:

9

"Striving to be European and Black requires some special form of consciousness."[23] Gilroy pointedly notes that the same can be said of Jews (pp. 208ff.).

This diasporic view of an existence at the margins was extremely attractive to Jewish men and women of letters who celebrated it as a sign of an advanced modernity. *The Jewess of Toledo,* a novel by the German–Jewish writer Lion Feuchtwanger published in 1955, embodies this outlook perfectly.[24] Like many of Feuchtwanger's earlier works, this novel deals with the Jewish predicament of being caught between universal claims and particular attachments, in this case framed by a love story involving a Christian king and a Jewess. The story is set in twelfth-century Spain, a country bordering both Christianity and Islam, and thus on the front line of the original Crusades and Jihads, in an age when those words were more than just metaphors. The hero of Feuchtwanger's book, Jehuda Ibn Esra, lives at the epicenter of these realms. He accepts the post of finance minister under King Alfonso – essentially the post of an economic czar, who takes a cut of the overall profit in return for personally putting up capital and bearing huge risks – because he sees this Christian country as having productive potential that he can bring to fruition, if, and only if, he can keep the country out of war. The king, a knight of the old camp, wants to go to war as soon as possible, since that is the only sure road to glory. He grudgingly accepts that he must build up the economic strength of his exhausted country first, and with the same unwillingness finally recognizes that Ibn Esra has a genius for peacetime management that he himself lacks. Thus the two struggle with each other for many years, in a partnership and a rivalry for very high stakes. Jehuda Ibn Esra has a beautiful daughter named Raquel who is every inch his child. She is as cultured as anyone in the realm, and she is just as ambitious as her father – ambitious not merely to get ahead in this dangerous world but to make it better: to soften it, beautify it, redeem it. She is even more deeply entangled in it, because King Alfonso falls in love with her, and she with him. This relationship keeps the entire kingdom in suspense for seven years. Enemies and allies and historical forces gather on every side, until the next crusade – and with it, the destruction of everything Jehuda Ibn Esra has built – seems to be hanging on the subtleties of love. The secularized Jewish elite (Feuchtwanger's projection, no doubt) sees Raquel as a civilizing influence on a man who is a force of nature. Jews and women, and in particular a Jewish woman, champion those civilizing influences over knightly ideals.

It is no accident that Feuchtwanger wrote this book just after the Nazis and their war destroyed his German–Jewish world of educated and wealthy burghers. For Feuchtwanger, the knightly ideals that would destroy everything that other people had built up were all too close to home. He contrasts them with the striving for wealth and commerce pursued by the citizens of the town, by Jews, and by women, who counteract the destructive force of knights and barons with the quiet pleasures of enjoying material things. In his Josephus trilogy, published between 1931 and 1941, Feuchtwanger, assuming the role of the Jewish historian Josephus Flavius, depicts the dilemma of a man torn between Jewish patriotism and Hellenist/Roman imperial cosmopolitanism. Feuchtwanger was trying desperately to protect a European cosmopolitanism composed of Jewish, Greek, Christian, and Muslim identities against the rise of National Socialism.[25] In Weimar Germany and Central and Eastern Europe, there were more such heroes trying to work out economic and political arrangements that would bind Germany to England and avoid war. European Jewish intellectuals lived between cultures and were regarded with suspicion. They saw themselves playing the same dangerous game for the same high stakes – namely, the preservation of civilization and all that they had built. These men's position between cultures is what gave them their sophistication, their breadth of vision, and their tolerance – in a word, their virtue. Their composite culture was ingrained in their character. The various cultural traditions they embodied all felt familiar, as though they belonged together. They personified the ideal of integration; this was inextricably part of their ideal of individual cultivation. In men and women like this, rootedness – being fixed in one place and submerged in one culture – was regarded as a limitation. They recognized that limited people could only extend their (mental and physical) boundaries by war. This is why their cosmopolitanism was always threatened by the warriors they tried to civilize. It also expresses a vision of multiethnic European civilizations. It is coextensive with Gerard Delanty's (2003) vision, discussed above, of a Europe based on multiple modernities and composed of three civilizational constellations: the Occidental Christian, the Byzantine-Slavic Eurasian, and the Ottoman/Islamic.

It is my intention to add the Jewish dimension to this civilizational equation. One way of doing this involves exploring memories of the Holocaust, which changes the relationship between universalism and particularism. These memories were organized around a dichotomy between universalism (the idea that the Holocaust was an assault on

11

humanity) and particularism (the recognition that it was primarily an attempt to exterminate European Jewry). As we will see in the following chapters, Hannah Arendt constantly tried to navigate between these two poles in her work. The Holocaust has not become one totalizing signifier conveying the same meaning for everyone. Arendt tried to demonstrate that memories of the Holocaust (even if she did not use the term) involve the formation of both nation-specific and nation-transcending commonalities. Thus, for her as for many other Jewish intellectuals, it is no longer the dichotomy but the mutual constitution of particular and universal conceptions that determines the ways in which the Holocaust can be remembered. One theme nevertheless is constant: the tension between the universal and the particular has become an inevitable feature of the cosmopolitan condition, and this is, of course, not merely an accident of intellectual history. As I show in the following chapters, the agonizing that Arendt and others went through – their inability to give up either their universalist dreams or their ethnic national identity – was not merely an indecisiveness born of trauma and exile. Questions of Jewish particularism and universalism within and beyond Judaism, and questions of individual independence and collective responsibility, are not only questions of particular concern but are theoretically relevant to cosmopolitan theory and praxis. The reason why this generation of Jewish intellectuals, who underwent their formative political growth in the interwar years, were pioneers in developing the concept of modern cosmopolitanism was that they were situated between worlds. Together with all the non-Jewish cosmopolitans, they left their imprint on a vision of postwar Europe.

Hannah Arendt used to call the era that challenged democracy and was at the same time deadly for European Jews "dark times," a term she borrowed from Bertolt Brecht's poem "An die Nachgeborenen" (To Those Born After Us), which Brecht wrote in 1939 in exile and which begins, "Truly, I live in dark times." In 1959, Arendt elaborated: "History knows many periods of dark times in which the public realm has been obscured and the world become so dubious that people have ceased to ask any more of politics than that it show due consideration for their vital interests and political liberty."[26] Arendt was looking for a new kind of language that could give expression to the predicament of Jewish and human existence in a post-Holocaust world. Existentially, the question for Jews was whether to assimilate or not. This was an intellectual puzzle. Can a Jew assimilate? Or is the idea of Jewish assimilation oxymoronic by definition? Because the more you assimilate, the less you are a Jew.

And if you still feel very much like a Jew, despite adopting the clothes and manners and way of life of the mainstream culture, then this proves that you haven't yet fully assimilated.[27] Arendt's basic answer is: if it is not possible to be both, it is not possible for the Jews to exist. The Holocaust made it impossible for her ever to consider her Jewishness something secondary. It was, indeed, a matter of life and death. Giving up her Jewish identity would be a betrayal of self and of millions.

As we will see, throughout her work Arendt explored the philosophical concept that the universal and the particular are mutually constitutive, the relationship between them one of inherent connection rather than opposition. For Arendt, the universal means what it does because the particulars are its background, and the particulars mean what they do because the universal is their background. When one changes, the other changes – but neither disappears. So when Jews become assimilated into Christian or secular culture, that culture becomes more Jewish, and Jewishness becomes more a matter of culture. They both change, and their relationship changes, but neither disappears. Again, the modern manifestation of this dynamic is cosmopolitanism. And Arendt was one of the first to attempt to transform cosmopolitanism and give it a modern sociological meaning. This need arose at precisely the moment when the Holocaust called the whole Enlightenment project into question. Arendt also argued that "dark times" demand a new epistemological responsibility to break through social scientific certainty and bring us back to experience.

This is not to say that this kind of thinking need be caught in a web of closed-off essentialism. Jonathan Sacks, the chief rabbi of the United Hebrew Congregations of the Commonwealth, observes that "universalism is an inadequate response to tribalism."[28] According to Sacks, five universalist cultures marked the history of the West – the Alexandrian Empire, ancient Rome, medieval Christianity, Islam, and the Enlightenment (61) – and Jews suffered under all of them. Thus universalism, although many consider it morally superior while others criticize its intolerance, was also historically a reaction to Jewish tribalism. For religion, one feature is absolute; all other social differences and oppositions are unimportant when compared to faith. The New Testament says, "All men are equal before God." This equality, this annulment of the boundaries between people, groups, classes, nations, societies, and cultures, is the social foundation of Christianity. "There is neither Jew nor Greek, there is neither slave nor free man, there is neither male nor female; for you are all one in

Christ" (Galatians 3: 28). But this belief has led to a further consequence. A fundamental new distinction has been established in the
world, and it is just as absolute as the social and political distinctions
that preceded it: the distinction between believers and nonbelievers.
The Pauline dictum of "oneness" was the first universal reaction
against Jewish tribalism.[29] These were the key debates between Jewish
and non-Jewish intellectuals[30] As we will see in chapter 5, through
trials like the one in Nuremberg where the Allied forces tried Nazi
criminals after the war, the destruction of the Jews was depicted as
a "crime against humanity," Jews symbolizing the universal concept
of "humanity." This is nothing new and is part of a long European
tradition that culminated in the Enlightenment. It was the Enlightenment that (after Christianity) emphasized the concept of humanity
(and crimes against it) and oneness. But it neglected those who did
not want to be a part of this kind of "humanity."

For Jews in Germany, the message came through loud and clear
in one of the key texts of the Enlightenment, Gotthold Ephraim
Lessing's "Nathan the Wise" (1779), which would become crucial
not only for German-Jews in general but also for Arendt's understanding of Jewish history. This late eighteenth-century story trans-
ports us back to twelfth-century Jerusalem during the Crusades.
Nathan, like Feuchtwanger's Ibn Esra, is a wealthy businessman who
negotiates between Christians and Muslims. In the iconic central
scene, the sultan asks Nathan which is the true religion, Judaism,
Christianity, or Islam. Nathan replies with the famous parable of the
ring. A ring has passed from father to favorite son for many generations. At one point a father has three favorite sons, and he promises
the ring to all three by having two replicas made. When the sons
argue about which one of them has the true ring, a wise judge tells
them that the true ring has to be deserved by the way we live. The
message, of course, is that there is no one true religion; all religions
can be equally true:

> How can I less believe in my forefathers
> Than thou in thine. How can I ask of thee
> To own that thy forefathers falsified
> In order to yield mine the praise of truth.
> The like of Christians.[31]

Anybody could join universal humanity when he was ready to leave
his particularity behind. Ulrich Beck (2009) shows that this can be
read in a different way and sees Lessing as the instigator of a new

14

religious cosmopolitanism. Truth is not what's at stake here, but humanity.

In Beck's view, Lessing chooses cosmopolitanism over absolute truth. Lessing is interested in certainty (religion), but not in truth. Arendt read Lessing differently and at different times. She first wrote specifically about Lessing in an essay published in 1932 entitled "The Enlightenment and the Jewish Question." Arendt was twenty-six years old at the time and deeply engaged in Zionist politics and ideas.[32] Many of her ideas during this period were developed under the influence of the German Zionist Kurt Blumenfeld, who introduced Arendt to the concept of cultural Zionism.[33] She was also working on her "habilitation"[34] about Rahel Varnhagen at this time. In this work, Arendt struggled with Jewish issues of assimilation and acculturation through an analysis of the struggles of a Jewish woman in Germany during the Enlightenment. Rahel Varnhagen tried to be both Jewish and German at once and attempted in vain to escape her Jewishness. Arendt tried to link Varnhagen's personal story with larger political issues of assimilation and emancipation.[35] In her biography of Varnhagen, Arendt first pursued the questions of Jewish identity that would occupy her throughout her intellectual career. Was the Enlightenment indeed the beginning of the successful integration of Jews into the larger society? Could Jewish emancipation provide the necessary protection for minorities?

Arendt's 1932 essay on the Enlightenment begins with a criticism of Lessing and Mendelssohn's view that Jews can be like anyone else – they just need to stop being Jewish. As Arendt points out, "Truth gets lost in the Enlightenment – indeed, no one wants it anymore. More important than truth is man in his search for it" (Arendt 2007: 4). For Arendt, "truth" was replaced by something better in the Enlightenment: the discovery of the purely human as an abstract notion. But, unlike Lessing, Arendt emphasized the contributions of another German philosopher who stood between the Enlightenment and Romanticism, Johann Gottfried von Herder. Arendt considered Herder the link to a historical (and, later, a political) vision of how to understand one's Jewishness. In Arendt's view, Herder rediscovered history, and with history, diversity and plural life-worlds (key concepts in Arendt's thinking) were restored to the Jews.[36] This was the beginning of Arendt's criticism of Jewish thinking about history. She recognized Jewish indifference to history (in her essay she identifies this indifference with the thought of Moses Mendelssohn) and related it to a Jewish diasporic tendency to which she was attracted as well. From Herder she learned that a universal history of humanity is impossible and that there is an alternative, namely, to think of human groups as collectivities and to see that Jews needed to be recognized as Jewish citizens. But Arendt also recognized the pitfalls of Herder's view of the Jews, pitfalls that became central in her later view of Jewish politics. On the one hand, Herder recognized that the Jews had their own history, separate from that of others; but Herder also insisted on Jewish secularization and the abandonment of their religious past. Arendt did not accept either the solution of Lessing or that of Herder. She was trying to find her own way. But this was no longer a theoretical problem for her.

With the Nazis' rise to power, Arendt herself was thrown into Jewish history. This short essay was written just before the Nazis came to power, and Arendt had to leave Germany for Paris and, later, New York. As a critic of the Enlightenment, Arendt accepted many of Herder's particular cultural commitments, but central for Herder was his belief that only a common language can humanize people. If language expresses thinking and feeling, and if it is possible through language to express universal values in particular ways, then Jewish multilingualism resolves this predicament.[37] The scholar of nationalism Ernest Gellner expressed this problem cogently with a metaphor from the arts. Gellner posited two ethnographic landscapes (evolving in time rather than in space). The prenationalist landscape resembles paintings by Kokoschka; there are no clear contours in the details, but there is the impression of a whole. Gellner believed that plurality and variation can be connected through diverse groups and languages. By contrast, the national geographic map – the other ethnographic landscape – resembles pictures by Modigliani: clear colors and even clearer forms, separated neatly from each other. Thus, state and culture are basically the same. Society is understood in terms of the nation.

Gellner (1983: 134–5), whose roots are like Kafka's in Czechoslovakia, did not think that culture is congruent with a homogenous language. The European-Jewish experience was multilingual, and this multilingualism became central to Jewish efforts at cultural reconstruction after the war. Two ideas are significant here: the idea that different cultures live in different worlds, and the idea, a variant of the first, that we live in a common world with one common history and narrative, which turns particular histories into relics of the past. There are those who emphasize the polis and those who emphasize the cosmos, those who stress the virtues of multiculturalism and those who advocate universalism. With the Enlightenment imperative hovering over this enterprise, the universalizing camp has a long tradition

16

of rejecting particular attachments as anachronistic.[38] In its contemporary manifestation, the particular is frequently perceived as an impediment, if not an outright antidote, to the cosmopolitan project. It is particularly important to emphasize the paradoxical results of a European cosmopolitan model based (for instance) on universalized memories of the Holocaust that leave out the particular experiences of its Jewish victims. By excluding the memories of Jews, Europeans inevitably fall back on a Kantian conception of cosmopolitanism rooted in a universalism that has no conceptual or actual space for the persistence of particular attachments. Therefore, a Jewish view can concretize the notion of "rooted cosmopolitanism." How do these values become the vantage point of the personal identity of human beings and thereby also politically significant? How do they acquire and renew their reality in rituals and take root in postnational communities?

I develop a genealogy in this book that allows me to recast the idea of rooted cosmopolitanism and place it in the context of the steady development of history, where it belongs. "Rooted cosmopolitanism" is not simply a recent trend that postulates that globalization has eroded our sense of place and that cosmopolitanism can restore it. Rather, this is an existential problem of how to reconcile the idea that people should be equal – one of the defining ideas of modernity – with the particularist identity that defines so many things that people, especially minorities, care about, and that seems to been present since the birth of nationalism in the nineteenth century, when it became one of the fundamental component parts of modernism, and when the nation-state became the template of "society."[39] Clearly, there are pitfalls in this approach. Is it possible to de-essentialize when one talks about ethnic identity? Is there something that all Jews share? If you look at Jewish worlds even before, but especially after, emancipation, you will find secular and orthodox Jews, West European Jews and East European Jews, all of whom inhabit different worlds. Naturally there are also Jews from Arab and North African countries. What do these people share, if anything at all?

This seems like a strange question, given that the question of Jewish identity is one of the most controversial within the Jewish community and that there exists a state that defines itself as Jewish. My interest lies not in determining "who is a real Jew," however, but in the meaning of Jewish existence – even in terms of performance and action, a pivotal question after the attempt to destroy Jewish life in Europe. Jewish identity can no longer be defined by the dichotomy of assimilation and Zionism. Jewish identity also means more than

17

lifestyle and culture. It is more than a product of its non-Jewish environment. There seems to be more, something that the "normal" tools of the social sciences cannot approach. It could be something physical and metaphysical at the same time. Arendt called it the "hidden tradition."[40]

Arendt returned to Lessing and to this hidden tradition twenty-seven years after she published her first thoughts on him, when she received the Lessing Prize in Hamburg in 1959. There she gave a talk on Lessing called "On Humanity in Dark Times: Thoughts about Lessing." Her thinking about Lessing had become reconciled. In this talk she considered Lessing's most important quality his capacity for friendship with people who were different from him. "He wanted to be the friend of many men, but no man's brother," she said (30). Arendt's thought had grown much more political by 1959 and giving up the search for truth had actually become a political virtue for her that approached Beck's cosmopolitan vision. "Because Lessing was a completely political person," she said, "he insisted that truth can exist only where it is humanized by discourse . . . but such speech is virtually impossible in solitude." She ended the talk by quoting Lessing: "Let each man say what he deems truth, and let truth itself be commended unto God" (31). Arendt made a point of speaking to her German audience as a Jew:

> In this connection I cannot gloss over the fact that for many years I considered the only adequate reply to the question, who are you? To be: A Jew. That answer alone took into account the reality of persecution. As for the statement with which Nathan the Wise (in effect, though not in actual wording) countered the command: "Step closer, Jew" – the statement: I am a man – I would have considered as nothing but a grotesque and dangerous evasion of reality. (17–18)

For Arendt, being a Jew was first of all a political stance, one that she developed while still in Germany through her intellectual connections with Zionism.[41] The Germans celebrated Arendt as a humanist and she responded as a Jew. When she was later attacked by many of her Jewish friends as a universalist, she responded as a humanist.[42] She was content neither to be a Jew nor to be a universalist. She wanted to be both. This is also the basis of Arendt's tense relationship with Jews and Judaism and of her search for a way to place Jewish identity within the modern nation-state. But emancipation (as Arendt knew very well), and above all the French Revolution, had changed all of this. European Jews started to feel the strain between citizenship and loyalty. Within the bounds of citizenship, Jews needed to find, determine, and maintain their Jewish identity. As we will see, it was this tension between citizenship and humanity that troubled Arendt so deeply in her analysis of human rights in her 1951 *Origins of Totalitarianism*. But the beginning of this modern story lies in France and its revolution. Arendt's life, as well as her work, takes us to France, her first stop after being forced to leave Germany.

One of the defining moments in the debate that took place in the French National Assembly during the French Revolution occurred over the question of whether Jews could be citizens of the French nation or should be treated like all other foreigners. Stanislas Marie Adelaide, Comte de Clermont-Tonnerre, a liberal aristocrat, argued for the inclusion of Jews and Protestants in the nascent French nation (he was killed during the storming of the Tuileries in 1792). On December 23, 1789, he gave a speech that became constitutive of Jewish modernity after the French Revolution in which he argued that citizenship should not be based on ethnicity, nationality, or culture:

> Every creed has only one test to pass in regard to the social body: it has only one examination to which it must submit, that of its morals. It is here that the adversaries of the Jewish people attack me. This people, they say, is not sociable. . . . But, they say to me, the Jews have their own judges and laws. I respond that is your fault and you should not allow it. We must refuse everything to the Jews as a nation and accord everything to Jews as individuals. We must withdraw recognition from their judges; they should only have our judges. We must refuse legal protection to the maintenance of the so-called laws of their Judaic organization; they should not be allowed to form in the state either a political body or an order. They must be citizens individually. But, some will say to me, they do not want to be citizens. Well then! If they do not want to be citizens, they should say so, and then, we should banish them. It is repugnant to have in the state an association of non-citizens, and a nation within the nation. . . . In short, Sirs, the presumed status of every man resident in a country is to be a citizen.[43]

These words are at once a hope and curse. The Jewish exile is over. Assimilation and civic equality can become keys to the end of exile. Jews can stop being wanderers; they can become equal citizens. This promise, especially in Western Europe, created the contradiction between nationalism as a universal force and the attraction of super- and supranational modes of belonging – the modern form of life in exile. Clermont told the Jews that there was no room for particular

19

wills within the general will of the nation. This was a truly revolutionary insight and has remained one of the integral aspects of being European; in fact, the European project of unity is based on it. Europe's universal pride allowed Jews to be part of it as equals, to become integrated as Germans, French, Spaniards, Norwegians – but not as Jews. France is exemplary here in that it became the classic locus of the translation of emancipatory ideas into politics. Jews were supposed to be like everybody else and not a "nation within a nation." Emancipation did indeed emancipate.[44] It released the Jews from the confines of their community and had them enter modernity as individuals and as individuals, moreover, who like all other citizens had to rely on the protection of the state. But from this moment on, Jewish "difference" became a modern problem that would have enormous political consequences in later centuries.[45] This was not only true for the Jews. The French Revolution did indeed try to dissolve all corporations in order to construct its new universal state. Citizenship promised to end the Jewish Diaspora and bring the Jews home, not as Jews but as citizens. Thus citizenship became part of the solution to the Jewish problem.[46]

The Jews were used to living in autonomous communities knit together by religious and community bonds. The revolution severed these bonds and provided universal citizenship in their stead, which is exactly where Arendt's criticism of abstract universalism starts. With the destruction of these bonds, the question of Jewish solidarity and belonging became a predicament. Jews were provided "exit visas" from their "national/corporate" existence but not "entry tickets" into the societies in which they lived.[47]

Arendt experienced this personally in France between 1933 and 1941. After being interned by the French as an enemy alien, she fled to the United States. Her first publication in America concerned France and the Dreyfus affair – for many observers, the beginning of the end of Jewish emancipation in the country of its invention. Alfred Dreyfus, a Jew and officer in the French army, was falsely accused of treason in 1894. The French army, the last bastion of French revolt against the "liberty, equality, and fraternity" of the French Revolution, attacked Dreyfus as a foreigner, a man without honor, and a traitor to the army and the French nation. The enemies of the Jews considered Jews the embodiment of the French Revolution, guilty of using notions like equality to dominate and subject the "true" French nation.[48] For many Jews (including the Zionists), the Dreyfus affair symbolized the beginning of the end of Jewish emancipation in Europe, more than three decades before the Nazis came to power.

Jews could not escape being a "nation within a nation." In an era when modernity also meant the transition from "community" to "society," this became an accusation against them; they were still a close-knit community and thus undermined universal claims of citizenship, but at the same time they took advantage of the increasing privatization and commercialization of society. Jews were caught in a double bind, seen as too particular to be universal citizens and as too universal to transcend the bounds of citizenship, too cosmopolitan to be particular citizens.[49] This was a predicament for Jews not only as citizens but, soon enough, also as socialists. A few years later, Karl Marx reflected on the political emancipation of the Jews and why it had to fail.[50] Marx did not believe that the Jewish problem could be solved through legal means. Equal citizenship was not the problem; capitalism was. "The social emancipation of the Jew is the emancipation of society from Judaism," Marx wrote, and this statement became a battle cry not only for the enemies of the Jews but for Jews themselves who saw in socialism a secular answer to the ancient Jewish longing for salvation, now termed "human emancipation." Jews as Jews undermined this universal claim. Marx put the Jews center stage in the European drama of modernity. Jews became the symbol of all modern paradoxes. As figures of particularity, they undermined the universal claim of the Enlightenment; they turned into the outsiders of the Enlightenment, still living in fantasy worlds of close-knit communities.[51] At the same time, Jews were also the symbol of community's opposite: transnationalism, homelessness, abstraction, multiple loyalties, and the money economy.

This defines the paradoxical situation of the Jews: their cosmopolitanism was particular and their particularity was cosmopolitan. Again, it was Arendt who tried to recast this predicament as a virtue. When she criticized the Enlightenment as being hostile to Jewish experience, she sought a political Jewish solidarity transcending the solidarity of the nation (perhaps modeled on class solidarity). She believed in the "nation within a nation" – not the nation in the old medieval corporate sense but in a new political sense.[52] She adhered to this line of thought in her later practical and theoretical works. As we will see, her *Origins of Totalitarianism* is about the Jewish condition in disguise and forms a bridge between her earlier works on Jewish issues and her later work on universal issues, culminating in an account that purports to be both: *Eichmann in Jerusalem* (1963a).

However, this theoretical argument needs to be historicized. The tension for Jews between being different and equal at the same time reflected their concerns until the time when Jewish life in Europe was terminated. This book follows these theoretical questions but also tries to demonstrate the possibilities of Jewish political action beyond the sovereignty of the nation-state. Chapter 2 contextualizes the life and thought of Hannah Arendt as part of a so-called hidden tradition of Jewish thinking that is suspicious of state politics and sovereignty. I look at Arendt in conjunction with Walter Benjamin, Franz Kafka, Gershom Scholem, Moritz Goldstein, and others who tried to come to terms with their Jewish identity in the age before the rise of Nazism. We will see how Arendt integrated much of their thinking about the Jews into her own work, but also translated some rather unpolitical thinking into political action and thought. For her, the political solution to questions of sovereignty was political federalism, a system that tries to keep sovereignty in check. We will follow her into exile in France and look at the foundation of the World Jewish Congress in 1936 in Geneva, in which Arendt participated as an observer. The politics of the World Jewish Congress was always something Arendt looked at, criticized, and participated in, but from a distance.

Chapter 3 deals with a part of Arendt's life that has not been central in the literature on her, namely, her work with Jewish Cultural Reconstruction (JCR), an organization dealing with the restitution of collective cultural property that belonged to Jews as private or communal property and was looted by the Nazis, partly recovered at the end of the war, and then restored to collective Jewish communal property. Arendt served first as the JCR's research director and then as its executive director, and we will see how her encounter with American and West German bureaucracy influenced her thoughts on the structure of totalitarianism and the role of bureaucracy, as well as restitution as the site where issues of private and collective property were debated and ethnic identity contested and formulated.

Chapter 4 deals with the politics of the transition from minority rights to human rights and locates Arendt's thinking on this issue within the struggles of Jewish organizations for minority rights in the newly constituted European states after World War I. Arendt was critical of both minority and human rights, and this chapter examines this struggle in relation to her thoughts on Jewish autonomy. It looks at Arendt's thinking in the context of Jewish thought on political and cultural autonomy in such thinkers as Simon Dubnow and Salo Baron. The chapter ends with Rafael Lemkin's attempt to create an international judicial framework to fight genocide, and with the commonalities and differences between Arendt and Lemkin.

Chapter 5 explores the subject of guilt and responsibility as part of post-World War II politics and looks at how Arendt responded to the Nuremberg Trials. Chapter 6 examines Arendt's reading of totalitarianism and the Eichmann trial in Jerusalem through the lense of Jewish politics and intellectual thought. It locates Arendt's view of totalitarianism within the framework of other Jewish thinkers on the subject. It also looks at Arendt's struggles with other intellectuals in the wake of the publication of her report on the Eichmann trial in Jerusalem. We will see that Arendt's view of these issues depended in part on whom she was addressing. In debating Jewish thinkers like Scholem, she took a more universalist stance, whereas in discussions with Germans like Enzensberger, her stance was a more particular Jewish one. The book concludes with a chapter on Arendt's critical thinking on Zionism and will then look in particular at the fate of the Polish Jewish writer and painter Bruno Schulz, who not only exemplifies issues of cultural property but serves as a fitting conclusion to the eternally complex issue of Jewish identity and belonging.

# — 2 —

# PARIS, GENEVA, AND PORT BOU:
# THE LAST EUROPEANS

For Arendt, the issues of universalism and particularism that she struggled with all her life were not abstractions. They were matters of life and death. When the French ceased to view Jews as citizens and saw them as Jews – as a nation within a nation – she felt that the entire revolutionary tradition of citizenship was at stake. This marked the beginning of her reckoning with that tradition.

"Dear Scholem – Walter Benjamin took his own life on September 26th at the Spanish border in Port Bou. . . . Jews die in Europe and they bury them like dogs,"[1] wrote Hannah Arendt on October 21, 1940, to Gershom Scholem in Jerusalem. It was she who informed Scholem that Benjamin had committed suicide on the border between France and Spain. He was on his way to America, a place he did not want to go. As she wrote in an essay on Benjamin almost thirty years later,

> How was he to live without a library, how could he earn a living without the extensive collection of quotations and excerpts among his manuscripts? Besides, nothing drew him to America, where, as he used to say, people would probably find no other use for him than to cart him up and down the country to exhibit him as the "last European."[2]

In May 1941, Arendt was able to flee France and Europe via Lisbon to the United States. After her arrival, she began her reckoning with her European past. In "Porvenir in Buenos Aires: A Way Toward the Reconciliation of Peoples," an essay published in 1942 in German in an exiles' magazine, Arendt expresses her deep disappointment and anger at what remained of the heritage of the French Revolution.

"On that day in Compiègne, when Pétain put his signature to the infamous paragraphs of the German–French armistice, which demanded that every refugee in France be handed over to the Nazis, even those who fought under the French flag – on that memorable day Pétain tore the tricolor to shreds and annihilated the French nation."[3] In Arendt's eyes, the French nation had perished, and with it the European tradition of citizenship. This also meant that "the Jewish question" has turned into a symbol for all of Europe's unresolved national questions. She considered the Jewish question purely a political one:

> Justice for a people, however, can only mean national justice. One of the inalienable human rights of Jews is the right to live and if need be to die as a Jew. A human being can defend himself only as the person he is attacked as. A Jew can preserve his human dignity only if he can become human as a Jew. For a Jew – in a time when his people are persecuted and the scraps of desert land that he has turned into fertile fields through the work of his own hands are threatened – that means fighting for the freedom of his people and the security of his land. ("Porvenir in Buenos Aires: A Way Toward the Reconciliation of Peoples": Arendt 2007: 261–2)

During the early years of World War II, Arendt continued to demand the formation of a Jewish army to fight the Nazis. Here also lie the perplexities of her reading of Jewish collective political action. She wanted the Jews to be "powerful" and to act as sovereign states, forming an army, recognizing and fighting one's enemies. She wanted the Jews to be a politically active people. At the same time, as she knew only too well from her own experience, the Jews were not a unified collective but a diasporic nation unable to act collectively.[4] Arendt was aware of this tension, and it may be no coincidence that she took Benjamin's last manuscript, "On the Concept of History," a document of "the last European" that slowly gained recognition over the years, with her to the United States.

The manuscript itself was the result of many conversations between Arendt and Benjamin in Paris. History did not play a role here; rather, it was turned into messianic hope. The manuscript was only published twenty-seven years later, in a Benjamin reader edited by Arendt. In the same collection, Arendt also published Benjamin's thoughts on Kafka.[5] Both Benjamin and Arendt considered Kafka a symbol of European Jewish identity unbridled by ethnic exclusiveness. Kafka was born in 1883 a subject of the Habsburg Empire and died as a citizen of Czechoslovakia in 1924.[6] He wrote in German and lived in Prague. Arendt was intrigued by Kafka's predicament.[7] She quoted a letter from Kafka to Max Brod in her essay on Benjamin: "Thus they [German–Jewish writers] lived among three impossibilities: The impossibility of not writing . . . the impossibility of writing in German . . . and the impossibility of writing differently," but Kafka also wanted to add another impossibility, "the impossibility of writing."[8] Arendt saw Kafka, Benjamin, and herself that way.[9] It was as impossible for her to be a Jew as it was for her not to be one, and she saw this problem as the predicament of an entire generation of Jews. The use of German was for Kafka (as for Benjamin and Arendt) the "self-tormenting usurpation of an alien property." Clearly, not only the language is at stake here but also the traditions, the politics, and everything associated with the language. For Jewish writers, language is always a foreign language – as are Hebrew and Yiddish for most Jews who assimilated in their countries in the western parts of Europe. The German-born Israeli poet Yehuda Amichai once wrote: "Hebrew writing and Arabic writing go from east to west, Latin writing, from west to east."[10]

These writers were aware that language is anchored in historical experience. Arendt and Kafka tried to learn Hebrew but never really mastered it. They may not really have wanted to. For them, being Jewish writers was expressed by Kafka's four impossibilities. In their opinion, Jewish nationalism did not need a unified language (as it did not need a unified territory). The hidden Jewish tradition has many layers, and Arendt developed them in her confrontation and reading of Benjamin, Kafka, and Scholem, the Jerusalem scholar of Jewish mysticism (their paths would cross many times over the course of their lives).[11] The question behind the "hidden tradition" of the Jews remained the question of political action. In Scholem's reading of Jewish history and in Benjamin's reading of Kafka's writing, Arendt discovered a "hidden tradition" that connects Jewish particularity to the general course of history. As we have seen, however, Arendt wanted to demystify this "hidden tradition" and give it a more heroic meaning of honor and struggle. At the same time, Arendt looks for this hidden tradition in Heinrich Heine, Bernard Lazare, and Charlie Chaplin. Once again she attempts to attain the human through the Jewish experience:

> It is therefore not surprising that out of their personal experience Jewish poets, writers, and artists should have been able to evolve the concept of the pariah as a human type – a concept of supreme impor-

26

tance for the evaluation of mankind in our day and one which has exerted upon the gentile world an influence in strange contrast to the spiritual and political ineffectiveness which has been the fate of these men among their own brethren. (Arendt 2007: 276)

The social sciences usually look at traditions as invented, imagined, or constructed. "Soul," "Essence," "Mysticism," and the "Non-Explainable" are not part of the social scientific toolbox. God does not play a huge role in these deliberations. Nevertheless, when we construct identity, we also create differences by working through the essence of our own identity. Thus one creates essence; this is what Arendt intended to do. There is no contradiction here. Clearly, the yearning for territorial independence and the universal message of Diaspora and exile are not only particular Jewish tensions but tensions around which citizenship, civil society, and cultural identity revolve. It is the Jewish experience, however (before and after the catastrophe), that constitutes these tensions as a condition of existence. It was the Jewish philosopher Franz Rosenzweig who claimed that Jews live in two dimensions: eternity and temporality.[12] The dimension of eternity never allows Jews to consider the state the last recourse of legitimacy. For "God's people," eternity is always present.[13] Thus language also plays a part. Hebrew is the holy language, the language in which Jews pray (and in which they conduct their daily affairs in the state of Israel today), but there is also the language used to communicate with others.

As Lowith shows in his comparative essay on Heidegger and Rosenzweig, Heidegger was caught up in temporality, whereas Rosenzweig could hold up the eternal truth of the Jewish god.[14] This seemed irrelevant to a nonbeliever like Arendt, but she approached this problem from a rather secular and political vantage point via her reading of Scholem, Benjamin, and Kafka. Her thought was always too political to consider their solutions theological. For her, the political solution to sovereignty was a plural and federalist structure. Her experience as a refugee and stateless person, the experience of the Diaspora, where rights no longer have meaning, and her life in exile turned her attention to the counterpoint of life in territorial and temporal history. In her 1943 essay "We Refugees," she writes about the worldlessness of the Jewish refugee:

remember that being a Jew does not give any legal status in this world. If we should start telling the truth that we are nothing but Jews, it would mean that we expose ourselves to the fate of human beings who,

27

unprotected by any specific law or political convention, are nothing but human beings. I can hardly imagine an attitude more dangerous, since we actually live in a world in which human beings as such have ceased to exist for quite a while. (Arendt 2007: 273).[15]

This view also informed her understanding of place not as territory but as politics, which always made her relation to Zionism extremely problematic[16] and which entered into her reflections on her friend Benjamin's suicide: "Yet our suicides are no mad rebels who hurl defiance at life and the world, who try to kill in themselves the whole universe. Theirs is a quiet and modest way of vanishing; they seem to apologize for the violent solution they have found for their personal problems" (Arendt 2007: 268). She depicted this "worldlessness" concretely once again when she reviewed the autobiography of Stefan Zweig, *The World of Yesterday,* also in 1943.[17] Zweig committed suicide in February 1942, in Brazil, in despair about the world he had lost; his autobiography appeared after his death. Arendt's reading of Zweig is bitter; she sees him as exemplary of the worldlessness of the Jewish literati, who do not acknowledge the political concepts of disgrace and honor.[18] The closing sentence of her review is a plea for a Jewish politics:

> When finally the whole structure of his life, with its aloofness from civic struggle and politics, broke down, and he experienced disgrace, he was unable to discover what honor can mean to men. For honor never will be won by the cult of success or fame, by cultivation of one's own self, nor even by personal dignity. From the "disgrace" of being a Jew there is but one escape – to fight for the honor of the Jewish people as a whole. (Arendt 2007: 328)

Thus, for Arendt, Zweig serves as a point of entry for criticizing the lack of political commitment and political action of the so-called man of letters. To Arendt's mind, Zweig represented an aesthetic way of being Jewish, whereas she was looking for something like Feuchtwanger's political reading of Jewish history.

In her *Origins of Totalitarianism,* published for the first time in 1951, Arendt developed this line of thought further, writing about the "perplexities of the rights of man" within the framework of a universal critique of human rights. Arendt knew from her own experience as a stateless person and prisoner in an internment camp in France that universal rights have no relevance if not guaranteed by particular institutions. People have no place in the world, and this is what defines the condition of statelessness. For those who lack rights, there is no law. Eight years separate the publication of "We Refugees" and *The Origins of Totalitarianism*. These eight years were critical in the development of her thought; her thinking on Jewish politics changed radically. At this time, she was working theoretically on Jewish subjects and was actively involved in Jewish politics. It is thus no coincidence that a historian of Soviet Jewry began his book on the history of the Jews in the Soviet Union by observing that "the modern age is the Jewish age" (Slezkine 2004: 1). Slezkine, writing from the Eastern European perspective, claims that the twentieth century was the Jewish century. He does not argue in terms of the Holocaust but bases his reasoning on Jewish dispositions and experiences, viewing Jews as carriers of modernity in terms of their literary orientation, mobility, and urbanity. Slezkine stresses the universal potential of the Jewish experience as a link to modernity. He demonstrates that the virtues of modernity, such as the intellectual achievement of globalization, are nothing other than Jewish virtues. In his view, Jews are not only revolutionaries but embody the qualities of modernity; like Feuchtwanger's Ibn Esra, they are urbane, mobile, educated, intellectual, and flexible. Slezkine describes a society of strangers who perceive their alienation as an opportunity for liberation. Jewish history is turned into universal history, but it is the refusal to succumb to an unconditional universalism and the preservation of particular attachments (even in terms of the eternal versus the temporal) that transformed Jews into exemplary carriers of cosmopolitanism.

This view corresponds with Benjamin's and Arendt's reading of Kafka. Thus Kafka's Jewish literature becomes universal literature the same way that Arendt's political theory becomes a universal theory. In her essay on Benjamin (and Kafka), Arendt mentions an event that took place in 1912 and caused quite an intellectual uproar: the so-called Goldstein affair.[19] The importance to Arendt of Goldstein's essay "The German–Jewish Parnassus" is readily apparent in a letter she wrote to Goldstein in December 1968, in which she calls his essay "paradigmatic."[20] In her essay on Walter Benjamin, Arendt spends almost eleven pages discussing Goldstein's essay, beginning with Goldstein's often quoted statement, "We Jews administer the intellectual property of a people which denies us the right and ability to do so" (Arendt 1968b: 183–4). Goldstein did not want and was not able to take the Zionist route out of this situation. He could no more become a Zionist than he could become a German. But this did not prevent him from becoming a "national Jew." For Goldstein, this was

29

clearly a cultural mode of being. He had no intention of relocating to Palestine, nor did he support political and territorial sovereignty. He wanted Jews to write as Jews, even if they wrote in the most beautiful German possible. He wanted to recover a Jewish voice in the German language. He was aware, and wanted other Jews to be aware, that most Jews in Germany were not able to write in Hebrew and that German was a kind of foreign language. Clearly, Goldstein's language was the language of culture and aesthetics and not the language of politics. But his politics of culture resonated with a minority politics that was already solidly in place among the Jews of Eastern Europe. There, questions touched on concepts of cultural autonomy in the political sense.[21]

Arendt saw a way out of her own (and Kafka's, and Benjamin's) predicament in Goldstein's thinking. As Jews, they must be both inside and outside, must continue to live as strangers (or pariahs), must speak and write in a foreign language. For Arendt, this recalled the impossibilities of writing that Kafka had articulated. Arendt, who edited Kafka's diaries for Schocken in the 1940s, knew that Kafka was aware that his own German could never be pure. Arendt also understood that all these considerations regarding language were not merely reactions to anti-Semitism. It was their awareness of the "insolubility of the Jewish question," as Arendt put it (Arendt 1968b: 190) that made these thinkers truly "Jewish." They knew that they could not return to the so-called ranks of the Jewish people or to Judaism because they understood that all membership was questionable. Becoming a Communist, a Zionist, an assimilated Jew, was impossible. Goldstein saw Jewish identity as based on a lack of roots. Arendt was aware that this view would turn Jews into defenseless victims. Almost in desperation, she quoted Kafka's diary: "My people, provided that I have one" (Arendt 1968b: 190). She also quoted a letter from Benjamin (reading Kafka) written in Paris and dated 1935:

> Actually, I hardly feel constrained to try to make head or tail of this condition of the world. On this planet a great number of civilizations have perished in blood and horror. Naturally, one must wish for the planet that one day it will experience a civilization that has abandoned blood and horror. . . . But it is terribly doubtful whether *we* [emphasis added by Arendt] can bring such a present to its hundred- or four-hundred-millionth birthday party. And if we don't, the planet will finally punish us, its unthoughtful well-wishers, by presenting us with the Last Judgment. (Arendt 1968b: 192)

Even in 1968, Arendt was still mourning her friend's suicide.

In Arendt's writings, Goldstein becomes a metaphor for how to write and which audience to address. The "affair" involved an essay Goldstein published in 1912 in a conservative German cultural journal called *Der Kunstwart* (The Guardian of Art), whose editor was considered a fierce German nationalist and its cultural critic an anti-Semite. *Der Kunstwart* at the time had the highest circulation among cultural magazines in Germany. Clearly, Goldstein was feeding anti-Semitic fantasies when he told his German audience that the Jews were masterminding German culture. But he was writing mainly for a Jewish audience, and his message was that Jews should find their separate ways and not succumb to the false promise of either of the two extremes, assimilation or Zionism. Goldstein wrote in two voices for two audiences, one Jewish and the other not, a device that became the hallmark of Arendt's writing as well.[22] Goldstein was attacked by assimilated Jews as well as by Zionists. His essay created an uproar among German readers as well, who expressed hostility toward Jews. Goldstein broke a discursive taboo (something Arendt understood intimately) by saying things that could also be uttered by anti-Semites.

The young Walter Benjamin (who was twenty when Goldstein's essay appeared) was well aware of this.[23] Benjamin exchanged letters with a young Zionist friend, Ludwig Strauss, about Goldstein's essay.[24] These letters reveal Benjamin's misgivings about assimilation, but at the same time showed him to be a true European: "It would be bad for Europe if the cultural energies of the Jews were to leave it," he wrote (Benjamin 1972: 834, my translation). Later in the correspondence he argued against the political face of Zionism as well, arguing that Zionism was first of all an "idea." The same could be said for Arendt: she embraced the idea but rejected the politics. Ironically, anti-Semites agreed with this analysis of the Jewish condition. More than forty years later, in 1957, Moritz Goldstein published an essay in which he was forced to defend his early essay from charges of anti-Semitism.[25] Goldstein began by quoting from a National Socialist book published in Germany in 1935, *The Jews in Germany,* which outlined in great detail the destructive influence of Jews on German culture. One chapter of this book dealt almost exclusively with Goldstein's 1912 essay, quoting it extensively. In the 1957 essay, Goldstein wrote in a rather apologetic tone about the circumstances of the earlier essay, pointing out that it had been written in any different historical context, before World War II and the Holocaust. But Goldstein understood that the Nazi arguments that Jews were outsiders who did not belong, who were not rooted in the soil, who were of but not in society, were nearly identical to the arguments of Jews who refused to assimilate and saw these attributes as virtues rather than vices. At the end of the 1957 essay, Goldstein closed the book on European Jewry. Two things, he argued, could end the curse of the wandering Jew. One was Israel – "it will give to world Jewry a new dignity, or rather restore its ancient dignity" – and the other was the United States (Goldstein 1957: 254).

It is ironic that two years after he published "German–Jewish Parnassus," Goldstein published another essay on the Jews and Europe, "Us and Europe"[26] In this essay, Goldstein emphasized that Jews were Europeans par excellence. They did not need nationalism in order to constitute a nation. Jews had no soil, no ground, no roots; the only thing they had was their book, which could be carried from one place to the other (Goldstein 1914: 200). His position that political Zionism was not the answer had not changed, and he expressed the hope that Jews could be Europeans and grow roots in Europe, the implication being that Jews were situated outside Europe and would have to become "hyper-European" (208). The essay ends with the hope that Jews, for a second time, would save the world and be a light unto the nations.

Arendt adopted many of these themes in her theoretical and political analysis of the Jewish condition, particularly in her attempt to define a "non-territorial" politics for the Jews. She emphasized "thinking" and "speaking" as the worldless virtues of the Jews and argued that these virtues were needed in times of political despair – "dark times." The abstract notion of a universal mankind was never Arendt's solution. She dreamed of a plural diversity of nations acting in cosmopolitan concert. Cultural cosmopolitanism, beyond nationalism and assimilation, was the Jewish (intellectual) ideal before 1939. But when this ideal could not be realized in Europe and died in the Holocaust, she settled for the pluralism of the United States of America. Thus, in her 1966 essay on Rosa Luxemburg, she pitied those Jews in Europe who truly believed they could become good Europeans.[27] At the same time, she never could make peace with "normal" politics, including the exercise of sovereignty and force.

Twenty years earlier she had worked as an editor for Schocken Books in New York, the self-proclaimed goal of which was to save Jewish-European culture and introduce it to an American audience. Part of her work there was to edit the diaries of Franz Kafka. While thinking through Kafka's life and work, she published two rather different essays on him, at exactly the moment when the fate of

32

European Jews was being sealed by the Nazis.[28] The essays are similar
yet different. One deals with the Jewish Kafka, whereas the other
tries to read him more as a universal writer and ends with the statement, "After all, this man of good will may be anybody and everybody, perhaps even you and I." In her "Jew as Pariah," essay, she
calls Kafka "the Man of Goodwill." He is the man who wants to
enter the Castle. For her, K. represents the dilemma of the "would-be
assimilationist" Jew, who does not belong to either the ruling or the
common people but is "involved in situations and perplexities distinctive of Jewish life" (Arendt 2007: 290). Arendt sees in K. the modern
Jewish dilemma. He acts as the world wants him to act, alone and
not in concert with other Jews. Thus K. is the "ideal" Jew, since he
wants to be like everybody else. But "everybody else" is also an
amorphous, indistinguishable mass. Thus K. desires only universals
– like a "good" Jew should. He wants to become a member of the
community and insists on his rights (this is an earlier version of
Arendt's criticism of "human rights"). K. dies a natural death: he
becomes exhausted (like Benjamin, who committed suicide on the
border between France and Spain).

When she wrote these lines, Arendt knew that the end of European
Jews had become a reality. She ends the essay by transforming Kafka
into her own kind of Zionist:

> In Zionism he saw a means of abolishing the "abnormal" position of
> the Jews, an instrument whereby they might become "a people like
> other people." Perhaps the last of Europe's great poets, he could
> scarcely have wished to become a nationalist. Indeed, his whole genius,
> his whole expression of the modern spirit, lay precisely in the fact that
> what he sought was to be a human being, a normal member of human
> society. It was not his fault that this society had ceased to be human,
> and that, trapped within its meshes, those of its members who were
> really men of goodwill were forced to function within it as something
> exceptional and abnormal – saints or madmen. (Arendt 2007: 295)

The final lines of this 1944 essay read like the exhaustion of Benjamin
put into words: "For only within the framework of a people can a
man live as a man among men, without exhausting himself. And only
when a people lives and functions in consort with other peoples can
it contribute to the establishment upon earth of commonly condi-
tioned and commonly controlled humanity" (297). Thus, as early as
1944, Arendt saw Kafka's reading as foreshadowing Jewish and
human fate. Her own readings of totalitarianism and the Eichmann

trial always refer to Kafka's world of "nobodies." She quotes from one of Kafka's early stories, "Description of a Fight": "I did wrong to nobody, nobody did wrong to me; but nobody will help me, nothing but nobodies" (289). Her notions of guilt and responsibility, as well as her analysis of the existence of a destructive order of modernity that will be deadly for the Jews, owe much to her reading of Kafka and her identification as a Jewish writer with him.[29] Her later work, which looks at the universal experience of the Holocaust through a Jewish lens, goes back to narrative strategies of Kafka (and Benjamin).

Thus the issues of universalism and particularism not only lie at the core of the current debate regarding the cosmopolitan moment but go straight to the heart of modern Jewish thinking. Cosmopolitanism, and this is of central significance, should by no means be equated with atheism and secularism.[30] In fact, the reverse is true: cosmopolitan theory does indeed have a transcendental horizon. At its crux are boundaries between the profane and the holy as well as the sacred character of existence. This is how monotheism has become part of the modern existence. Arendt, Kafka, and Benjamin are part of a long-standing Jewish tradition that holds that modernity must become aware of its inherent self-consuming threats. Barbarism is part of modernity, and the only countermeasure against it is a transcendental perception of human sacredness. This raises the question of a transcendental horizon, which protects autocratic humankind from itself. This horizon connects Arendt's ideas to those of Rosenzweig, but she was also always looking for ways to politicize these theological concepts. In her analysis of concentration camps in *The Origins of Totalitarianism,* she writes, "The concentration and extermination camps of totalitarian regimes serve as the laboratories in which the fundamental belief of totalitarianism that everything is possible is being verified" (437). The possibility of everything (corresponding to Kafka's world of nobodies) is a key concept for Arendt. It speaks directly to the lack of transcendence and faith in authority and religion, which, she believed, needs to be restored. It also corresponds to her readings of the camps as "useless" and to her many references to theological concepts like purgatory and hell, not to mention the concept of evil. "It is inherent in our entire philosophical tradition that we cannot conceive of a 'radical evil,'" she writes, "and this is true both for Christian theology, which conceded even to the devil himself a celestial origin, as well as for Kant" (459).

Questions of universalism versus particularism became questions of survival for Jewish thinkers like Arendt and Benjamin. They tried to think beyond principles of liberalism or Marxism (in theory as well as in practice), to avoid the "either–or" and achieve the "both–and." This stance also makes clear the distinction between Jewish and non-Jewish experiences, which includes the refusal to recognize that Jews were targeted as Jews and was part of a universal imagination in its liberal or socialist form. It was even considered a concession to Hitler.[31] Thus, when we talk about memories and experiences, particularism cannot be subordinated to universalism. The specific Jewish dimension of the Holocaust was not only dissolved but even delegitimized as part of the Nazi racist project. After the Jews were killed simply for being Jewish, they were elevated to the status of "human beings." It almost seemed that to emphasize their Jewishness would be a concession to racist thinking.

A cosmopolitan politics needs to recognize that distinctive memories are not always sharable. Yes, they can be universalized, and this has happened in the past. The question is not about the "otherness of the other" but about concrete historical experience. The issue is not only theory and theoretical debates but the ways in which Jews lived before and could live after the Holocaust. This is one of the reasons why Arendt and Benjamin always drew on literature and poetry. Storytelling provides the best way of reaching an understanding of the human condition – especially the human condition in the dark times in which, and about which, Arendt wrote.[32] Arendt, Benjamin, and Kafka were first of all Jewish thinkers. In Benjamin's "Theses on the History of Philosophy," which Arendt literally transported out of Europe and into the United States, Benjamin writes of a dying European Judaism, "The true picture of the past flits by. The past can be seized only as an image which flashes up at the instant when it can be recognized and is never seen again."[33] Here Benjamin expresses the loss European Jews had to endure. This statement echoes his essay "The Storyteller" (Benjamin 1970: 83–107), in which he reflects on the storyteller as someone who narrates from afar things that are near.

As we will see, Arendt's theoretical and professional work attempted to give this "flitting by" of the past a new meaning. Again, this is also about the multilingualism of the Jews. Yiddish, for instance, the language of most Eastern European Jews before the Holocaust, was not bound to territory or national borders. Jewish languages undermined the affinity between culture, language, and territory praised by many

Romantic thinkers. This, too, was considered part of the Jewish "hidden tradition." Benjamin was very familiar with an essay by the important Hebrew poet Hayim Nachman Bialik, translated by Gershom Scholem into German and published in the magazine *Der Jude* (The Jew) in 1919. The essay explored the relationship between law and legends in Jewish thought, a relationship in many ways parallel to that between theory and narrative.[34] Arendt wanted to combine both facets of Jewish identity, especially in her book on the Eichmann trial, whereas Benjamin privileged legend over law. In his essays on Kafka, he constantly returns to the distinction between the two and relates Kafka to Bialik's distinction: "This does not mean that his [Kafka's] prose pieces belong entirely in the tradition of Western prose forms; they have, rather, a similar relationship to doctrine as the Haggadah (legend) does to the Halakah (law)."[35] Bialik emphasized that Judaism is composed of both the order of the law and the mercy of the legend. For Bialik, the mixture of legend and law is also expressed in the many languages in which Jewish books are written (see also Suchoff 2007). Two different orders compose Judaism, the preservation of tradition and constant renewal. Law and legend stand for determinism and freedom, and Judaism is made up of both. Benjamin read *The Castle* less politically than Arendt did. For him, the village of the story came from Talmudic legend. Benjamin writes of a legend in which a princess languishes in exile, where the language spoken is incomprehensible. The Messiah is on his way to save the princess. For Benjamin, the princess represents the body, and the Messiah – the soul – is supposed to save this body. When exile has gained control over man, this becomes impossible (Suchoff 2007: 122).

Arendt, who edited this essay of Benjamin, was not Jewish in the traditional orthodox sense – for her, Jewishness was a political identity – but she had read enough of Scholem and Benjamin to adapt this kind of thinking to her own needs. While working on her essay on Benjamin in 1968, she was also teaching a seminar at the New School of Social Research in New York called "Political Experience in the Twentieth Century," in which she asked her students to read literature and forget theories in order to come to terms with the twentieth century.[36] The students were asked to put themselves in the place of an imaginary person born around 1890 (Benjamin was born in 1892) and to relive the events of the century through that person's eyes and emotions. The project was her own version of "law and legend" applied to politics.

But something else haunts Bialik's essay. He discusses an ancient dispute about whether Jews are allowed to save a book from burning on the Sabbath. If so, should only Hebrew books be saved, or books in other languages as well? Bialik seems pleased that the sages decided that books written in any language can be rescued from a burning synagogue. We thus come full circle to the issue of Jewish multilingualism, but this time expressed in terms of rescuing this tradition from the fire. In 1934, Bialik wrote a Hebrew poem about the book-burning frenzy in Germany in which "flying letters" are presented as symbols of eternal Jewish redemption leaping from the ashes of catastrophe, represented as "burning scrolls." Bialik's language is the language of the Talmud. "Burning scrolls and flying letters" are indeed taken from the Babylonian Talmud, Tractate Avoda Zarah 18a, where the story of Rabbi Haninah ben Teradion is told. The rabbi was wrapped in a Torah scroll and set on fire, and when his disciples asked him what he saw, he replied, "I see the parchment burning while the letters of the Torah soar on high."

Hannah Arendt clearly reflected the German–Jewish sensibility in her attempt to see Jewish sources through the lens of modernity and to endorse the predicament of being an insider and an outsider at once. She politicized this sentiment, however. During her exile in France, she lived through a particular politics of minorities that was part of Jewish thinking and action that originated east of Germany, in the regions of the former Habsburg and Russian empires. There, politicized Jews developed notions of autonomy and minority rights that still have meaning today. Thus Arendt should be read not simply as a German Jew but as one who through her work in Paris became familiar with the politics of Eastern European Jewry and tried to integrate the sensibilities of both Western and Eastern European Jews.[37] During her years in France she was involved in Jewish politics and defense organizations, worked for the Zionist youth movement, visited Palestine, participated in the founding meeting of the World Jewish Congress in Geneva, and was even interned in a camp in 1940. The founding of the World Jewish Congress in the summer of 1936 was a defining moment for Arendt and for Jewish politics before the Holocaust. The Congress was initiated by the Comité des Délégations Juives, an organization formed on March 25, 1919, to coordinate the activities of several Jewish organizations at the Peace Conference in Paris; it also grew out of the American Jewish Congress. It was composed of delegations from Palestine, the United States, Canada, Russia, the Ukraine, Poland, East Galicia, Romania, Transylvania, Bukovina, Czechoslovakia, Italy, Yugoslavia, and Greece claiming to represent more than 10 million Jews.[38] The Congress was founded with the intention that it would be dissolved after the Peace

Conference in Paris, but Jewish delegates understood that it needed to be institutionalized. One can rightfully claim that this transnational organization, which coordinated American and European Jewish political activities, inaugurated twentieth-century Jewish cosmopolitan politics. This was the beginning of Jewish minority politics.

The Congress also cooperated with other ethnic minorities in the years between the world wars. Arendt was part of this effort, and the experiences of those years became the theoretical anchor for her analysis of minority and human rights in *The Origins of Totalitarianism*. But this first meeting of the World Jewish Congress was the impetus for more than the issue of minority rights; the concept of "totalitarianism" also dates to this time. There was, of course, no Jewish delegation from Germany one year after the passing of the Nuremberg Laws, but Soviet Jews were also prevented from attending.[39] It was clear to the delegates that there was "an essential oneness of the problems and difficulties of the Jews. . . . Jews are a people; they are neither a church, nor a creed" (Institute for Jewish Affairs 1948: 48). Nahum Goldmann, one of the delegates, later president of the Congress, declared, "The new Moloch of totalitarian Statism is preparing brutally to subordinate to itself all the richer, higher, and holier values of human culture" (49), adding, "The international safeguard of minority rights, guaranteed by the League of Nations, hardly amounts to anything now" (49).[40] Totalitarianism was not yet the analytical tool it would become in the 1950s, but it was nevertheless part of a collective Jewish experience. Before the rise of the Nazis in Germany, the chief physical danger to Jews came from the Soviet Union. The Bolshevik revolution in particular had dire consequences for one of the largest Jewish communities in Russia.

Little is known about Arendt's attendance at the Congress, but she clearly took away a political vision of Judaism.[41] Her future husband wrote to her that he thought the Jewish cause should be combined with the cause of the oppressed peoples of the world, and that the Jews should fight in Spain on the side of the international brigades. Arendt replied, on August 24, 1936, that the Jews were unlike any other people, a people without territory (Arendt and Blücher 2000: 14–18). She clearly believed at the time in the national revival of the Jews, which would also frame her demand for a Jewish army to fight the Nazis five years later. When Arendt emigrated to the United States a few years later, she put these ideas into practice. Her first paid position in the States was with a Jewish organization called Jewish Cultural Reconstruction. Its task was to rescue the physical remains of

Jewish culture (books, manuscripts, scrolls, and other artifacts, both religious and secular) confiscated by the Nazis.

In her work with the JCR, first as research director and then as executive director, Arendt was able to translate her Jewish political theory into lived practice. Over time, delving into the past became a theoretical as well as a practical task. Her approach to the past drew heavily on her reading of Benjamin. She ended her essay on Benjamin and his gift for thinking poetically with a statement that could just as well describe her own method of thinking:

> And this thinking, fed by the present, works with the "thought frag-ments" it can wrest from the past and gather about itself. Like a pearl diver who descends to the bottom of the sea, not to excavate the bottom and bring it to light but to pry loose the rich and the strange, the pearls and the coral in the depths, and to carry them to the surface, this thinking delves into the depth of the past – but not in order to resuscitate it in the way it was and to contribute to the renewal of extinct ages. What guides this thinking is the conviction that although the living is subject to the ruin of the time, the process of decay is at the same time a process of crystallization, that in the depth of the sea, into which it sinks and is dissolved [in] what once was alive, some things "suffer a sea-change" and survive in new crystallized forms and shapes that remain immune to the elements, as though they waited only for the pearl diver who one day will come down to them and bring them up into the world of the living – as "thought fragments," as something "rich and strange," and perhaps even as everlasting Urphänomene. (Arendt 1968b: 205–6)

Let us turn now to the translation of those theoretical issues into practical politics.

# — 3 —

# FRANKFURT, JERUSALEM, OFFENBACH, AND NEW YORK: JEWS AND EUROPE

Jewish multilingualism is one of the keys to understanding a critical historical episode in Jewish politics following World War II and the Holocaust. At stake was the future of the Jewish past. The Nazis looted Jewish cultural materials, and after the war, when most of the former owners (whether individual or collective) had perished, the problematic question of "who owns Jewish culture" arose. Hannah Arendt played a significant role in this episode. For a book-centered people like the Jews, the destruction of culture meant first of all the destruction of books.[1] The connotation of the Jews as "the People of the Book" means, of course, the centrality of the Bible, but also more than that. Books were part of Jewish social structure in the absence of state and territory.[2] The Nazi attempt to destroy the Jewish people was thus deliberately accompanied by the destruction of its books as well.[3] This was not even done secretly but was part of a proud material and cultural eradication. On March 28, 1941, the *Frankfurter Zeitung* reported on the destruction of the largest Talmudic library in Poland, the famous Lublin Library. "We threw the huge Talmudic library out of the building and carried the books out to the market place, where we set them on fire," the article read. "The fire lasted twenty hours. The Lublin Jews assembled around and wept bitterly, almost silencing us with their cries. We summoned the military band, and with joyful shouts the soldiers drowned out the sounds of the Jewish cries" (quoted in Friedman 1957–8: 5–6).[4]

The destruction of someone else's culture is perpetrated not only through the obliteration of physical artifacts; it can also be accomplished through appropriation. Ironically, part of the Jewish cultural heritage survived, and it was centralized and catalogued because

40

many agencies of the National Socialist project worked to preserve these objects with the same thoroughness and diligence that other agencies devoted to destroying the humans who created them. Various Nazi agencies and institutions were involved in so-called *Judenforschung* (research on Jews),[5] and several institutions, at times with conflicting goals, were founded for this purpose. Organizations such as the Institut der NSDAP zur Erforschung der Judenfrage (National Socialist German Workers' Party Institute for Research on the Jewish Question) and the Forschungsabteilung Judenfrage (Research Branch for the Jewish Problem) were set up to study Jews and Judaism and began to loot Jewish libraries in Germany and in Reich-occupied countries during the war. Another important agency, the Einsatzstab Reichsleiter Rosenberg (ERR), was created in July 1940 and coordinated by Alfred Rosenberg, who also founded the Institut der NSDAP zur Erforschung der Judenfrage in Frankfurt the following year.

At around the same time that Arendt arrived in the United States, in March 1941, Rosenberg convened a conference to open the Institute.[6] In Rosenberg's view, the so-called Jewish question was first of all a European question, and it called for a European "solution." It was clear to the attendees that Jews could no longer remain in Europe. Rosenberg's keynote address, "The Jewish Question as a World Problem," emphasized that research on Jews was indeed possible and that whoever denied this was simply expressing the weakness of liberalism itself.[7] The speech was designed as an attempt to negate the French Revolution and the Jews allegedly responsible for it. In a manner by this time familiar, Rosenberg went on to depict the Jewish influence on the United States, comparing research on Jews to research on poisonous plants: one needed to understand poisons in order to counteract them. Rosenberg assured his audience that the inevitable German victory would make it possible to "secure" important Jewish documents. And indeed, Rosenberg's ERR confiscated one of the most important Jewish collections in Germany, the Judaica Collection of the City Library of Frankfurt. Rosenberg planned to open a library on world Jewry as part of the Hohe Schule für Nazi Kultur und Weltanschauung (Advanced School for Nazi Culture and Ideology), which was designed to inculcate in the party elite its anti-Semitic ideological foundations.

Jewish books and manuscripts were plundered all over Europe. By 1944, Rosenberg and his staff, together with other institutions, had looted more than two hundred Jewish library collections and confiscated more than three million books from some one thousand libraries throughout Europe. This was one of the largest cultural

41

despoliations in history.[8] In Poland alone, before 1939, there were more than 250 Jewish libraries housing 1.6 million books.

Arendt was well aware of these efforts through her practical and theoretical work. In 1946, she reviewed Max Weinreich's book on Hitler's professors and argued that Weinreich took them too seriously. "Their shame is pettier than that and they were hardly ever guilty of having 'ideas,'" she wrote.[9] The purpose of this kind of pseudoscience lies, of course, in its rationales. The Nazis wanted to destroy the Jews, and in order to do so, they felt they had to study the so-called enemy. The British Jewish historian Cecil Roth (1899–1970), who was active in the process of Jewish cultural reconstruction, described the Nazis' approach in 1944: "What use are Nazis to likely make of such material? Some of you may wonder. The answer is very simple. They are among the very few persons in the world today who take Jewish scholarship seriously."[10]

It may strike the twenty-first-century reader as strange that Arendt would even consider some of this so-called research for her study on totalitarianism, but her work on restitution made her familiar with the various institutions in Nazi Germany in charge of research on the Jews. Thus in a footnote she mentions Walter Frank, a notorious Nazi historian (who committed suicide on May 9, 1945) as someone who, "in spite of his official position under the Nazis, remained somewhat careful about his sources and methods" (Arendt 1951: 21n14). If we see the Nazis' rationale as emphasizing difference, it can have a positive bent. In this sense, all preoccupations with difference can serve different ideological functions. The language of "race," for example, can be used either positively or negatively.

This point is directly linked to restitution. Before claims for restitution could be made, a legal framework had to be formulated. International law, according to which only states could claim restitution, had to be modified. Formerly private property needed to be transformed into collective property as a consequence of historical catastrophe.[11] Thus the legal status of the Jews had to be changed from "minority" to "collective." This was done first on a legal, theoretical level through two groundbreaking studies, both published in 1944: Siegfried Moses's *Die Jüdischen Nachkriegsforderungen* (Jewish Claims after the War), and Nehemiah Robinson's *Indemnification and Reparations: Jewish Aspects*.[12] These texts laid the foundation for one of the most influential legal rulings in the history of the Jews. The law was changed to allow the property of murdered Jews and obliterated communities to be redefined as the property of a legally recognized stateless collective – the Jewish people – whose claims were not only equal to, but in many cases emerged as superior to, the claims of nation-states. These two books reflected two approaches to the future of the Jewish people and its claim to heirless Jewish property. Siegfried Moses was one of the leaders of the German Zionist movement (he later became Israel's first state comptroller), and his account was based on the Zionist assumption that the Jewish Agency should be put in charge of these processes. Nehemiah Robinson, for his part, demanded the creation of a new transnational federation of agencies representing Jews from all over the world. Robinson's ideas bore fruit in the form of the legal incorporation of several Jewish successor organizations that considered themselves the legal representatives of the Jewish people.

Just as Moses' legal framework was based on his Zionism, so Robinson's grew out of his political and ideological background. Robinson was a lawyer from Lithuania; he served as head of the Institute of Jewish Affairs, the research wing of the World Jewish Congress. The Institute of Jewish Affairs was deeply involved in the politics of Jewish minority rights in the period between the two world wars. As mentioned above, a form of collective Jewish politics emerged during this period to defend Jewish interests that were different from but parallel to Zionism. This difference in political attitude carried over into the immediate aftermath of the Holocaust, when efforts focused on restitution for the Jewish people. Once again, Zionists and Diaspora Jews had to coordinate their perceptions and aims and cooperate in early restitution efforts. Together they had to convince the rest of the world – especially America – of the claims they both took as a starting point: that the "Jewish people" had the same rights to restitution as nation-states and that any Jewish organization speaking on their behalf could legally claim to be the lawful successor to Jewish property holders.

It may be difficult to conceptualize questions of restitution, justice, redress, suffering, forgiveness, and even morality in collective terms. This may be due to two very different systems of behavior, differentiated both in our historical memory and in social theory. On the one hand, economic behavior is supposed to be self-regarding, rational, and calculating; on the other hand, moral behavior is supposed to be undertaken without thought of gain, based on intrinsic values, and altruistic. To act morally is to override one's personal interest and act "on principle." Restitution, however, by its very nature, combines the economic and the ethical. The Holocaust constitutes a particular moment, an epoch-making event that over the past six decades has become a defining moment in the self-understanding of the western world, often making it difficult to understand in the West that this is not universally understood (Levy and Sznaider 2005). The Holocaust has gained this symbolic stature not only because of the astounding number of people killed but mainly because of its genocidal intentions and the use of industrialized modes of mass extermination. By raising basic questions of morality, reason, and humanity, the Holocaust constitutes a paradigmatic case for the relation between modernity and social theory. Modernity, the primary analytic and normative framework for social theory, itself is not spared. From this perspective, the mass murder of European Jews by the Nazis is not only a German–Jewish tragedy but a tragedy of modernity itself.[13] Jews were supposed to be equal, but the Nazis brought back a world of social hierarchies that we had thought no longer existed.

It is important to emphasize how the concept of honor is inextricably linked to inequality. Charles Taylor (1992) makes this point quite clearly: for some to have honor, others must not. When the currency of social life was honor, Jews were among the excluded. They were *unehrenhaft*, "not honorable," and therefore *satisfaktionsunfähig*, or "incapable of giving satisfaction," that is, of demanding a duel to prove their honor. The bourgeois concept analogous to honor is "dignity." Unlike honor, it applies to everyone. Everyone can have it, everyone can lose it, and everyone can fight for it. It is an egalitarian concept, and it is therefore compatible with democratic society. Dignity is a universalist concept that is therefore compatible with equal citizenship. Universality was anathema to the Nazi mind precisely because it obliterates distinctions, which for them constituted the ultimate social reality. If every individual is unique, then any attempt to generalize is doomed to eradicate precisely what is most important about people. In political terms, distinctions that matter cannot be changed by human effort. This is like saying that virtue is a function of blood alone. In many ways, this is also the source of modern anti-Semitism. It created an untenable dilemma for the Jews after the Holocaust because all collective efforts to restore honor and property had to accept the definition of the Jews as a collective, which included the danger to collectivize individuals, which is exactly what the Nazis did to individual Jews. Part of this quandary arises from the circumstance that there is no unitary Jewish language. Jews are multilingual by definition. Some of them, of course, speak the holy language of Hebrew, which later became the national language of Israel. But most Eastern European Jews spoke Yiddish, which varied from region to region, while others spoke the language of the countries in which they lived.

After the war, many of the books and manuscripts the Nazis had confiscated ended up in a depot in Offenbach under the control of the US Army, where more than three million books and manuscripts the Germans had amassed were processed. This situation was rendered even more paradoxical in that the Nazis in many ways "saved" Jewish artifacts as a matter of official policy.[14] Whenever prior ownership could be established, the Americans shipped the materials back to the country of origin in probably one of the largest restitution efforts ever carried out. In an ironic twist of poetic justice, the sentencing and execution of Alfred Rosenberg by the International Military Tribunal in Nuremberg took place on October 16, 1946, even as the Allies were undoing his wartime work. He was also hanged for the organized plunder of both public and private property throughout the occupied countries of Europe, which the Tribunal defined as "a crime against humanity." The International Military Tribunal's definition of Rosenberg's crimes against Jewish life and culture as heinous contraventions against all humanity had enormous consequences for the future memory of the Holocaust. The fate of Jewish cultural property, however, was in jurisprudential limbo at the time. It was unclear what constituted Jewish property as compared to the property of various nations whose legal systems had remained intact. The idea of Jewish collective property had to be legally formulated and fought for, and these battles pitted groups with different agendas and resources against each other. For instance, certain American-Jewish organizations, such as the Hebrew University in Jerusalem, considered themselves as eligible to represent the collective claims of the Jewish people. Americans, as the occupying power in large parts of Western Europe, were put in charge of huge depots of heirless cultural property (aside from books), much of it originating in the Jewish communities of Eastern Europe. The American authorities had to maneuver between the interests of the Hebrew University, the interests of American-Jewish organizations, those of newly emerging Jewish communities in Germany and Europe, and, lastly, their own political interests, especially in relation to the claims and demands of the Soviet Union against the backdrop of the emerging Cold War.[15] After the actual picture of the Jewish catastrophe in Europe became clear, Jews in the United States, Palestine, and elsewhere realized that they had to take responsibility for the postwar fate of European Jews.

Emissaries of the Hebrew University in Jerusalem, among them Gershom Scholem, Avraham Yaari, Hugo Bergmann, and Shlomo Shunami (all prominent members of the Hebrew University faculty),[16] traveled to Europe to sort and salvage Jewish books and take them back to Jerusalem. At the same time, American-Jewish organizations were active in similar efforts; the most important of these was Jewish Cultural Reconstruction (JCR), under the leadership of Salo Baron, a Jewish historian at New York's Columbia University, and, of course, Hannah Arendt, the JCR's research director at the time. Because Arendt was a research director of the Jewish Cultural Reconstruction Commission in the late 1940s, she was familiar with the organizational structure of the different agencies dealing with Jewish cultural property.

At times, the emissaries from Jerusalem and New York cooperated, especially when it came to forming a common front against the German bureaucracy or the newly established Jewish communities in Germany, who had their own property claims. At other times, however, they competed not only over books but also over the moral high ground and the right to the "true" representation of the Jewish people as a collective entity.[17] Thus Jews (but not only Jews) faced a conceptual dilemma after the Holocaust. The Nazis categorized Jews as a separate nation, regardless of their citizenship. In contradistinction, classical international law did not recognize nations without territory. There were no legal categories that could provide the Jews, as Jews, with a lawful right to make collective claims for their looted property.[18] How could stateless and exiled people come forward and file legally recognizable claims?

This is, of course, not a Jewish problem alone, but one of general significance in the study of the aftermath of genocide: is the entirety of a people, as a collective to whom a destroyed minority belongs, entitled to the property left by its kin? This was the major question confronting the Jews as a people without a state of their own after World War II.[19] The question of equal citizenship lost its relevance. After the Holocaust, the political thinking of the Jews was organized around Jews as a collectivity and their rights as a collectivity. But it also became clear to organized Jewry (in the form of organizations like the World Jewish Congress) that the restoration of Jewish life in Europe to a kind of status quo ante was no longer possible. Many Jewish refugees refused to be repatriated to Eastern European states. As a result, Jewish organizations, including the Hebrew University of Jerusalem before the establishment of the state of Israel, pressed their case and demanded to be legally treated as though they were states. Had they failed in this project, heirless Jewish property would have either remained in Germany or been returned to Eastern Europe, where almost no Jewish communities remained.

Today's definition of "minorities" can be misconstrued as reflecting a long-standing universal phenomenon. This ahistorical perception has frequently led to a misreading of human rights terminology that stems from events during the second half of the twentieth century. In fact, the distinction between nations (majorities) and minorities is a rather recent one. Jews as a collective had to maneuver around these issues and thus created the situation of collective ascription. The Nazis targeted the Jews as such at a time when many Jews did not define themselves collectively anymore.

Salo Baron, a specialist in Jewish history at Columbia University in New York, played a major role in this effort.[20] Baron was born in Tarnow, Galicia, in 1895. He studied in Vienna when Tarnow turned from a Habsburgian into a Polish city, and he left for the United States in 1926. Shorty after his arrival, he published his paradigmatic article titled "Ghetto and Emancipation,"[21] in which he presented a critique of modernity and Jewish emancipation from a Jewish histori-cal angle. This was in many ways the historical version of Arendt's philosophical essay of 1932, "Enlightenment and the Jewish Ques-tion." Baron also suggested a different historical timeline. He criti-cized the view that emancipation was positive gain for the Jews as a collective, thus challenging the position shared by most Jewish histo-rians of his time. For Baron, the Middle Ages were actually a favor-able era for the Jews. He rejected as ahistorical the view that Jews lacked equal rights: "In the Jewish 'Middle Ages,' it is said, the Jews did not have 'equal rights.' But to say that pre-Emancipatory Jewry did not have equal rights with the rest of the population does not mean that Jewry was the subject of unfavorable discrimination. The simple fact is that there was no such thing then as 'equal rights'" (Baron 1964 [1928]: 51). Jews – like other corporations – enjoyed a certain measure of autonomy, which could provide protection at times. The modern state, which according to Baron needed Jewish emancipation more than the Jews needed it, made assimilation a prerequisite. This situation rendered Jews, as individuals, dependent on the state for protection.

This was not necessarily a Zionist position. Baron believed that Jews could live in the Diaspora (although he thought that after 1945 the European Diaspora was no longer viable). Baron argued for an active minority politics that demanded equal rights without assimila-tion. He believed that only Jewish autonomy could limit the power of states over Jews. Writing five years before the Nazis came to power in Germany, he argued that it was clear that

47

Emancipation has not brought the Golden Age. While Emancipation has brought a reduction of ancient evils, and while its balance sheet for the world at large and for the Jews is favorable, it is not completely clear of debits. Certainly its belief in the efficacy of a process of complete assimilation has been proved untenable. Autonomy as well as equality must be given its place in the modern State, and much time must pass before these two principles will be fully harmonized and balanced. Perhaps the chief task of this and future generations is to attain that harmony and balance. Surely, it's time to break with the lachrymose theory of pre-Revolutionary woe, and to adopt a view more in accord with historic truth. (63)

Baron reconstructed Jewish history before the French Revolution as a history of autonomy and political action. His argument was not for universality but rather for autonomy and privileges.[22] Baron's criticism of the "lachrymose" version of Jewish history (a history of suffering and martyrs) became the foundation for his political and cultural work, in which the Jews as an autonomous collective, rather than a territory, were at the center. Baron was also convinced that the Jews as a transnational people were always in need of a transnational order for their protection.[23] Baron was convinced that the Jews would do better if their status was guaranteed by an international order. He always believed that the so-called Jewish problem transcended national boundaries and therefore needed an international political agency. It is thus not surprising that Baron viewed the anti-Jewish legislation passed in Nuremberg in 1935 not as a return to medieval barbarism but as a product of the modern age.[24] Indeed, Baron saw the Nuremberg laws as unprecedented: "The Nazi attempt, consequently, to place the non-Aryans and a number of professed political and religious dissenters outside of the pale of a united German citizenry is not a re-erection of the medieval legal structure, but the establishment of a new, unprecedented legal status" (Baron 1935: 1). This argument anticipated Arendt's insight, after the war, that totalitarianism and the concentration camps constituted an unprecedented phenomenon of the modern age.[25]

The year Arendt arrived in New York, she paid a visit to Salo Baron (they had mutual friends) to discuss the situation of the Jews in Vichy France.[26] Apparently Arendt told Baron that she believed in the continuity of anti-Semitism in France from Dreyfus to Pétain. Baron encouraged her to write, and Arendt's first academic publication was the result.[27] This was the beginning of a lifelong friendship between Baron and Arendt.[28] Baron belonged to a group of Jewish intellectuals in New York (most of them with Eastern European backgrounds) who devoted themselves to researching and understanding the consequences of Nazi policies toward Jews in Europe and the United States (see Liberles 1995: 221ff.). In 1936, they established an organization called the Conference on Jewish Relations, which positioned itself as a response to Nazi research on Jews. In 1937, the conference founded an academic journal, *Jewish Social Studies* (still published today), with Salo Baron as its editor; Arendt wrote for it frequently after arriving in America. Significantly, American-Jewish intellectuals felt responsible for the fate of their brethren in Europe, and felt a common bond with them that transcended the bonds of citizenship. Furthermore, they were concerned that the anti-Semitic messages coming out of Germany would somehow poison public opinion in the United States as well. One of the conference's first studies was a book that examined the international dimension of Germany's racial laws and provided a wide-ranging discussion of national sovereignty and what states could do to/with their own citizens.[29] The book also stressed that attacks on Jews were attacks not only on them but on humanity as a whole, thus making an argument that would later become crucial in connection with the Holocaust. Were the Nazi atrocities crimes against humanity or crimes against the Jewish people? This question was also central to Arendt's later work.[30]

In 1944, the Conference on Jewish Relations founded the Commission for European Jewish Cultural Reconstruction; initially its mission was defined as reconstructing Jewish life in Europe, but the Commission soon realized that it needed to salvage the remainder of Jewish material culture from Germany and wider Europe.[31] In an article published in *Commentary* in November 1945, Baron mentioned the large collections of Judaica assembled by the Nazis and argued that it was the task of Jewish organizations to ensure that these materials be returned to the Jewish people as a collective.[32] Baron also criticized the beginning of the human rights regime as insufficient to the task of protecting Jews as Jews and made the case for upholding the minority rights of Jews.

Thus, overall, the intellectual affinity between Baron and Arendt led to a professional and intellectual cooperation that lasted for several decades. Both thinkers shared a critical view of Jewish history and modernity, and both were critical when it came to Jewish emancipation and its call to abandon Jewish distinctiveness. Both were convinced that the Enlightenment and Jewish emancipation posed a problem for Jewish tradition and history that could not be solved by the conferral of equal citizenship alone. More important, neither Baron nor Arendt believed that Jewish history was a history of

49

suffering alone. Rather, they felt that Jews were more than the objects of history and that there was a hidden tradition of Jewish activism that needed to be rediscovered and reclaimed. Thus, when Arendt reviewed Gershom Scholem's book on Jewish mysticism in 1948, in which Scholem attempted to recover the "hidden" Jewish tradition of political action – hidden in the sense that although it was a tradition of glory and honor visible in the public word, also it was at the same time hidden from the public eye – she wrote about the mainstream of Jewish history: "In sharp contrast to all other nations, the Jews were not history makers but history sufferers, preserving a kind of eternal identity of goodness whose monotony was disturbed only by the equally monotonous chronicle of persecution and pogroms" (Arendt 2007: 303).

This claim came straight out of Baron's attacks on the "lachrymose" version of Jewish history. Given their intellectual kinship, it was only natural that Baron would hire Arendt in 1944 to be the research director of the JCR, her first paid position in her new country and a position that would lead to her first journeys back to Europe. Arendt's theoretical and practical work began to merge around this time, informed as it was by activism, volunteerism, and the desire to act politically. In addition, Arendt did not want to perceive herself as a helpless victim. This was a position that would often put her on a confrontational course with other Jews. Arendt's work during this period became engaged, more journalistic than philosophical, reflecting her desire to combine theoretical and practical concerns.

Her work with the JCR became a gateway for her thinking on matters Jewish. She published many of her essays in these years in Jewish publications like *Aufbau* (literally, Reconstruction), *Jewish Social Studies*, the *Menorah Journal*, the *Contemporary Jewish Record*, *Commentary*, *Partisan Review*, the *Jewish Frontier*, and others.[33] Her politically most engaged essays were published in *Aufbau*, a German-language newspaper written and published by Jews who had emigrated from Germany.[34] It was in the pages of *Aufbau* that Arendt advocated the formation of a Jewish army that would fight the Nazis. At around the time when German Einsatztruppen were slaughtering tens of thousands of Jews, Arendt wrote emotionally charged articles for *Aufbau* in which she demanded that Jews make themselves into a nation: "A Jewish army is not utopian if the Jews of all countries demand it and are prepared to volunteer for it," she wrote in November 1941, in an essay called "The Jewish Army – The Beginning of Jewish Politics?"

But what is utopian is the notion that we could profit in some way from Hitler's defeat, if we do not contribute to it. Only the real war of the Jewish people against Hitler will put an end – and an honorable end – to all fantastic talk about a Jewish war. An old and very contemporary Zionist proverb says that freedom is no gift. Freedom is also not a price for suffering endured. One truth that is unfamiliar to the Jewish people, though they are beginning to learn it, is that you can defend yourself as the person you are attacked as. A person attacked as a Jew cannot defend himself as an Englishman or Frenchman. (Arendt 2007: 137)

This is a fascinating demand, coming on the heels of the Nazi attack on the Soviet Union at a time when the slaughter of Jews had reached unheard-of proportions in Europe. How could Arendt see Jews as a people who could form an army, when they were neither a sovereign nation nor yet a collective, when indeed, they were at their most powerless?[35] Arendt's answer was that the Nazis' attack on the Jews *created* that collective, created a mirror image of anti-Semitic fantasies, which she completely recast. She truly believed that the Jews could be among those actively engaged in fighting Hitler in Europe. Her essays for *Aufbau* were more emotionally charged than any of her other writing. Her criticism of the Enlightenment and "the Jewish question" had come full circle and now encompassed not only Salo Baron's conception of Jewish history but also the Nazi slaughter of the Jews. Arendt was not talking about territorial sovereignty – that was not her point – but she wanted the Jews to be a political people. In one of her later essays in *Aufbau* (September 8, 1944), she reported proudly that Jews were fighting as Jews in partisan units under a Jewish flag (Arendt 2007: 221–4). A few months earlier, on April 21, she wrote a very emotional piece commemorating the anniversary of the Warsaw ghetto uprising, in which she said, "Honor and glory are new words in the political vocabulary of our people" (Arendt 2007: 199). As usual, she moved constantly between the particular and the universal.

Arendt tried to formulate a political space located between the particular, belonging to a people, and the universality of humanness, without relinquishing either one. For her, Jewish fate lay in the tension between these poles. Assimilated Jews no longer had a collective history, which made them easy targets of anti-Semitic resentment. At the same time, anti-Semites fantasized about Jewish collective power, which was exactly what Arendt demanded. Clearly, she did not want to sacrifice Jewish particularity for universal

51

equality, especially not when the Nazis were attacking precisely that kind of equality. Since Arendt did not want to be identified with right-wing Zionist attempts to form a Jewish army, she founded her own Jewish group in 1942, Die Jungjüdische Gruppe (the Young Jewish Group), as a forum for public discussion of the future of Jewish politics.[36] Its meetings were conducted in German.[37] The invitation to the first meeting, held on March 11, 1942, already read like a political platform: "The Jungjüdische Gruppe invites those individuals to a meeting who do not consider themselves arbitrary victims of a catastrophic event, but rather feel co-responsible for the future of the Jewish people" (my translation).

At the first meeting Arendt and her co-founder Josef Maier gave a paper on the "theoretical foundation of politics" in which they argued that Jewish identity has clear political and historical dimensions: "The subject of Jewish politics is not an arbitrary concept or some kind of empty definition of a Jewish human being, but solely and uniquely about real Jewish people who actually exist – the people whose enemies want to destroy it" (my translation). Because Arendt had started to think about these issues before the catastrophe of Nazi Germany and the war (in her essay on the Enlightenment, for example), this argument reinforced her belief that the only viable answer for modern Jews is politics – not necessarily Zionist politics, but collective politics of some kind.

That Arendt's thinking had also come full circle is also reflected in an essay she published in the Zionist newspaper *Jüdische Rundschau* on April 7, 1933, a few months after the Nazis came to power, called "Original Assimilation," which she began with the statement: "Today in Germany it seems that Jewish assimilation must declare its bankruptcy" (Arendt 2007: 22). It was as though she was challenging Herder in her belief in the distinctiveness of peoples. The Jungjüdische Gruppe was an attempt to kindle an intra-Jewish debate regarding questions of Jewish nationalism and Zionism, which for Arendt were not necessarily the same thing. She saw criticism as an internal affair. As she wrote on April 3, 1942, in *Aufbau*, "The criticism the Jewish patriot offers his own people is intended to prepare them better for the struggle" (Arendt 2007: 152). Her criticism of territorial Zionism was internal criticism, just as, I would argue, *Eichmann in Jerusalem*, written roughly twenty years later, was intended as internal criticism.

But this kind of criticism was already present in her writings in the 1940s, in her work for the JCR and also as an editor for Schocken Books. While living the life of a Jewish official – actually something like a civil servant – Arendt criticized Zionist politics. Again, this was criticism from within, since she always respected the Zionists for their political activism. This criticism culminated in her famous essay "Zionism Reconsidered," published in the *Menorah Journal* in 1944 (Arendt 2007: 343–73), the opening salvo in years of arguments with her Zionist friends that reached its peak with the Eichmann book. She rejected the Zionist movement's claim that the only way to meet the challenges of Nazism was the foundation of a Jewish sovereign state. Even in 1944, she still believed in a transnational Jewish politics independent of the big powers. She also believed that Zionism was based on obsolete nineteenth-century ideologies like nationalism and socialism.

Arendt was looking for a cosmopolitan Jewish politics in the depths of the Jews' darkest hour. The Zionist belief at the time was that Jews needed their own sovereign state to protect themselves. In Arendt's view, this was an admission of weakness that she was not willing to make. She thought the Jews were stronger than they actually were at the time. At the same time, she had set the terms of the debate, distinguishing between politicized Jews who understood themselves as cosmopolitan actors and Jews who believed that only the sovereignty of a state could protect them. She concluded that the Zionists were wrong to trust in the national state as a guarantor of security. Instead, she introduced her hope for a federal principle of political organization, not only for Jews but for all European peoples. Thus, she wrote in "Zionism Reconsidered," for Jews, "there is only too little reason for rejoicing in the decline of the national state and of nationalism. We cannot foretell the next steps of human history, but the alternatives seem to be clear. The resurgent problem of how to organize politically will be solved by adopting either the form of empires or the form of federations" (371). She expressed her hope that federalism could be a sound alternative to what she considered an outdated nationalism.

Scholem, in many ways an "outdated" nationalist himself, disagreed, and wrote a rather lengthy letter from Jerusalem dated January 28, 1946, when both were working for the JCR and it had become painfully clear what had happened in Europe. Scholem expressed his bitter disappointment in Arendt's position.[38] He made his point quickly: "your article has nothing to do with Zionism but is instead a patently anti-Zionist, warmed-over version of Communist criticism, infused with a vague galut nationalism" (330). Scholem was wrong that Arendt's criticism was communist, but he was right in accusing her of *galut* (i.e., diasporic) nationalism. Arendt could not

53

have defined her position better than by calling herself a Diaspora nationalist. Scholem was, of course, debating within an inner Jewish circle and could not relate to any other views of Diaspora nationalism.[39] Scholem accused Arendt of denouncing Jews for fending for themselves in their darkest hour and emphasized his own unabashed nationalism: "I am a nationalist and am wholly unmoved by ostensibly 'progressive' denunciation of a viewpoint that people repeatedly, even in my earliest youth, deemed obsolete" (331). But Scholem went even further, reminding Arendt again of the concept of the Jews' hidden tradition: "I do not give a rap about the problem of the state, because I do not believe that the renewal of the Jewish people depends on the question of their political or even social organization. My own political credo is, if anything, anarchistic." He went on to argue a point that seems to have been debated in 1946 as well as in 2010: "But I cannot blame the Jews if they ignore so-called progressive theories which no one else in the world has ever practiced." Scholem was actually part of a small political group called Brith Shalom (Covenant of Peace) which in the 1920s and early 1930s was not interested in sovereign statehood but had other political concepts in mind. He belonged to a group of Jewish cosmopolitan nationalists before the concept even existed. They advocated an idea they called "binationalism" in Palestine, which was based on the sharing of sovereignty.[40] The members of Brith Shalom did not want to transplant European modes of ethnic domination to the situation of Jews and Arabs in Palestine. Arendt, who supported Brith Shalom from afar, would probably have agreed on these issues until the mid-1930s, but the rise of Nazism also changed the makeup of Jewish nationalism. The Arendt–Scholem controversy is part of the Jewish political reaction to the threat of Nazism.

Arendt did, of course, answer Scholem (as she did again seventeen years later, when the two clashed again over the Eichmann book).[41] First of all, she rejected being labeled a communist, concluding her letter, "I have always considered your position as a Jew to be a political one, and I've always had the greatest respect for your decision to take the political reality of Palestine seriously." She admired Scholem for his Jewish politics, and even learned about the hidden tradition of the Jews from his work. But she did not like his Zionism. At approximately the time that World War II ended, Arendt published an essay in the *Jewish Frontier* in which she talks about the transnationalism of anti-Semitism and rejects nationalism as the answer. "Thus the 'national state,' having lost its very foundation, leads the life of a walking corpse, whose spurious existence is artificially prolonged by repeated injections of imperialist expansion."[42] And in 1950 she published an article in *Review of Politics* called "Peace or Armistice in the Near East?" in which she again proposes federalism as the solution for the Near East.[43] This essay concludes with the claim that "national sovereignty, which so long had been the very symbol of free national development, has become the greatest danger to national survival for small nations" (450). Arendt refused to see sovereignty as the solution for the Jewish homeland.[44] The distinction between homeland and sovereign nation-state separated her national sentiments from those of Scholem. Around the same time, both Arendt and Scholem were thrown into Jewish politics and agreed on the need to save Jewish books in order to redefine Jewish culture after the war. Their personal fates became intertwined, but this was not only about personal fate. Their lives expressed different Jewish political options at the most critical juncture in the collective life of the Jews.[45]

Arendt's work for the JCR was a translation of her theoretical thoughts into political praxis. Her first task as research director – this was around the same time she was writing about Kafka and the meaning of language for Jewish writers (Young-Bruehl 2004: 189ff.) – was to compile an inventory of Jewish cultural artifacts. She accomplished this task with the help of a network of European-Jewish refugees in the United States, England, and Palestine, and published the first list under the title "Tentative List of Jewish Cultural Treasures in Axis-Occupied Countries."[46] Four more lists followed between 1946 and 1948. These lists are usually not included in the Arendt canon, but they are among her important publications on Jewish matters and should be considered as such. Arendt cooperated with many Jewish archivists and librarians to compile these lists, and they served as an efficient countermeasure to the plunder of Rosenberg and his cronies. It is no surprise that the first list starts with a list of the the major anti-Semitic research institutions, many of which benefited from the robbery.

These were the same lists used by the Jewish organizations (and especially by the American military) to reconstruct the losses and try to obtain restitution. In 1974, Salo Baron summed up the contributions of these lists as follows:

> The Commission prepared a number of studies surveying the Jewish cultural treasures preserved in libraries, museums, and archives, Jewish educational institutions, the Jewish press, and the Jewish publishing firms which had existed in Nazi-occupied Europe before the War. On the basis of these studies, which appeared as supplements to our

quarterly, we could not only demonstrate the vast and irretrievable losses suffered by the world Jewish community, but also place in the hands of the various military administrations in Germany reliable reference works for whatever was still salvageable of that millennial heritage.[47]

The authors of the lists were aware that what remained of Jewish material culture in Europe had to be redistributed. Millions of books and manuscripts (roughly 3.5 million books from 430 libraries) found their way onto this list through listings from Jewish congregations, institutions, libraries, schools, publishing houses, newspapers, and journals. They came from all over occupied Europe and were written in all the European languages Jews employed. The list amounted to an alphabetical inventory of Jewish culture that cut across the various national boundaries of Europe. It included the Jewish community library of Vienna, the library of the "Consistoire Israelite" in Sofia, the community library of Tallinn in Estonia, small Jewish libraries in Venice, large libraries in Riga, a very large library in Kovno, Lithuania, the so-called Mapu Library (containing more than fifteen thousand volumes). These lists are like a shrine, preserving the Jewish culture that might have been lost for ever.

It must have been fascinating for Arendt to see the list of Jewish cultural institutions in Eastern Europe, institutions that demonstrated the cultural autonomy and rejection of assimilation. Nearly all the European languages were represented, testifying to the variety of languages in which Jews read and wrote. The lists enumerated 854 newspapers, magazines, and journals and 643 Jewish publishing houses.[48] The lists are a testimony to the tension between place and nonplace in Jewish culture; the same theological tensions mentioned in chapter 2 were manifested in material culture as well. The lists were arranged by territory, but cultural artifacts are not territorial; they are at once super- and supranational. They illustrate the exilic culture of the Jews, not the confinement of territory. The people who compiled these lists were, of course, aware of this. They wanted to prevent these cultural items from returning to these territories. The lists undermined a spatially fixed understanding of culture that was taken for granted; this was what made them revolutionary. The inventory of Jewish cultural treasures was triggered by the catastrophe of the Holocaust, but the nonspatial aspect of Jewish culture clearly goes back further than that. The lists countermanded a conception that accompanied the formation of nation-states in the eighteenth and nineteenth centuries. The Jewish catastrophe undermined the triumph of this national imagination, which in many ways also triggered the Holocaust. For the Jewish activists of the JCR, the nation-state had ceased to appear as a natural development.

The lists also included the German institutions in which looted material was housed. Arendt could see, up close, not only the rich culture of the Jews in Europe and the various languages they employed in expressing this culture, but also how various Nazi agencies operated to either destroy or appropriate this culture. The lists were an expression of the richness and variety of universal Jewish culture, but at the same time its cemetery, an instance of the "burning scrolls." Many of these treasures ended up in the Offenbach depot.[49] The committee members working in Jerusalem felt strongly that the cultural artifacts should go to Jerusalem. But, whatever their difference, both sides agreed that these books and religious artifacts and other treasures could not be returned to their countries of origin. In this sense, both sides undermined the territorial linkage to culture.

The lists also connoted death, especially the death of European Jewry and with it the death of the European-Jewish Diaspora. The restitution committees were aware that books were representative of people as well. And books were not the only thing to "resist" repatriation; many now stateless Jews resisted as well. Arendt wrote a short article in 1945 in which she talked about this resistance of Jewish refugees to repatriation.[50] She thought that many of these stateless people would insist on keeping their status as refugees in order not to return "home." The members of the JCR were aware of this type of resistance and reassigned the new Jewish locations to either the United States or Palestine (after 1948, Israel), a reassignment that meant a constant conceptual shifting between the universal and the particular in terms of the Jewish experience. This was not a recovery of the Jewish tradition in an intellectual or theological sense (and was thus unlike Rosenzweig, Scholem, Benjamin, or even Kafka). Rather, it was recovery in the mundane sense of physical repossession of lost culture, which was then remitted to new owners. Baron wanted the JCR to become the body (legally and culturally) with the right to administer these cultural goods. When Jewish organizations whose members came primarily from Europe claimed this property, it ceased to be determined territorially and became defined ethnically.

Much legal maneuvering had to occur before this could be accomplished. First, American-Jewish organizations had to persuade the American administration to support them. Jerome Michael, one of the founding members of the JCR and a professor of law at Columbia

University, wrote a very long letter – a legal brief, really – to General J. H. Hildring, in early June 1946, explaining the Jewish position after the war.[51] Michael first introduced the organization and then described Jewish culture in Europe before the war. He told Hildring about the German plunder of books and his concern with their preservation:

> They must, in the first place, be so disposed of that they can never again be misused to make war upon the Jews. . . . This implies that, to the extent that they exceed the religious and cultural needs of the Jews who may continue to reside in the countries of their origin . . . as the result of the annihilation of millions of European Jews, including most of their religious leaders, scholars and teachers, and of the dispersion of the survivors . . . they must be removed there from . . . Europe is no longer, and it is very unlikely that it can ever become, a center of Jewish spiritual and cultural activity. The great centers of such activity are now, and will continue to be, Palestine and the United States, where so many thousands of the survivors of European Jews have found refuge.

This, in a nutshell, was the thinking within Jewish circles with respect to the Jewish cultural heritage.[52] Europe had ceased to be the center of Jewish life. Thus the legal correspondence between Michael and the State Department actually had a tacit subtext, namely, the future of Jewish life in Europe. Appended to Michael's letter was the "Tentative List," so that the American administration could have some sort of grasp of the cultural treasures the organization wished to safeguard. But it was not until 1949 that the American administration accepted this argument about Jewish claims and allowed the JCR to act as the trustee of looted Jewish cultural property.

That same year, Hannah Arendt went to Germany to handle the organization's affairs, which required cooperating with the Hebrew University emissaries there. The Hebrew University, with its own organization – the Committee for the Saving of the Treasures of the Diaspora, founded in 1946 – saw fit to follow suit. At the same time, the Hebrew University in Jerusalem published a legal memorandum stating clearly that the Hebrew University should be the sole repository, thus fueling further debate over how "to make whole what has been smashed."[53] The American-Jewish organizations agreed with their Jerusalem colleagues that the sites of destruction would never again be viable places for Jews to settle. They also feared that Jewish cultural materials would again be used to "study" the Jews as enemies. Both Jerusalem and New York concurred that Europe had been reduced to a Jewish graveyard, but they disagreed on where the new nucleus of Jewish life should be located. The American members of the JCR felt that America was a viable alternative to Jerusalem. In the end, however, the Hebrew University cooperated with the JCR. This meant that the university had to renounce its claim to be the sole representative of the cultural future of the Jewish people. The university's representatives reached an agreement that 40 percent of the materials would be shipped to Jerusalem, 40 percent to New York, and the remainder to other countries in the West. Scholem and his Jerusalem colleagues, as well as Arendt and her New York colleagues, negotiated in Germany not as citizens of a state but as emissaries of the Jewish people. It is clear from their correspondence and reports that both were very conscious of the symbolism of their task. Both were intellectuals who were deeply invested in theories they had developed in which Jewish identity was not simply a function of territory but, far more so, of political action and recognition. For them, negotiating with American and German officials as equal partners – achieving that equal status – was a hugely significant step. It was an action that would reestablish the Jewish people after the catastrophe as a recognized entity in modern terms.[54] The JCR became the trustee for Jewish cultural materials.

It was clear that the organization could deal only within the American Zone of occupation in Germany and that the depot in Offenbach should be cleared out no later than 1949. The Hebrew University in Jerusalem sent a delegation to Offenbach to represent the interests of the Hebrew University as the representative of Jewish culture, the most prominent member of which was Gershom Scholem, who had left Germany in 1923 for Jerusalem and was one of Walter Benjamin's closest friends. Scholem spent several months in Europe, visiting the Offenbach depot to supervise the work of the organization.[55] Like Baron and Arendt, Scholem was a fierce critic of assimilation and favored the Zionist solution. Both Scholem and Arendt were pillars of Jewish life after the Holocaust; their cooperation and debate were typical of Jewish intellectual life after the Holocaust.[56] They agreed that what was at stake was more than so-called equal rights and involved the particular claims of a collective. Arendt and Scholem went to Germany not as "former German Jews" but as Jews who were negotiating with the Germans on behalf of the Jewish people.[57]

Scholem wrote very detailed descriptions of the pillaged libraries, documenting the ways in which the Nazis had classified and collected the stolen books. He also expressed his belief that Nazi officials had hidden many more books. Like Arendt, he had begun to realize more fully what had happened in Europe, and his report reflected his growing melancholy. Arendt wrote him from the United States on May 20, "You must be in Frankfurt by now. The sadness in Paris must have been a nightmare. I wish I could have been with you, which wouldn't help much. But at times, a witness of days past can help to get over the unreality of melancholy."[58]

We can partially reconstruct Arendt's first visit to Germany in 1949, when she was not yet an American citizen. She was stateless, and she negotiated as such with the German authorities.[59] More than 500,000 items remained behind in Offenbach. Thousands of books, manuscripts, Torah scrolls, and other artifacts of Jewish culture could not be returned because their owners had died or been murdered, and the Jewish communities that could have claimed these objects in their owners' stead no longer existed. The people in charge were well aware that they were dealing with Jewish cultural property. Their rightful owners gone, these objects became the collective property of the Jewish people. To have returned them to their countries of origin, where Jewish populations had been decimated, or – worse – to allow them to remain in Germany, would have been a travesty. Heirless cultural property became the basis for collective legal claims after the genocide. Thus the Jews not only reclaimed some of their stolen property but were also able to assert their collective rights. By 1952, the JCR had removed 439,263 items from Germany. Of these, 191,423 went to Jerusalem and 169,013 to the United States and Canada; the rest were shipped to different countries. For example, JCR staffers gathered many Torah scrolls, Torah covers, silver pointers, and other objects from destroyed Jewish communities in Europe and brought them via the Offenbach depot to the United States. There they handed them over to the Synagogue Council of America, which distributed them to Jewish congregations. Through this symbolic act, American Jewry forged a living bond with the destroyed communities of Europe.[60]

In November 1949, Arendt returned to Europe for the first time since the end of the war; she stayed until March 1950. Her correspondence with her husband, Heinrich Blücher, reflects her agitated emotional state during the visit to Germany, where she negotiated with both library directors and politicians.[61] Blücher tried to calm her, closing a letter of December 8, 1949, "Don't over-exert yourself – they are only books" (103). But Arendt could not take his advice. These were not only books for her; she was on a journey of redemption. "Almost every day I've been in a different city," she wrote Blücher on December 14, "and had appointments literally from morning to night" (Arendt and Blücher 2000). As for Scholem, confronting Germany and Germans was very difficult for Arendt. Her letter to her husband continues, "Do you know how right you were never to want to come back here again? The lump of sentimentality that begins to rise gets stuck in one's throat. The Germans are living off lifelong illusions and stupidity. . . . When I get tired, I feel completely lost. And yet there's this descriptive familiarity in everything, above all the landscape" (103–4).

Arendt went to visit her mentor Karl Jaspers, who in the meantime had left Germany and was living in Basel, Switzerland. From there she wrote another lengthy letter to her husband on December 26, in which she went into more detail about her work.

> I must probably have accomplished too much, I myself don't know. The Society of German Librarians will send an appeal to their members, and the same will happen with the museums. So far so good. But then, the president of this society in Munich told me he thought it would be good also to put out a governmental regulation, and I'm now preparing it, i.e., a regulation by the German state governments. After all, I didn't come to Germany to change German legislation. But now the strangest thing of all: One of the museum guys, a charming art historian, told me full of outrage that I should go to Heuss[62] and demand not only that items be returned, but also that reparations be made. This is an old idea of Baron's which we had given up because the American government refused point-blank to have anything to do with it. So what should I do? I imagine I'll go to Heuss. I have a good relationship with most of them – they trust me, after all we speak the same language. Dreadful are only the so-called German Jews, the communities are bands of robbers, everything uncouth and totally vulgar and nasty. When I can't handle it anymore, I escape to the Jewish American organizations. (111)

Apparently Arendt felt that she had ceased to be a German Jew altogether after she arrived in the United States. This contradicts the many clichés about her as a German Jew, an identity she refused, as we see in her speech accepting the Lessing Prize almost ten years later.[63] Arendt went beyond the aesthetic politics of Moritz Goldstein and others. She found comfort in American-Jewish organizations because these organizations represented the kind of active politics she respected. For the same reason, she resented the new Jewish communities in Germany, in which she saw people with no self-respect, people who did not act but were acted upon. This is not the snobbery of a former German Jew toward Jews from Eastern Europe but the view of someone who insisted on the importance of acting politically in a world in which most Jews had been reduced to passive victims. Her political activities in Germany were her response to what the Nazis had done to the Jews, as she wrote in her chapter "Total Domination" in *The Origins of Totalitarianism*. "Total domination," she wrote, "which strives to organize the infinite plurality and differentiation of human beings as if all of humanity were just one individual, is possible only if each and every person can be reduced to a never-changing identity of reactions, so that each of these bundles of reactions can be exchanged at random for each other" (Arendt 1951: 438). This was Arendt's dispassionate view of victimhood, something she wanted to escape through her own political activity in Germany. Unlike many of her friends from Germany, who shied away from politics, Arendt considered redemption not only in theological but in political terms. For her, the JCR was about politics, not religion. In this respect, she also accepted the resolution of the World Jewish Congress, which convened in the summer of 1948 in Montreux, Switzerland, and proclaimed "the determination of the Jewish people never again to settle on the blood-stained soil of Germany."[64] Arendt believed that the JCR would be the representative of the Jewish people as a collective and not of Jews as citizens of their respective countries. For her and her colleagues, the days of being German Jews were over. This is why she resented the attempts of Jews in Germany after the war to consolidate themselves as autonomous Jewish communities.[65] Arendt was *in* Germany but no longer *of* Germany. Her work with the JCR also points to internal Jewish conflicts about the future of Jewish life in the former sites of the Holocaust.

The field reports Arendt sent to JCR headquarters provide some details about the concrete work she conducted in Germany.[66] These reports are very businesslike; in documenting her attempts at political negotiation, she tried to refrain from injecting personal impressions. Given that many of the plundered cultural materials had ended up in German libraries, the cooperation of librarians in reclaiming them was clearly necessary. As Arendt wrote in her December 1949 report, "Without active cooperation from the German librarians nothing can be achieved" – but she was also aware that an appeal might not be enough and that a decree from above might be required. To that end, Arendt met in Munich with Dr Gustav Hoffmann, the director of the Bavarian State Library. It was Hoffmann who told her that relying on voluntary cooperation would not be enough and that the JCR should try to get the government to issue a decree mandating the return of the stolen items. Although he was skeptical that it would produce results, Hoffmann published an appeal in a librarians'

journal he edited, asking German librarians to report plundered artifacts to the JCR.[67] Although, as we have seen, Arendt had told her
husband that she had not come to Germany to change its legislation,
she nevertheless made the Tentative Lists part of every memorandum
she wrote to the politicians involved.

Arendt was constantly afraid that there could be a revival of
Nazism in Germany. On December 30, 1949, Arendt wrote to Baron,

> on the other hand, the renazification of Germany is frightening. SS
> people who are now returning from the internment camps have great
> amounts of money in their pockets – nobody knows where this money
> comes from and nobody dares to investigate. . . . This does not mean
> that I believe in a real revival of Nazism in Germany, but the atmo-
> sphere is frightful.[68]

Arendt and Scholem were corresponding on the same issue at this
time. Scholem wrote to her on January 20, 1950 that he had read
her field reports and hoped she would get a government decree, but
he also expressed his doubt. He added that he had talked to many
officials and had concluded that no one could be trusted.[69] Arendt
replied on February 5. She tried to argue with him, claiming that
there was such a thing as blind mistrust, which was as bad as blind
trust, and that not all Germans were untrustworthy; some were
people of good will who wanted to help. Arendt was perhaps recall-
ing her own 1944 essay on Kafka, in which she analyzed K., the man
who wants to enter the castle, as a man of goodwill who dies of
exhaustion. "The whole struggle remains undecided," she wrote in
that essay, "and K. dies a perfectly natural death; he gets exhausted.
What he strove to achieve was beyond the strength of any one man.
But though his purpose remained unaccomplished, his life was far
from being a failure."[70] The same could be said of the work of Arendt
and Scholem in Germany.

Scholem's mistrust appeared to be justified. The German authorities were not interested in issuing a decree.[71] The work of the
JCR came slowly to an end. Scholem and Arendt were probably
closer in their distinctive approaches to Jewish politics than they later
became in their period of mutual animosity, prompted by Arendt's
book on Eichmann. For both, the European chapter of Jewish existence had drawn to a close. Both were seeking out new models of
Jewish existence. Scholem decided to go the route of national sovereignty, while Arendt became an American Jew who believed in
the viability of diasporic life. She wanted to continue to live out the

tensions between particularism and universalism without ever really resolving them.[72] For both Arendt and Scholem, Jewish politics meant first of all speaking as a Jew, in a Jewish voice, and addressing Germans on an equal basis with Jews.[73] Melancholy suffused their attitudes and decisions. Scholem, like Arendt, rejected a post-Holocaust German identity. "After having been murdered as Jews," he wrote, "the Jews have now been nominated to the status of Germans, in a kind of posthumous triumph; to emphasize their Jewishness would be a concession to anti-Semitism. What a perversion in the name of progress, to do everything possible to avoid facing the realities of the Jewish–German relationship!" (Scholem 1976: 72). Arendt shared this attitude. She wanted to speak to Germans as a Jew. Her position was not that of a universalist but of a Jewish pariah confronting a dominant society. Arendt's work with the JCR was a Jewish answer to Zionism, which insisted that a truly Jewish life was possible only in Israel. Through her work on the lists, Arendt saw concretely that Jewish cultural property was bound not to territory but to transnational ethnicity. From there on out, the tension between Jewish culture and Jewish modernity would be played out in the tension between American and Israeli Jews. As Scholem put it, there is no language between the dead. To receive trusteeship over the cultural property of the Jews as Jews not only opened the doors to later claims of restitution but also functioned as a belated recognition of the Jews as a collective. This was equally important to both Scholem and Arendt.

Arendt published a "Report from Germany" when she returned to the United States. She never mentioned her work with the JCR, but she reflected on Germany and Germans; indeed, this essay was her personal reckoning with Germany.[74] She observed the European indifference, heartlessness, and refusal to face the events of the recent past. "The sight of Germany's destroyed cities and the knowledge of German concentration and extermination camps have covered Europe with a cloud of melancholy," she wrote (Arendt 1993c [1950]: 248–9). She mourned her Jewish identity and expressed her frustration that the Germans she met did not. Arendt also remarked on something that fifty years later would become part of Germany's past: "a deluge of stories about how Germans have suffered" (249). She offered a number of ideas about responsibility and attempts to evade it on the part of individuals, organizations, and official bodies. And she hinted presciently at a process that would also assume more organized and conscious form later: "The reality of the death factories is transformed into a mere potentiality."

This essay is written in a sad and melancholic tone, reminiscent of Scholem's reaction when he wrote about the Germans, and of Kafka's in describing K.'s travails and demise. Both Scholem and Arendt were like K., the land surveyor, in their desperate attempts to save Jewish patrimony. They knew that there was neither a way back nor a clear way forward. Both were aware that Jewish and non-Jewish memories of Europe were going their separate ways. Even when they argued about the future of the Jews, they had more in common than Jews and non-Jews did. They shared an unbridgeable memory; the bridge had been blown up by the Nazi mission to destroy the Jewish people and their culture. The JCR was an organization of American Jews, former German Jews, and former Eastern European Jews, Zionists and Jewish nationalists who opposed Zionism. But despite their disagreements, this diverse group of Jews shared a common purpose: the conduct of Jewish politics. This division between Zionist politics, which concentrated on nation-building, and Jewish Diaspora politics was carried over to the United States. This was not an abstract metaphysical issue; it was the continuation of a long Jewish tradition of minority politics in Eastern Europe. Arendt was no longer a German Jew espousing emancipation; she had become part of a tradition with roots in Eastern Europe. She was on her way to becoming an American Jew, trying to balance universal and particular identities. As she wrote in a 1947 essay for *Commentary* called "Creating a Cultural Atmosphere,"

> The Jewish people of America, on the other hand, live a reasonably safe and reasonably free life that permits them to do relatively what they please. The central and strongest part of Diaspora Jewry no longer exists under the condition of the nation-state but in a country that would annul its own constitution if it ever demanded homogeneity of population and an ethnic foundation for its state. (Arendt 2007: 302)

Arendt arrived at this American-Jewish position via the Eastern European Jewish experience. As I write, sixty-six years after the Holocaust, this Eastern European Jewish experience is identified primarily with territorial Zionism. Arendt, through her practical work, was very much aware of other Eastern European Jewish experiences and the active political struggle against what would come to be called genocide. She was very much a part of this Jewish struggle, which embodied the tension between universalism and particularism not as theoretical problems but as part of Jewish life in postwar Eastern Europe. But Arendt could never really escape her ambivalence about being Jewish and European, even German. This identity continued to influence her work, even if she was no longer primarily concerned with matters Jewish. The JCR was first of all a countermeasure against cultural genocide before the term existed. The concept of genocide as we understand it today grew first of all out of the Jewish Eastern European experience. It was coined by the Polish Jew Raphael Lemkin, who came to New York around the same time that Arendt did. Lemkin's and Arendt's intellectual projects intersected, though we do not know whether the two ever met. What we do know is that Arendt, although she used the concept of genocide, never mentioned Lemkin in her work, and Lemkin never mentioned her in his.[75] Their thoughts clashed on Jewish questions, however. The issue was not that Arendt's ideas derived from liberal and individualistic reasoning on German–Jewish emancipation, or that Lemkin was an Eastern European Jew thinking in collective and ontological terms (Benhabib 2009a: 349). Rather, both viewed the Jewish fate as a point of departure for their analyses of the fate of other ethnic and minority groups. Both saw the world through the lens of ethnic collectivities, and both were very much concerned with the struggle over minority rights in Europe between the world wars. This is the period that formed their respective worldviews, inasmuch as it was the worldview of politically minded Jews that translated Jewish thinking into cosmopolitan terms. This period, and the transition from minority to human rights, is the subject of the next chapter.

# — 4 —

# THE VIEW FROM EASTERN EUROPE:
# FROM WARSAW TO NEW YORK

Some people view the Holocaust as the culmination of the history of anti-Semitism, some see it as the apogee of the history of racism, and some consider it a crime against humanity. The differences between these points of view are subtle but crucial. Anti-Semitism is suffered only by Jews; racism, a broader category, can be experienced by anyone who is different or other; crimes against humanity are broader still, and may even be considered as crimes against the human condition. The Holocaust (the term was not used until several years after the war) constitutes an epochal break with the past, regardless of the scope of the definition. It thus has the potential to challenge basic assumptions – about the sovereign law of nation-states, for example – and to create a cosmopolitanized public and political space that reinforces moral interdependencies. This emergent cosmopolitanism exemplifies a dynamic through which global concerns become part of local experiences. My choice of the term "cosmopolitanism" as a new moral and political idiom in this connection is not arbitrary. It relates to political and intellectual trends predating the era of the nation-state. In this chapter, I show how these political and intellectual developments changed in the period between the world wars and were first of all part of Jewish lived experience, an experience in which Hannah Arendt played a crucial intellectual role at various junctures. Before the concept of the Holocaust as a description of the Nazi murder of the Jews came into being, Raphael Lemkin gave the world the concept of genocide.

In 1939, the concept of genocide did not yet exist. Raphael Lemkin, a Polish Jewish lawyer, coined the term in 1943, two years after his arrival in the United States. The concept of genocide then took on an intellectual and conceptual life of its own. Clearly, it was and is related to the destruction of European Jewry (later called the Holo-caust) but today it also means more than that.[1] The relationship between the concept of the Holocaust and the concept of genocide is also the relationship between a unique event and a more general crime.[2] Arendt did not use the term "genocide" until the 1960s. She described the tension between uniqueness and generality when she wrote of "a crime against humanity committed on the bodies of the Jewish people."[3]

Raphael Lemkin, who was six years older than Arendt, was born in 1900 in a small locality called Bezwodne, which was then part of tsarist Russia and became part of Poland after World War I. His home town was typical of places where Eastern European Jews lived in that it was partitioned, and the changes in its territorial status constantly created new allegiances and minorities. This is the context in which the term "genocide" was born.[4] Lemkin studied law and worked as a prosecutor in Warsaw; he became an expert in international law. The term "genocide" first appeared in print in 1944 in a classic study by Lemkin that has now reached legendary proportions as the seminal text of genocide studies: *Axis Rule in Occupied Europe: Laws of Occupation, Analysis of Government, Proposals for Redress*. When the book was published, by the Carnegie Foundation in Washington, DC, the mass killings of Polish Jewry, including Lemkin's own family, had already taken place. The book was Lemkin's attempt to come to terms with the unprecedented crimes of the twentieth century. In this respect it was path-breaking, not unlike Arendt's *Origins of Totalitarianism*, published seven years later but conceived and planned at around the same time as Lemkin's book. *Axis Rule in Occupied Europe* is very different from *Origins* – not a sweeping attempt to understand the twentieth century but a lawyer's almost desperate effort to come to terms with the Nazi genocide. In its structure and tone (even in its name), it is much more similar to the "Tentative List of Jewish Cultural Treasures in Axis-Occupied Countries" published two years later (see chapter 3).

Lemkin's book deals first with German techniques of occupation and reviews the laws and legislation of the occupation. The second part of the book provides an alphabetical list of the occupied coun-tries (very much like the tentative list) showing how the administra-tion of these countries was subordinated to Nazi laws. The third part consists of another alphabetical list of countries and the wording of the laws of occupation. As a lawyer, Lemkin saw the struggle against genocide first and foremost as a legal problem. He believed that in defining genocide as a crime subject to prosecution under international law, he would find a mechanism for the international protection of national and ethnic minorities.

The legal aspects of Nazi rule make up the bulk of this book, but this is not what it is remembered for. The book endures because of one short chapter, "Genocide," which took up only sixteen of the book's 674 pages. In this chapter, Lemkin conceived – one might even say invented – a new way of looking at the unprecedented. People today know, or think they know, what genocide is all about and to the extent that they do, this is largely thanks to Lemkin. Lemkin begins this chapter with the statement that "new conceptions require new terms" and that "by 'genocide' we mean the destruction of a nation or ethnic group" (Lemkin 1944: 79). From Lemkin's Jewish perspective, it was clear that the world was divided up into nations and/or ethnic groups. "The objectives of such a plan [i.e., genocide]," he continues, "would be disintegration of the political and social institutions, of culture, language, national feelings, religion, and the economic existence of national groups, and the destruction of the personal security, liberty, health, dignity, and even the lives of the individuals belonging to such groups." Lemkin's historical scope is broader than the Nazi murder of the Jews, but he always comes back to the Nazis. He is concerned primarily with wars against populations rather than against sovereign states and focuses on what would later be codified as "crimes against humanity." In the second part of the book, Lemkin writes about the techniques of genocide, its political, social, cultural, economic, biological, physical, religious, and moral aspects. Under the "cultural" heading he includes the destruction of libraries, archives, and museums. Like the members of the JCR, he singles out the burning of the great library of the Jewish Theological Seminary in Lublin, Poland, and even quotes the same German article from the *Frankfurter Zeitung* of March 28, 1941, celebrating the burning of this great Talmudic library (85).

Lemkin always returns to the assault on Jews and Jewish culture, although he tries to go beyond them. He was aware that he was confronting a new type of crime, writing that the "techniques of genocide represent an elaborate, almost scientific system developed to an extent never before achieved by any nation" (90). At the end of the chapter, Lemkin refers to the protection of minorities as the crux of his concept of genocide, as a problem not only of war but of peace. In his view, older systems for the legal protection of minorities could not deal with the crime of genocide, which, he argues, should be considered a universal crime. Lemkin's concept of genocide would become very significant in later debates regarding the Holocaust. For him, genocide was a heuristic concept that included the Holocaust, and his argument initiated a debate about whether the Holocaust was a unique event, a chapter of Jewish history alone, or whether the Nazi atrocities could be generalized and universalized – in which case the destruction of European Jewry becomes an example within the broader framework, whether called genocide, ethnic cleansing, or crimes against humanity. Lemkin's position was that the destruction of European Jewry constituted a particular example of a broader general phenomenon.[5]

Lemkin tried to be both a Jewish and a Polish patriot, and he saw the Nazi occupation of Poland as a catastrophe for both groups, even though 90 percent of the 3.5 million Jews of Poland were killed.[6] The debate on the uniqueness of the Holocaust thus began, even before it was so called, with the concept of genocide. Arendt later built on this concept, but without explicitly relying on Lemkin's work. Lemkin felt that it was very important that the concept of "cultural genocide" be included in the UN Convention on Genocide (1948), which he worked very hard to get enacted and which was finally voted on four years after his book came out, during the same week in which the UN issued its Universal Declaration of Human Rights. But the term "cultural genocide," as a subcategory of "genocide," was considered a moral rather than a legal category. The framers of the post-World War II order chose to exclude "cultural genocide" from the 1948 Convention on the Prevention and Punishment of the Crime of Genocide when it was ratified by the United Nations on December 9, 1948. Cultural rights were excluded from the ratification because they were presumed to be subsumed under individual or collective rights. As we saw in the previous chapter, the JCR dealt in practical terms with cultural and collective rights without ever naming them as such.

Current debates about "cultural rights" and the recognition of particularism and minority status can benefit from a historical perspective which allows us better to grasp why universalism triumphed over particularism after World War II and enables us to learn from the Jewish experience. The issue of Jewish cultural genocide is no longer reflective solely of a particular group at a given time but of contemporary dilemmas faced by liberal societies when dealing with multiculturalism. The historical episode of the Holocaust is not just part of Jewish history; it also informs contemporary debates on cultural rights and their perceived challenge to universal human rights. Universal human rights and cultural rights are not the same thing. The problem that Raphael Lemkin faced when he formulated his notion of genocide was how cultural pluralism and human diversity, coupled with respect for culture, can be combined with a commitment to norms and ideals that are binding for all humankind. As a lawyer, he tried to formulate this problem in legal terms. The contextualization of Lemkin's ideas within Jewish history exemplifies the ways in which the notion of culture has become a contested concept in the discourse on rights. "Cultural rights" (like "cultural genocide") and minority rights are not natural derivatives of human rights: they have been defined in different ways at different times. But both notions were part of an inner Jewish political debate on how to face the challenges of modernity. Both Lemkin and Arendt (and they are, of course, not alone in this) stand as exemplary actors in these debates in that their different answers were mustered within the same universe of discourse.

Lemkin left Eastern Europe in the winter of 1939. In his unpublished autobiography, he tells the story of how he left Riga for Latvia just in time (Jacobs and Totten 2002: 365–99, esp. 374ff.). While Lemkin was waiting for a plane to Sweden, he went to visit the most famous Jewish historian of that time, Simon Dubnow (1860–1941), who was living in Latvia. "There I turned the conversation to my plan to outlaw the destruction of peoples," he wrote.

His reaction was vivid.

*Dubnow*: "The basic value of your plan lies in the legal recognition of the act. Obviously if killing one man is a crime, killing of entire races and people must be an even greater one."

*Lemkin*: "Killing an individual is a domestic crime. Every nation deals with it through its courts and on its own initiative, but murder of a whole people must be recognized as an international crime, which should be condemned not just by one nation, but by the entire world. Nations will have to cooperate in punishing such criminals to prevent future mass murders. Should such a thing start again, the nations would have to act. Moreover, the offender will face judgment, also by history."

*Dubnow*: "The most appalling part about this type of killing is that in the past it has ceased to be a crime when large numbers are involved and when all of them happen to belong to the same nationality, or race, or religion. These things must be discussed openly. Let nations take their choices whether they want to belong to civilized world community. I have always felt that history must sit in judgment." (377–8)[7]

About eighteen months later Dubnow was killed by the Nazis in the Riga ghetto. Lemkin's account of this conversation may not be a verbatim transcription, but it is emblematic of the link between Lemkin, who would coin the term "genocide" a few years later, and Dubnow, one of the most important historians of the Jewish people of the time and also a politicized Jew, who not only affirmed the viability of the Diaspora but also championed the fight for the rights of the Jews as an autonomous people. In this respect, there were many similarities between Salo Baron and Simon Dubnow. It could even be claimed that Baron finished what Dubnow had begun. Their encounter reflected a tendency among Jewish intellectuals to reject assimilation and to subordinate ethnic identity to national identity. Dubnow clearly rejected the assimilation of Jews within their host societies.[8] He argued for what he called "autonomism," under which people could be equal and different at the same time, and through which particular forms of membership were considered part of modern existence for minority groups, foreshadowing recent debates on multiculturalism.

Dubnow developed his ideas on cultural autonomy around the same time that Lemkin came of age, a time when the problem of minorities had become a crucial one in Eastern and Central Europe. Of nationality he wrote, "A nationality, in its over-all development, is a cultural-historical collectivity whose members are united originally by common descent, language, territory and the state, but who after some time reach a spiritual unity based upon a common cultural heritage, historical traditions, common spiritual and social ideals and other typical characteristics of development" (Dubnow 1958: 98). For Dubnow, as for many others at that time, nationalism and universalism were not mutually exclusive. In Dubnow's view, "It is our duty to fight against the demand that Jews give up their national rights in exchange for rights as citizens" (110). Dubnow rejected universal assimilationism as a condition for citizenship and insisted on the unique national and cultural features of ethnic groups. His position anticipated conflicts not only between the notion of genocide (cultural and otherwise) and that of universal human rights but also, more poignantly, the European world in which both he and Lemkin lived – a world based on territorial sovereignty whose bricks and mortar were ethnicity and minorities. It was a world of population transfer and minority rights in a Europe that emerged out of the ruins of World War I and was created on paper by the Paris treaties of 1918 and 1919.[9] But it could be argued that when Dubnow was killed by the Nazis in Riga in 1941, the Jewish idea of autonomism died with him. Before the Nazis occupied Eastern Europe and murdered most of its Jewish inhabitants, the idea of a Diaspora nationalism that rejected assimilation, accepted Jewish nationhood, but did not grant territorial sovereignty seemed like a viable solution for a middle way between the stark choice of assimilation or Zionism. Dubnow tried to translate the ideas of cultural and national autonomy into a Jewish political program that would provide a Jewish identity that went beyond religious affiliation.[10] Dubnow also gave political meaning to the idea of a people without a state. This, of course, also negated key concepts of sovereignty, such as internal and external affairs. In Dubnow's thinking, state and nation became two different concepts, neither able to conquer the other.

Dubnow's view on Jewish statelessness greatly influenced political Jewish thinking on minority rights and territoriality. His work can be seen as the Eastern European version of Benjamin's and Rosenzweig's thinking about the atemporality of the Jews. Both Benjamin and Dubnow lost their lives within a year in the Nazis' attempt to wipe out all Jewish life in Europe. Both men saw Jewish existence as distinct from that of other minority groups in Europe. Both tried to translate powerlessness into power and looked at history from the point of view of the weak. Theirs was a politics of difference, minority rights, and multiculturalism at a time when people were unfamiliar with these ideas and larger forces were on the verge of destroying them. Theirs is a history of Europe's defeated.[11] Whereas Benjamin and Rosenzweig came to their stateless vision through a romantic religion of redemption, Dubnow and Lemkin came to it through the experience of the Jews in Eastern Europe, trying to maneuver their lives as empires fell around them. Arendt's views on Jewish politics alternated between these two poles and at times even tried to reconcile them.[12] Both visions were aimed at giving meaning to a powerless people in a time of crisis. They were utopian when they were formulated, yet in many ways they have survived the test of time.

The Paris Peace Conference was crucial for Jewish politics. News of the massacre of Jews in the hinterland between the future Poland and the future Ukraine began to filter into the conference and affect the deliberations of the participants. Ethnic minorities needed protection from ethnic nationalism. Jewish activists believed that this kind of protection could be internationally guaranteed through a new transnational politics. Clearly, the Jews as a transnational people favored a transnational legal system of protection.[13] More than seven million Jews lived in Eastern Europe at the time of the Peace Conference. Jews who took part in the conference were fighting for legal recognition as Jews without a state. Its general secretary, Leo Motzkin (1867–1933), a Russian-born Jew, published a collection of documents demanding exactly that. Motzkin wanted a kind of new and revolutionary kind of citizenship for Jews – a stateless citizenship, a citizenship that would cut across territorial nations and recognize Jews as citizens of Europe even if they did not belong to a particular state.[14] He and his fellow politicians insisted on the kind of personal and cultural autonomy that had existed in the former European empires, a theoretical notion that had been translated into political practice. He and his allies rejected the notion that Judaism was "only" a religion; they insisted on the status of Jews as a people, and on this basis the forerunner of the World Jewish Congress, the Committee of the Jewish Delegations, demanded recognition as the bearer of collective rights and acknowledgment of the Jews as a national minority with rights of language and culture.

These efforts were dominated by anxiety over loss of protection and loss of culture on the part of Jewish participants who were in fact diplomats without a state and were working to develop a de-territorialized conception of rights. Although the League of Nations rejected most of their demands (including the demand that Jews have a seat on the League as Jews per se), it created an environment in which Jews could act politically as a collective. This status also functioned as a middle way between the options of assimilation or Zionism; it acknowledged a collective political Jewish identity that did not seek territorial sovereignty. But these politicized Jews did not understand their Judaism as a private identity complementing their citizenship. The Jewish minority status was different from that of other minorities. There were others who demanded rights, but these other minorities could always fall back on a mother country somewhere else.[15] Other minorities (Germans, Hungarians, Bulgarians, and Turks, for instance) were represented at the Peace Conference by the spokesmen of the defeated states, whereas Jews could find representation among the victorious states.[16] Yet it was extremely important to the Jewish representatives that their concerns be defined not in exclusive terms but in conjunction with those of other minorities.

Clearly, the collapse of the European order had created a new category of people, the ethnic minority living within a nation-state's borders. This was crucial for many minorities, but especially for homeless Jews. Thus the concept of minorities was born in Europe out of this ethnic and national situation. The Jewish delegates did not speak with one voice, however; Jewish politics was already divided.[17] French Jews, for instance, came to Paris in the French republican tradition. They were French nationalists and wanted their

Jewish brethren to be nationalists as well. In the tradition of emancipation, they were Jewish in religion only. They wanted (despite Dreyfus) to see the achievements of French emancipation spread to the East. The British delegation did not think much differently and were no more sympathetic to minority rights than the French. Then there were Zionist Jews, who were pushing their views on territorial rights in Palestine. The whole gamut of Jewish politics, begun in the nineteenth century, was on display at the Paris Peace Conference. Zionists and Jewish nationalists worked closely together.[18] The separation between Zionism and Jewish nonterritorial nationalism started later, when sovereignty became an explicit goal of the Zionist movement.

The debates at the Paris Peace Conference form the background for Arendt's critique of Zionism, which was part of an internal Jewish debate often misinterpreted as a debate between universalism and particularism. It was actually a debate between two forms of particularism. Whether working in concert or in opposition, these Jews approached politics as transnational Jews and not only as citizens of their respective countries. They fought for group rights and as such laid some of the groundwork for the rights of diasporic peoples today.[19] The Peace Conference also put an end to Western European notions of civil equality that treated Jewishness as a religious affiliation alone. Group rights meant rights with respect to the autonomy of religion, language, education, and culture. Such far-reaching demands for recognition as autonomous national minorities ran counter to the sovereign European spirit of the times; nevertheless, the Jewish delegates were convinced in the years following the Paris Peace Conference that the Jewish situation had improved. Thus Janowsky concluded his 1933 study on the subject by quoting Jewish leaders to the effect that the minority treaties had "at least absolved the Jews of Eastern Europe from the serious disabilities from which they have so long suffered" and predicted that the treaties would "forever end the grave abuse of the past. They will enable the Jews as well as other minorities to live their own lives and develop their own culture" (Janowsky 1933: 389). Polish Jews believed that a better era was now dawning. Janowsky's conclusions were published at around the same time that Nazi Germany was invading Poland, which, of course, undermined the relevance of the Paris Peace Conference completely. That Poland was the first state to sign the treaty also points to its later failure. But failure does not negate relevance.

The minority treaties, like the other achievements of the Jewish delegation, reflected a cosmopolitan nationalism of the kind that

Jewish historians like Dubnow and Baron conceptualized and that formed the background for Arendt's and Lemkin's own identities as Jews who were constantly struggling to translate this cosmopolitan nationalism into ways of acting beyond the borders of Jewish ethnicity. The treaties also constituted an illusory attempt to save Jewish imperial identities (see also chapter 1) in the age of the ethnic nation-state. The Jewish delegates tried to make "statelessness" a virtue, something that Arendt would criticize after World War II. This was an attempt to translate Dubnow's ideas into politics. As Dubnow observed in his essay "The Jews as a Spiritual Nationality," "The view that since the Jews were exiled from their ancient homeland in Asia Minor they have no moral or legal right to European territory is so widespread that it is used not only by anti-Semites but also by political Zionists" (Dubnow 1958: 104). What made the Jewish delegates' demand revolutionary was the recognition of statelessness as a new form of citizenship. Arendt did something similar in her attempt to translate worldlessness into worldly politics. Arendt would come to see statelessness not as an opportunity for cosmopolitan politics, but as worldlessness, but this view took shape only after she became aware of the horrors of the Holocaust (see chapter 2 and Arendt's 1943 essay "We Refugees": Arendt 2007).[20] Like many others, she understood that international guarantees were not enough to save the Jews. In Jewish memory, the destruction of European Jews and the failure of international systems of protection are closely connected. This is why the sovereign state has become so significant in Zionist thought.

Arendt's reading of minority politics was always extremely ambivalent. On the one hand, minority politics was the kind of active politics in which she wanted to see Jews engage; on the other, she always saw minority politics as impotent and as not sufficiently political. Nevertheless, the idea of minority politics gave Jewish organizations an opportunity to try to translate theology into politics.[21] It also meant shifting between essentialism, and constantly constructing anew what it meant to be Jewish. And it meant confronting failure.

Although it was imposed on the new states rather than embraced by them, national sovereignty won the day even before Poland cancelled its official obligations toward minorities in 1934. In principle, one could argue that the collective protection of religious and linguistic minorities (the official language shied away from the term "national minorities," though this was exactly what the term referred to) became part of international law. Jewish organizations also tried to become part of an organizational network outside the League of Nations. This was perhaps the first time that Jewish minorities took part in an attempt to organize European minorities in Europe within a common frame. This common network operated from the mid-1920s and called itself the European Congress of Nationalities (or Congress of European Minorities). This Congress was a truly nongovernmental organization in every sense of the term. At its inaugural event in Geneva in October 1925, fifty delegates from thirty-four national groups from fourteen different countries represented forty million people in Europe. It was heavily dominated by the German minorities, who also ran its monthly publication, called *Nation und Staat,* which began publication in 1927. Thus German was the de facto language of the organization. The Jewish delegation took part in the Congress until 1933, when the Nazis came to power, and the German delegation identified with the fascist and anti-Semitic program. The years 1925–33 witnessed an interesting example of cosmopolitan minority politics, but at the same time revealed the dangers of minority politics and how it can lead to exclusive ethnic essentialism. In the first years of its existence, the European Congress of Nationalities tried to lobby the League of Nations to create a pan-European guarantee of cultural autonomy and minority rights.[22] The key idea was a federation of cultural autonomy. This was also an attempt to resuscitate the idea of a benign empire in the age of the nation-state.

An analysis of the issues of *Nation und Staat* between 1927 and 1933 shows how the concept of multiple cultures was slowly displaced by a monolithic concept of race.[23] There is, of course, a certain irony in the fact that between 1925 and 1933 Jewish and German delegations worked side by side on a common project of minority politics. An even greater irony lay in the fact that the Jews from Germany had no intention of including themselves, and even after 1933 saw themselves not as a minority but as Germans who happened to be Jewish. Arendt was clearly not part of that dream, but she could not embrace an ethnic politics originating in Eastern Europe, either. Even then, most official German Jews held fast to the dream of assimilation. In this respect, they were in tune with the dominant thinking of the time which believed that assimilation was the solution to the so-called national question. But the dark side of assimilation is dissimilation. When *Nation und Staat* published an article on international law and minorities by the National Socialist international legal expert Norbert Gürke, in which he attacked the Jews, the cooperation between Jews and Germans was practically over.[24] In this

77

article Gürke used the common clichés of anti-Semitic propaganda. The Jews were not only a religious minority but were of different blood and hostile to the German nation; they could not be considered Germans. That this article appeared in the monthly publication of the Congress spelled the end of the Congress's mission to promote transnational politics. This short-lived and basically failed episode of a joint politics of minorities clearly provided an alternative to exclusive ethnic nationalism. It was a unique chapter in transnational politics, but it was soon buried by the tragic events that followed.

There is a lesson to be learned from the attempts of Jewish politicians to take part in a transnational minority politics, and it applies to today's minorities as well. Clearly, the Jews were among the first to see that the promise of the Enlightenment had passed them by. For Jews, minority politics was a combination of particularism and cosmopolitanism – not a normative political theory but something that emerged organically from their life experience. It also foreshadowed questions of humanitarian interventionism (or the lack thereof). One reason for the collapse of minority politics was that the League of Nations had no instrument of intervention. The principle of territorial sovereignty was still inviolable and always acted as a hegemonic counterweight to autonomism and minority rights. Jewish politics, however, provided for restrictions on sovereignty, at least in principle. The Peace Conference served as a catalyst for renewed efforts to preserve the nation-state as an international principle. It also inaugurated the contemporary political trend in which international politics is informed by moral and legal principles and in which, by extension, abuse of minority rights is subject to international treaties. This is true even though the system did not work, because these measures were designed to support the nation-state, leaving the sanctity of national sovereignty untouched. It took the catastrophe of the Holocaust, which targeted precisely that group which counted most on this kind of cosmopolitan protection, to change matters after 1945.

The Jewish delegation at the Paris Conference, as well as Jewish participation in the Congress of European Minorities, was indeed an attempt to practice Jewish politics. Thus, when Arendt complained in *The Origins of Totalitarianism* about Jewish worldlessness and Jews' refusal to participate in politics, she may have overlooked this particular instance of minority politics or judged it in terms of its later failures. She may have also viewed Jewish politics from a Western European angle, even though she was familiar with Jewish politics in Eastern Europe as well. Arendt was very much aware of the work of the Congress of European Nationalities, although she was ambivalent about it.[25] She was already viewing Europe through American eyes, and she had realized that the minority treaties did not work or, as she put it, "that the transformation of the state from an instrument of the law into an instrument of the nation had been completed; the nation had conquered the state, national interests had priority over the law long before Hitler could pronounce 'right is what is good for the German people' " (Arendt 1951: 275).

But Arendt was, of course, also aware that the Jews were at the head of the minority movement because "they formed a majority in no country and therefore could be regarded as the minorité par excellence, i.e. the only minority whose interests could be defended by internationally guaranteed protection" (289). It is interesting to note that she used Janowsky's 1933 book as one of her sources but did not actually discuss the activities and politics of the Jewish delegation. Janowsky's book still lies in the shadow of Western European Jewish "non-understanding" of politics and moves constantly between worldlessness and worldly politics.[26] In a letter she wrote to Erich Cohn-Bendit in the summer of 1940, Arendt went even further in her reading of Jewish politics at the Peace Conference.[27] She told Cohn-Bendit that the Jewish delegation, though it presumed to represent the Jews of Eastern Europe, was not actually rooted in the Jewish people (though she did not explain what she meant by "rooted").[28] She thought that the legislation concerning minorities was designed to depoliticize them, and she did not believe that minority politics is truly politics, since it was really only demanding "cultural autonomy." She considered this "culture without politics – that is, without history and a national context" (128). She also made it very clear that she did "not believe in any improvement in the minority rights of Jews," adding, "to me it seems absurd to demand 'better guarantees' " (129). She called the Committee of the Jewish Delegations a "complaint office" (125), something completely different from the active politics of the Zionists (she might have overlooked the fact that the Committee of the Jewish Delegations and the Zionists were not only competing but also cooperating).

In any case, she felt that the only hope for Jews lay in a concerted European politics, a European federal system that could provide an opportunity to all European minorities. Jews could only succeed if they worked together with other small European nations, she argued. This is exactly what the Congress of European Nationalities had tried, and failed, to achieve several years earlier. Clearly, the Jewish diplomats at the European Congress of Nationalities and the Paris Peace Conference were more rooted in the Jewish masses than the "pariah" Jews she so admired. But "rootedness" in the people was actually never a criterion for Arendt. Her own work with the JCR was certainly not rooted in the Jewish people, but it was definitely political work. Jews were more deeply involved in political struggles (Arendt's own included) than she gave them credit for. Again, Arendt was perhaps looking at the issue from the perspective of the German–Jewish experience, but definitely not from the Eastern European Jewish one, which tried as well as it could to stand up to the Nazi threat.[29]

It was precisely this point that would explode in the debates over the Eichmann book more than a decade later. For Arendt, this was more of a theoretical than an empirical historical problem. It was her rejection of the Enlightenment that led her to view Jewish politics since emancipation as a politics of passivity. She shared this attitude (as so many other aspects of Jewish history) with the Zionists. Nevertheless, or perhaps even because of this view, she identified many of the weaknesses of the minority treaties very clearly. She also articulated the basic distinctions between Eastern Europe and the rest of the western world.[30] She recognized that the conditions required for unity among a people, a territory, or a state were lacking, and that the whole system was thus destined to fail. In one of the strongest parts of her book on totalitarianism, she analyzed this failure as the consequence of a failed politics of ethnic nationalism, which was practically destined to create minorities, refugees, and stateless people. At the same time, she was not willing to recognize the efforts of Jewish diplomats to engage in meaningful Jewish politics. This may help explain why she never wrote about the efforts of Raphael Lemkin to achieve the passing of the Genocide Convention.

The political translation of worldlessness is statelessness, exactly the feature of modern life that Dubnow saw as redeeming but that proved to be futile for the Jews. Arendt's judgment of the Jewish lack of political savvy informed her analysis in *The Origins of Totalitarianism,* where she writes, "Ignorance or misunderstanding of their own past were partly responsible for their fatal underestimation of the actual and unprecedented dangers which lay ahead" (Arendt 1951: 8). In nearly the same breath, however, Arendt adopts the Zionist perspective in her analysis of anti-Semitism: "But one should also bear in mind that lack of political ability and judgment have been caused by the very nature of Jewish history, the history of a people without a government, without a country, and without a language" (8). Above all, she disdained Jewish leaders as self-serving parvenus.[31] Arendt was torn between the world of ancient warrior

80

virtues, which also meant being fixed in place and time, and the worldlessness of liberal society. This distinction also corresponds to her dichotomy between Jewish pariahs and parvenus (Arendt 1951: 56–68). In many ways, Arendt had trouble comprehending the virtues of so-called soft power, but she was judging this, of course, in the context of trying to comprehend the catastrophe that had befallen the Jewish people. Opposed to the parvenus stood the Jewish pariahs, Jews like Lazare, a French-Jewish author and lawyer during the Dreyfus period,[32] and other writers, such as Heine or Kafka. She did not include Eastern European Jewish intellectuals and political activists like Dubnow or Motzkin, who were actually much closer to her own view of Jewish politics. Like the Zionists, she thought that standing outside history weakens Jews, and not only Jews, as a collective entity like a people, which is why she advocated a Jewish army in the 1940s. Jewish diplomacy had no place in the kind of activist politics she supported, although she herself was a Jewish politician in Paris when she worked for several Zionist organizations, and although she worked as a Jewish diplomat for Jewish Cultural Reconstruction in the United States.

The Peace Conference in Paris also created a world of winners and losers, those who acquired national sovereignty and those who were forced to become minorities within the boundaries of their respective sovereign states. After World War I, minority treaties were signed by the newly reconstituted states of Poland, Czechoslovakia, Romania, Yugoslavia, and Greece, and by the defeated states of Austria, Hungary, Bulgaria, and Turkey. The winner states, of course, had no intention of signing these treaties.[33] For the loser states, the signing of the minority treaties was part of the formal ending of World War I. For the newly defined states, the signing of the treaties was a condition either of formal recognition or of expansion of old territories. Other new states that wanted to be admitted to the League of Nations, including Albania, Lithuania, Latvia, Estonia, and (outside Europe) Iraq, had to commit to minority protection. Thus, the same procedure that had created minorities in the first place, vis-à-vis majorities, tried to create the protection of minorities as well.

Dubnow, Lemkin, Arendt, and other Jewish intellectuals were concerned with juggling particularism and universalism and collective and individual rights. Clearly this balancing act took on more urgency after the Holocaust, when Jewish intellectuals had to come to terms with what had happened. But the sources of the problems of universalism and particularism go back further.[34] They emerged out of the decline of empires and the rise of ethnic nation-states in their place.

These Jewish activists were grappling with the question of the degree of specificity of the Jewish problem and the type of solution it required: should there be a solution for the Jewish people alone, or a more universal one? They were clearly "groupists" who believed in deep roots and culture.[35] From their perspective, the issue was not merely a matter of giving the subaltern a voice or engaging in a counter-memorial project, to use two fashionable terms for challenging dominant memory cultures.[36] Rather, this was strategic essentialism before the concept became known in postcolonial literature. What this Jewish minority politics tried to convey was that the universalist narrative obliterates the cosmopolitan potential of the Jewish experience, which straddles the interstices of universal identifications and particular attachments. Universalism was identified with assimilation, which was associated with giving up one's own cultural identity. This view goes against the grain of current sociological scholarship on ethnicity and nationalism, which is usually terrified by accusations of racism and essentialism and tends to maintain a firm grasp on a constructionist view of group belonging.[37] But in fact this view simply means that minorities are only constructions.

As an Eastern European socialized between the two wars, Lemkin, for instance, did not look on ethnic groups as socially and culturally constructed. Although he was concerned about colonialism and the situation of blacks in the United States, Lemkin's thinking and political activities almost always remained centered on Europe. He may have shared this orientation with Hannah Arendt, whose thinking was also informed by the European Jewish situation before the Holocaust and then by the Holocaust itself. Lemkin and Arendt enlarged their views, but they always came back to their original concerns. Thus, it would be difficult to call them universalists. Curthoys and Docker (2008: 21) argue that through a position such as theirs, "cosmopolitanism was defeated by profound persisting Eurocentrism." But the cosmopolitanism of Lemkin and Arendt was not defeated by their Eurocentrism. Lemkin, Arendt, and others took their fate and personal experience as European Jews as their starting point and broadened their stance to other cases in Europe. And their analysis went beyond Europe; both Lemkin and Arendt connected their reading of modernity to questions of colonialism as well.[38] Minority rights were thought to be enacted to protect helpless minorities from strong majorities, and it was generally expected that genocide would be declared a crime by international law so as to protect the most vulnerable.[39] Dubnow and Lemkin drew on their Eastern European experiences in reaching these conclusions. Their meeting took place on the eve of the destruction of European Jews, most of whom were Eastern European. They came from multiethnic communities that exploded into interethnic violence.[40] Lemkin came from the borderland of central Eastern Europe, a region of shifting sovereignty where the presence of what came to be called minorities constantly undermined the congruence of ethnic and political borders. When Dubnow wrote about autonomy and Lemkin about the prevention of genocide, both had a rather narrow definition of minorities in mind, namely, national or ethnic groups. Their definition, however, went beyond physical destruction to cover cultural and spiritual eradication, although their intent was overshadowed by the events of World War II. Dubnow, for instance, believed that the assimilation of Jews was tantamount to their cultural and spiritual destruction. In this, his thoughts paralleled Baron and Arendt. All three believed that Jews do not need territorial sovereignty in order to express their status as a people. In his definition of cultural genocide, Lemkin included the imposition of the national pattern of the oppressor on minorities. Their mindset was born in Central and Eastern Europe and reshaped by World War I, and none of them perhaps fully realized the power of their premonitions. It was clear that the minority protection system worked out by the League of Nations had failed those it was supposed to protect. This system guaranteed a right to life, as formulated in the treaty with Poland in 1919: "Poland undertakes to assure full and complete protection of life and liberty to all inhabitants of Poland without distinction of birth, nationality, language, race or religion" (quoted in Schabas 2000: 23n63).

When Lemkin wrote about protection, he meant national groups, and when he wrote about national groups, he meant first of all minorities.[41] Thus cultural and ethnic groups played a large part in Lemkin's thinking, and Lemkin paid close attention to the dangers of cultural destruction.[42] But it was precisely the connection between "cultural genocide" and minority rights that delegitimized the latter in the eyes of the key framers of the new order after World War II and that explains why, when the genocide convention was drafted nine years after the Dubnow–Lemkin meeting in 1948, "cultural genocide" was excluded from the final version.[43] Ethnic Germans who had been living for centuries in regions of Eastern Europe, rather than the Jews who were the primary victims of the policies of destruction during World War II, became the example of the destructive nature of the presence of minorities. Ethnic Germans were also the ones who pushed the Congress of European Minorities into the hands of National Socialism. Their presence became the model par excellence of an irredentist Fifth Column that destabilized Europe in the 1930s.[44] Ethnic Germans also served as a primary example of the way in which minorities are remembered after 1945 more as perpetrators than as victims. A policy of universal human rights was expected to adjudicate the special protection of minorities in the international arena. No doubt the destruction of European Jewry was the trigger for Lemkin's efforts to alert the world to systematic attempts to annihilate specific groups.

Today's definition of "minorities" can be misconstrued as reflecting a long-standing universal phenomenon. This ahistorical perception has frequently led to misreadings of human rights terminology that stems from events during the second half of the twentieth century. In fact, the distinction between nations (majorities) and minorities is a rather recent one. When the nation-state (a western principle) was introduced in the former territories of nineteenth-century empires throughout Eastern, Central and Southern Europe, the creation of large contingents of minorities became inevitable. The winner states thus imposed a system of minority protection on these new states – a feature resented from the start by new nation-states such as Poland and Czechoslovakia.[45] The minority rights protection system was prompted by the desire to make international relations conform to a higher morality. The League of Nations sought to create a political structure that would come to terms with national aspirations but not surrender to them completely; international law was supposed to keep these aspirations in check. This was Lemkin's moral impetus as well. In current debates, minority rights are often equated with human rights, but the contrary was true when human rights were codified in the wake of World War II: human rights were the "correct" answer to the pervasive memories of the failure to protect minorities. In the memory of those who tried to hammer out a new order after World War II (especially in Europe), minority rights were the perceived evil of the interwar period, and were even cast as partly responsible for Hitler's aggression and the outbreak of the war. Jewish diplomatic activities during the Peace Conference in 1919 foreshadowed problems to come. When Wilson and the Allies offered national liberation to the peoples of Eastern and Southern Europe, the fate of Central and Eastern European Jews depended on international guarantees. The lives of these Jews had been shaped by centuries of communal life; their integration into the modern world of nation-states had mostly failed in Europe (though not, of course, in the United States and Australia, among other countries). If they were to evolve, the Jewish communities of Eastern and Central Europe had to depend

84

on the niches provided by the multiethnic diversity of the now extinct large empires.[46] This fact informed Arendt's view of minorities and human rights, as she formulated it in her work on totalitarianism. Thus the genocide convention constantly wavered between the universal and the particular, and this helps explain why "cultural genocide" was considered too particular to be included in the final draft. Hence it was at the same time a philosophical and a geopolitical problem.[47]

Let us step back for a moment and look at Lemkin's first formulation of "cultural genocide," before the term was actually coined. In October 1933, just a couple of months after the Nazis came to power, at a conference in Madrid on the unification of penal law, Lemkin presented a paper in which he attempted to define the crimes of "barbarity"and "vandalism."[48] "Barbarity," in his view, constituted one of the first formulations of genocide, and "vandalism" was related to the destruction of culture. This is how Lemkin defined it:

## Acts of Vandalism

*(Destruction of the culture and works of art).*

AN ATTACK TARGETING A COLLECTIVITY can also take the form of systematic and organized destruction of the art and cultural heritage in which the unique genius and achievement of a collectivity are revealed in fields of science, arts and literature. The contribution of any particular collectivity to world culture as a whole forms the wealth of all of humanity, even while exhibiting unique characteristics.

Thus, the destruction of a work of art of any nation must be regarded as acts of vandalism directed against world culture. The author [of the crime] causes not only the immediate irrevocable losses of the destroyed work as property and as the culture of the collectivity directly concerned (whose unique genius contributed to the creation of this work); it is also all humanity which experiences a loss by this act of vandalism.

In the acts of barbarity, as well as in those of vandalism, the asocial and destructive spirit of the author is made evident. This spirit, by definition, is the opposite of the culture and progress of humanity. It throws the evolution of ideas back to the bleak period of the Middle Ages. Such acts shock the conscience of all humanity, while generating extreme anxiety about the future. For all these reasons, acts of vandalism and barbarity must be regarded as offenses against the law of nations.[49]

Culture in this sense (especially world culture) was always central to Lemkin. The link between the physical destruction of a people and its culture was part of his agenda from the early 1930s on. To Lemkin's mind, genocide was by no means synonymous with the extermination of the Jews. In fact, Lemkin justified his efforts with references to genocidal activities that took place before and after the Holocaust.[50] He was determined, like so many others, not to present the Holocaust, a term he did not use, as an exclusive threat to European Jewry, as he made clear when he wrote, "The Nazi leaders had stated very bluntly their intent to wipe out the Poles, the Russians; to destroy demographically and culturally the French element in Alsace-Lorraine, the Slovenians in Carniola and Carinthia. They almost achieved their goal in exterminating the Jews and Gypsies in Europe."[51]

In the end, the Convention on the Prevention and Punishment of the Crime of Genocide defined genocide in the broadest possible terms, as any of a number of acts "committed with intent to destroy, in whole or in part, a national, ethnical, racial or religious group."[52] When Dubnow appealed in 1891 to Jewish communities all over Eastern Europe to collect all possible documents related to their institutions, he was preventing a "memoricide" several decades before the Nazi regime decided to either destroy or collect Jewish cultural property.[53] As noted above, the 1948 UN Convention on the Prevention and Punishment of the Crime of Genocide did not include "cultural genocide." The United States and the Soviet Union, the two victors in World War II, represented two versions of universalism in 1945. The former stood for the universalism of individual liberties and a market economy and therefore showed an elective affinity with the basic contours of a universalism that excluded special consideration for minorities, while the Soviet system could not accept a minority-based rights regime as emancipatory, since this was counter to its socialist ideology of human emancipation.

I showed in the previous chapter how a particular Jewish political practice addressed cultural genocide on its own terms. Its main protagonists were Jews who saw Jewish politics within a larger framework.[54] Like the Jews who were engaged in minority politics after World War I, the members of the Jewish cultural reconstruction movement had a collective understanding of their political and cultural existence. Lemkin and Arendt are good examples of how one starts with the fate of one's own people but goes beyond it. Lemkin's notion of genocide, including cultural genocide, typifies this attitude. Lemkin was concerned about the fate of Jews as well as Poles, while recognizing the difference between them; thus he transformed Jewish memory into European memory. Lemkin and Arendt turned first to their own Jewish experience but understood that universalism and particularism are neither mutually exclusive categories nor moral categories to choose between but are first of all a matter of lived experience. Universal aspirations and particularistic ethnic identification are not only part of Jewish history but are part of a larger framework where universal and cultural rights compete with each other. An enlarged mentality is based on and woven into history and experience. It is grounded on a historical approach that includes a dual strategy that recognizes the contingency of foundational assumptions as well as the malleability of ontological principles. Clearly, "cultural genocide" was not accorded legal recognition because of anxieties about the subversive roles minorities can play when it comes to peace and stability, as they did in the 1930s. Nevertheless, minorities like the Jews succeeded in defining themselves as groups and legal entities. As we have seen, heirless cultural property became the basis for collective legal claims after the Holocaust. Thus the Jews not only reclaimed some of their stolen property but also succeeded in claiming collective rights and property. This is an important point in our understanding of the historical transition from minority to human rights. The minority rights protection system had a moral impetus, namely, the desire to make international relations conform to a higher morality rather than be governed by amorality. As the Jews quickly discovered, the primacy of national sovereignty trumped the rights of minorities, and the League of Nations had few instruments with which to enforce compliance of any sort. Politically minded Jews had to reorient themselves in order to cope with this state of affairs. The Jewish struggle for human rights was their attempt to do just this. Jewish political organizations understood that the minority rights struggle had failed and that the focus needed to be shifted to human rights, which were now supposed to be the solution to protecting the life and liberty of Jews. We see the same thinking at work in the distinction between the broad concept of genocide and its particular historical manifestations. The concept of genocide universalizes the experience of the Holocaust, which is but one instance of a class of (by definition comparable) phenomena.

The UN Declaration against Genocide, in which this idea first took clear shape, was the product of a period during which the Holocaust, a term not yet in use, was still considered part of a larger class of atrocities. The UN declaration's framing of human rights as universal codified the view that a moral world cannot stand idly by while genocide is taking place. The concept of human rights, whose modern legal roots stem from the same set of 1948 UN declarations, is in practice tied up with the even stronger assertion that the Holocaust is a slippery slope – that every act of ethnic repression, if left unchecked, can pave the way for the next Holocaust. This is exactly the argument that Lemkin tried to make and that Arendt later emphasized. The key (Jewish) problem, as they saw it, was how to make sure that the genocide convention, with its concept of universal human rights, would fulfill its mission: to prevent minorities from being exterminated.

Jewish diplomats took up this quest and became deeply involved in questions of human rights on the theoretical level and in the politics of the UN declaration. One of the leading figures in this struggle was the Jewish Lithuanian lawyer and legal scholar Jacob Robinson. Born in 1889 in Lithuania, Robinson came to New York in 1940, at around the same time as Arendt and Lemkin.[55] Robinson was very active in minority politics and represented the Jewish minority of Lithuania in the European Congress of Nationalities. In the 1920s and 1930s, he became an expert in minority rights legislation, and as early as 1928 he published a bibliography on minorities that surveyed the field up to that point.[56] After his arrival in New York in 1940, he founded the New York-based Institute of Jewish Affairs, sponsored and financed by the World Jewish Congress, where he worked with a group of Jewish social scientists, among them Max Laserson, Jacob Lestschinsky, and Arieh Tartakower.

The institute was supposed to conduct research on the status of Jews but rapidly became a clearinghouse of information on the Nazi attempt to destroy the Jews of Europe. It also researched the legal basis of demands for reparation and restitution of lost Jewish lives and property after the war. In many ways, the institute established the legal and ideological foundation for the work of the JCR in the 1940s. Robinson attempted to exert the institute's influence on the legal proceedings of the Nuremberg Trials and to have the Jews represented there as a collective victim. He was active in human rights legislation, served as a legal advisor to the newly founded state of Israel, and even acted as legal counsel for Israel's trial of Eichmann 1961. He was one of the most active Jewish diplomats spanning the era between the wars and the postwar order.

Robinson had a very Jewish Eastern European understanding of the concept of the nation, which was very much in tune with that of Dubnow, Motzkin, and Lemkin. These men shared the understanding that the system of minority protection had broken down; in a memo dated April 29, 1939, Robinson observed, "The Versailles system is in a state of dissolution. It was at the time an attempt to solve the Jewish problem. What have been the results for the Jews? What lessons can we learn from the collapse?" In fact, the Institute of Jewish Affairs was conceived independently by Robinson and Dubnow in 1939, on the eve of war.[57] "A knowledge of the facts is the prerequisite of any planned directed policy," Robinson's memo continued. "The collecting, sifting and ordering of the facts as well as their pragmatic interpretation would be one of the most important duties of such an institute." Robinson wrote another memo in 1940 in which he anticipated a future peace conference and told the Jewish people to be prepared:

> What we aim at is nothing less than the creation of a Jewish political science. That means that we want to limit ourselves to a study of all the problems pertaining to Jewry and abstain from political action, which remains a matter for political bodies. . . . The Jews in a changing world – that is the subject of our job. (The World Jewish Congress Collection", Series A: Central Files, Subseries 2: Executive Files, Box A9, File 6: Proposals for Institute to Study Jewish Situation, American Jewish Archives, Cincinnati, USA)

Robinson also raised the question of the relationship between Jewry and "the anti-nationalistic and super-nationalistic forces in Europe and the world," between "internationalism and cosmopolitanism."

At exactly the same time – April 1939 – Simon Dubnow composed a document for the World Jewish Congress called "The International League for the Protection of the Jewish People against Attack." Dubnow wanted to set up some kind of protective body to ward off the assault on the Jews. The institute began its work in February 1941, three months before Arendt arrived in the United States.[58] Its objective was to secure Jewish rights and the Jewish future in a postwar settlement of the world. But the institute also published one of the first books on the Nazi assault on the Jews, *Hitler's Ten Year War on the Jews*, which Lemkin used as a source of empirical evidence for his own study on genocide. This country-by-country study on the Nazis' attempt to wipe out the Jewish population of Europe, the first of its kind, also served as a basic document at the Nuremberg Trials. The leaders of the Institute of Jewish Affairs, aware that the era of minority rights was over, tried to influence international law and legislation in the belief that Jewish politics would be guided by questions of sovereignty and the future of the state of Israel. Arendt's slim relationship with the institute was not very cordial. In an article in the *Aufbau* dated April 10, 1942, slightly more than a year after the institute was founded, she criticized it in the context of her demand for a Jewish army. "While we have been busy making sure that the demand for a Jewish army remains on paper," she wrote,

> we can console ourselves that four institutions have, with scientific meticulousness, been busy preparing us for peace: the Institute of Jewish Affairs. . . . And so we are being prepared "unpolitically" for peace. . . . But so far no people has ever come up with the idea of trying to replace participation in a war with dreaming in advance about participation in a peace conference. This is a scholarly idea, and we like to hope that our scholars will not succeed in turning a "people of the book" into a people of papers. (Arendt 2007: 153)

This was one of Arendt's parting shots in her long internal struggle with the Institute of Jewish Affairs. She argued with its directors about minority rights, human rights, the Nuremberg Trials, and, especially, the Eichmann Trial. One of her last essays on Jewish matters is a reply to Jacob Robinson's criticism of her own book in 1965, twenty-three years after her *Aufbau* article appeared. After the war, Jewish politics took a turn away from minority rights and became engaged in questions of human rights, accountability, guilt, forgiveness, and responsibility – subjects to which we now turn.

# — 5 —

# ZURICH, VILNA, AND NUREMBERG: GENERALIZED GUILT

Hannah Arendt was in constant dialogue during the 1930s, 1940s, and 1950s with a real and imagined Jewish audience with whom she discussed Jewish politics, including the questions of how Jews should enter politics and how they should view themselves in history. She also communicated with non-Jewish German friends and acquaintances, among them her former teacher and dissertation advisor, Karl Jaspers. Jaspers and Arendt, in a renewed attempt at a German–Jewish dialogue, reflected on postwar Europe, German guilt, and "the Jewish question."[1] The correspondence broke off in 1938 and was resumed in October 1945, around the time that Jaspers, together with the political scientist Dolf Sternberger, founded a journal called *Die Wandlung* (Transformation), which was aimed at giving Germany a new intellectual direction after the war. The journal lasted from 1945 to 1949, and Arendt published several of her early postwar essays in German there, in spite of some initial reluctance.[2] On December 2, Jaspers had proposed to Arendt to be part of the journal: "Would you like to write an essay for us? . . . Perhaps you could write something on what truly unites us across all the barriers between us – and by us I mean Americans and Europeans, including Germans" (Arendt and Jaspers 1992: 26). She was initially reluctant to do so. As she wrote to Jaspers on December 6, 1945, in response to his invitation that she contribute to the journal,

> I have refused to abandon the Jewish question as the focal point of my historical and political thinking. And this brings me to your question about *Die Wandlung*. Need I tell you how much your request that I contribute pleased me? . . . I know you will not misunderstand me when I say that it is not an easy thing for me to contribute to a German journal. At the same time, I am unhappy about the desperate resolve of the Jews to leave Europe (you are probably aware of the mood in

91

all the refugee camps both in and outside Germany; and that mood cannot be ignored). I am also more anxious than I care to say about the frightening possibility of further catastrophes, particularly in Palestine, given the behavior of other governments and our own suicidal tendencies in politics. Yet one thing seems clear to me: if the Jews are able to stay in Europe, then they cannot stay as Germans or Frenchmen, etc., as if nothing had happened. It seems to me that none of us can return (and writing is surely a form of return) merely because people again seem prepared to recognize Jews as Germans or something else. We can return only if we are welcome as Jews. That would mean that I would gladly write something if I can write as a Jew on some aspect of the Jewish question. (Arendt and Jaspers 1992: 31–2)

Arendt was not interested in transcending barriers in the name of some fictitious "unity"; she would write only as a Jew. This was a difficult decision for her, for it takes the failure of the Enlightenment as a given. Her position coincided fully with Scholem's stance on the Jewish–German relationship. As he put it in a public lecture twenty years later, "I deem it important that Jews, precisely as Jews, speak to Germans in full consciousness of what has happened and of what separates us."[3] In spite of their differences, Arendt agreed with Scholem on this point and addressed Germans as a Jew; she used a different voice entirely when talking to fellow Jews or Americans. At around the same time she was writing her very critical articles about Zionism and Jewish politics in mostly Jewish journals in the United States, she was moving intellectually in a different direction when addressing a German audience. She had ceased to be the "Herr K." of Kafka's *The Castle*, she wrote about two years before her correspondence with Jaspers began. "K." wants to be let into the Castle but dies of exhaustion. "What Kafka depicts," Arendt commented, "is the real drama of assimilation, not its distorted counterpart. He speaks for the average small-time Jew who really wants no more than his rights as a human being: home, work, family, and citizenship. He is portrayed as if he were alone on earth, the only Jew in the whole wide world – completely, desolately alone" (Arendt 2007: 291). Arendt came to this realization before 1933, but the facts became much clearer, painfully so, after 1945. The Enlightenment principles of universal reason made no room for Jews to enter the family of universal humankind. Jews had to remain alone and unprotected. In Arendt's view, reconciliation after the Enlightenment had to include the risk of irreconcilable memories.

Arendt thus began a transformative process in which we can detect hints of cosmopolitan modernity, a condition in which a compromise is achieved that, although fragile, is sustained by the mutual recognition of the Other's history. This connection of perspectives makes acts of reconciliation a key component of memory. It is not so much the original crimes that are on the agenda but the question of how descendants should deal with history and memory. In other words, the inclusion of the Other softens the distinction between the memories of perpetrators and victims. What remains is the memory of a common history that, paradoxically, cannot be shared. That was part of Arendt's message to Jaspers. The cosmopolitan memory of the past emerges from the conscious and deliberate inclusion of the Other's (in this case the concrete Jew's) suffering – not from the idea of some community of fate inspired by mythical delusions and serving some false historical continuity based on "equality" or other universalist promises of the Enlightenment.[4] For Jewish intellectuals, this was no longer possible; the Holocaust had decisively and forever exposed the sham of Enlightenment principles.

A new moral and political field of action and responsibility thus emerged from risky communication and interdependence. The early correspondence between Arendt and Jaspers mirrored some of the larger issues involved. Especially in West Germany, a growing majority felt morally committed to reconnect with the West, which was both a consequence of the defeat of 1945 and the ensuing reeducation by the Americans. In this respect, *Die Wandlung* was exemplary. For the editorial board, radical distancing from the Nazi past was the most important priority of politics and remembrance. This was also the beginning in Germany of remembering the Holocaust as part of the project of moving from "Germanizing Europe" to "Europeanizing Germany." Naturally, Arendt was also aware that the Germans of *Die Wandlung*, with all their goodwill, could view things only from their own national perspective of "Never again fascism." It is through the question of guilt that these issues became most explicit. Arendt and Jaspers's discussion about guilt, responsibility, and reconciliation began immediately after the war. They thus set the parameters for a much wider conversation about the link between collective political responsibility and personal guilt.[5] Their exchange also highlighted the differences between Jewish and European memories of the destruction of the Jews. In many ways, Jaspers's book on German guilt[6] heralded the beginning of both the European Union and Jewish separation from Europe.

Following the defeat of Nazi Germany in 1945, one of the first tasks undertaken by the United States was the rebuilding and westernizing of its sector of Germany. The goal was to initiate a process of change whereby the Germans' worldview would be transformed; it would repent of its departure from the West and rebuild an ideological kinship with the United States via a renewal of the Enlightenment concepts of universal reason, justice, and equality. The broader cultural landscape of which National Socialism was a part constituted a radical critique of the modern West. The public debates that ensued in postwar Germany from 1945 to 1947, fueled by the Nuremberg Trials, were the first milestone in the process of cultural and political transformation. These debates dealt with questions of individual guilt and collective responsibility, issues fundamental to western thinking, and endeavored to reestablish an ethos of free speech and public responsibility in Germany.[7]

Jaspers's book, which provided a starting point for a debate whose ramifications extended far beyond Germany's borders, was unlikely to make for comfortable reading for Jewish audiences, something of which Arendt was painfully aware. The book deals with German guilt but not with the Jewish catastrophe. But how could a book on German guilt so blatantly ignore Nazi Germany's Jewish victims? One answer is that Jaspers's book is a product of its times. It demonstrates how little people were concerned with the destruction of European Jewry in the immediate aftermath of the Holocaust. Jaspers had every claim to legitimacy in publishing this little book, which was based on a course he taught at the newly reopened University of Heidelberg from late 1945 to early 1946.

When the Nazis came to power, Jaspers was already a well-established philosopher, having developed an existentialist philosophy of psychiatry. He labored continually, however, in the shadow of a bigger celebrity, Martin Heidegger, whose metaphysical broodings on modernity propelled him into Hitler's open arms. Jaspers was not so inclined: not only was his thought firmly anchored in western humanism, but his wife, Gertrud, was Jewish. For Jaspers, who refused to leave his wife's side, this meant dismissal from his post at the university. His books were banned. Because of their "mixed marriage," Gertrud and Karl were both in immediate danger of arrest by the Gestapo; the two even vowed to commit suicide together in the event of their capture. The couple lived a life of seclusion and they were spared only by the American occupation.

After the war, Jaspers joined forces with the American administration to reopen the universities; *The Question of German Guilt* was a step toward the reestablishment of academic life in Germany. Jaspers's book is more than a contemporary example of the way in which Germany confronted its past; it has recently become a paradigmatic benchmark in the political and philosophical analysis of guilt. This is especially true of Jaspers's distinction between criminal, political, moral, and metaphysical guilt. Here, the book departs from its specific political and historical context and becomes a paradigmatic treatise on reconciliation and guilt. "Criminal guilt," Jaspers wrote, refers to those acts for which one may be held accountable in a court of law; "political guilt" to the responsibility one bears for the political system in which one lives and in which one is thus, by definition, complicit.

Jaspers distinguishes between these two forms of guilt, which are public and external, and moral and metaphysical guilt, which are private and internal.[8] In the case of moral guilt, the individual must come to terms with the breakdown of his or her conscience ex post facto; moral guilt refers to whatever personal failings one demonstrates and can be judged only by one's conscience. This is the guilt that results from the decision to make one's conscience subservient to the state. Metaphysical guilt lies even further outside the human realm. It refers to the cherishing of one's guilt as part of a quasi-religious experience through which one can reach greater spiritual heights. In the case of metaphysical guilt, one is answerable only to God. Reaction to the book was harsh. Many considered Jaspers too "pro-American," and by 1948 both Gertrud and Karl Jaspers had left Germany for Switzerland, where Karl continued teaching and writing.[9]

The correspondence between Arendt and Jaspers on this issue became paradigmatic of Arendt's communication with German non-Jews. Frequently, Arendt tried to articulate the Jewish position on many issues. When it came to the *Question of Guilt*, she could not countenance Jasper's attempt to communicate to Germans alone, without clearly addressing their victims. Indeed, Jaspers's notion of metaphysical guilt struck Arendt as apolitical. Yet the virtual absence of the Jewish victims of National Socialism in Jaspers's book was no coincidence; the book was primarily an appeal to Germans to accept the legitimacy of the Nuremberg Trials, and to view them as a first step toward a new and more cosmopolitan Europe.[10] Jaspers envisioned this cosmopolitan Europe as the political mirror image of nationalistic Europe and the physical and moral devastation to which nationalism had led.[11] He consciously sought to reach beyond the mass graves to the European history of ideas. Jaspers viewed his ideal of a cosmopolitan Europe as a response to the traumatic way in which the Nazis, and those who cooperated with them, had perverted European values beyond recognition.

For Jaspers, the Nuremberg Court created both legal categories and procedures that extended beyond the sovereignty of any particular nation-state. It did so for practical reasons; this was the only way to grasp the historical atrocities committed by the Nazis. But Jaspers saw an opportunity for a new, cosmopolitan legal and moral category that would recognize the individual accountability of all perpetrators; the basis for this accountability would lie not within any particular nation's legal system but rather in the family of nations, such that what had in the past been considered crimes against the state now became crimes against humanity. Thus, if a state were to become a rogue, criminal state – for Jaspers, the distinction between a criminal state and a state that commits crimes was crucial – the individuals who served it could still be tried and sentenced for their deeds by an international court of law. This cosmopolitan legal principle was designed to protect the civilian population not from violence on the part of other, hostile states but rather from violent acts committed by their own state, whether against its citizens or, more important, its non-citizen residents, as well as people deemed to fall outside its legal jurisdiction despite living within its borders.

Jaspers saw the postwar era and the Nuremberg Trials as the dawning of a new transnational world. Yet this begs a deceptively simple question, which Jaspers found quite difficult to answer: who are the victims of crimes against humanity? Did the Nazis commit crimes against the Jews, or against humanity? Both Jaspers and Arendt tried to come to terms with these questions in their subsequent works, and both oscillated between universal and particular understandings of the Nazis' crimes. In fact, the kind of crimes at issue here, which are related to historical injustice, were crimes committed by political groups, collectives, against other members of groups. This is true even of crimes against humanity and genocide. Thus, especially for Jews after 1945, it was difficult to universalize these matters. Arendt seemed to be aware of this basic truth, and she reminded Jaspers of it in her letters.

In her own work on these issues, she preferred to use the distinction between guilt, seen as an inner attitude, and responsibility, which she saw as external and connected to the political public domain.[12] In her 1945 essay, she argued that it was practically impossible under the Nazis to distinguish between the guilty and the innocent: "These are the real political conditions which underlie the charge of the collective guilt of the German people" (Arendt 1997: 124). But she closed the essay with a more universal message: "Upon them and only upon them, who are filled with a genuine fear of the inescapable guilt of the human race, can there be any reliance when it comes to fighting fearlessly, uncompromisingly, everywhere against the incalculable evil that men are capable of bringing about" (132).

Arendt and Jaspers continued to discuss the question of guilt and responsibility in the following years, and Arendt helped Jaspers get his book on German guilt published in English. At the same time, she continued to press Jaspers to see the Jewish side of his thinking about guilt. In a letter of August 17, 1946, she wrote to him about the book from the perspective of the Germans who in her mind were truly responsible: "Mindful of what Germans have inflicted on the Jewish people, we will, in a future republic, constitutionally renounce anti-Semitism, stipulating, for example, that any Jew, regardless of where he is born, can become a citizen of this republic, enjoying all rights of citizenship, solely on the basis of his Jewish nationality and without ceasing to be a Jew" (Arendt and Jaspers 1992: 53). Arendt was in a sense resurrecting Motzkin's ideas about transnational Jewish citizenship in a different context.

But the same letter foreshadowed the debate that would surround the Eichmann trial fifteen years later. In particular, Arendt rejected Jaspers's reading of "criminal guilt," writing, "The Nazi crimes, it seems to me, explode the limits of the law; and that is precisely what constitutes their monstrousness. For these crimes, no punishment is severe enough. It may be essential to hang Göring, but it is totally inadequate" (54). Arendt also hints at her later analysis of the unprecedented nature of the Nazi crimes: "And just as inhuman as their guilt is the innocence of the victims." Jaspers disagreed, arguing that the Nazis should be considered common criminals. He answered her on October 5, 1946:

> You say that what the Nazis did cannot be comprehended as a "crime"
> – I am not altogether comfortable with your view, because a guilt that
> goes beyond all criminal guilt inevitably takes on a streak of "greatness" – of satanic greatness – which is, for me, as inappropriate for
> the Nazis as all the talk about the "demonic" element in Hitler and so
> forth. It seems to me that we have to see these things in their total
> banality. (62)[13]

Arendt replied on December 17, "There is a difference between a man who sets out to murder his old aunt and people who without considering the economic usefulness of their actions at all (the deportations were very damaging to the war effort) built factories to produce corpses" (69).

The Nuremberg Trial indictment stated in Article 7, "The official position of defendants, whether as Heads of State or responsible officials in Government departments, shall not be considered as freeing them of responsibility or mitigating punishment" (International Military Tribunal 1995 1:12). It thereby introduced the notion that international law has the authority to hold individuals acting in their official capacity responsible for certain violations. The indictment also introduced the idea of "individualized guilt" and its counterpart, "collective guilt." In thus individualizing guilt the Nuremberg tribunal showed that certain perpetrators, rather than an entire people, were guilty of the Nazi atrocities. The German nation was not guilty, but rather ordinary and extraordinary Germans. This distinction – in fact, all of the distinctions and dimensions and nuances of later debates about banality versus monstrosity, continuity versus unprecedentedness – were addressed in the exchange between Arendt and Jaspers in 1945–6.

Arendt made her argument even more clearly in her letters to Gertrud Jaspers, a fellow Jew with whom she felt more comfortable discussing Jewish issues. She wrote to Gertrud on May 30, 1946,

> What you wrote about "our problem"[14] moved me very much. Of course we're not fit for polite society – praise, glory, and hallelujah for that. . . . But I don't know either how one can stand to live there as a Jew in a society that doesn't even deign to speak about "our" problem – and today that means our dead. (41)

Arendt saw no place for metaphysical guilt in postwar politics; she felt that Nazi Germany's particular kind of guilt was concrete and unprecedented. Her chief concern was with "our" dead, but this of course was a Jewish agenda. Germans and other Europeans needed another agenda, which Jaspers could symbolize.

Jaspers's primary concern, as we have seen, was to connect Germany to a Europe in which it could reestablish its historical continuity and perceive itself as part of the West. Germany needed to reach back to its Enlightenment roots if it was to succeed in defining the Nazis' "final solution" as an aberration. Reconnecting with Enlightenment roots would also allow Germany and Europe to construct forms of memory that could counter myths of nationalism and warfare. But this agenda did not resolve or even address the issue of the Jews as a nation within a nation, and it constituted a throwback to the French Revolution and Nathan the Wise (see chapter 1). It was no coincidence that Jaspers envisioned a Europe in which Jews could become universal citizens. The postwar thinking of intellectuals like Jaspers was emblematic of the Eurocentric universalism that has characterized much of the core European postnational discourse of late. In the aftermath of World War II, Europeanization primarily meant the rebuilding of Western Europe with a pacified Germany at its center, as well as establishing the United States as a counterweight to Soviet influence in the East. Germany had to be westernized by way of integration into a newly formed system of interdependent Western European states. The intellectual debates on guilt and responsibility in Germany, spearheaded by Jaspers, as well as the question of the recognition of Nazi atrocities before and during the war, would go on to become paradigmatic European debates on the guilt of nations in general. Jaspers believed that the postwar world (including the Nuremberg Trials) had to be based upon a universal Kantian cosmopolitanism – had to become a world without borders or "Others." Arendt, given both her theoretical background and her practical work with the American-Jewish organizations, could not agree.

The English translation of Jaspers's book attracted a certain amount of attention in Jewish circles in the United States. Ben Halpern, an American Zionist, wrote a critical essay in which he accused Jaspers of trying to avoid admitting guilt and argued that only the victims, primarily the Jews, insisted that Germans accept responsibility and the guilt that went with it.[15] Ironically, Halpern noted that the Christian world faulted Jews for their unwillingness to forgive the Nazis for their crimes. Halpern, much like Arendt, saw Jaspers's "metaphysical guilt" as a form of apolitical escapism and an attempt to ennoble the Germans. Like Arendt, Halpern emphasized the concreteness of man's breach of the law. Halpern also shared Arendt's outrage that Jaspers ignored the Jews in his account of guilt.

Arendt and Halpern agreed about Jaspers, but they disagreed about Zionist politics and the state of Israel.[16] Just as Europe set about reorganizing its postwar order, the Jews of Palestine were fighting for their territorial sovereignty. Arendt was involved in both debates. In her debate with Jaspers, she sounded much like her Jewish colleagues in America, except that she did not embrace the Zionism that most of them did. While she understood that most American Jews had become Zionists and saw Arab and Jewish territorial claims as irreconcilable, and, although she acknowledged the "intimate connection between this mood on the part of the Jews everywhere and the recent European catastrophe" (391), she rejected the argument that Jews had to fight for their own state, no matter the cost. She also lamented the lack of "loyal opposition" and tried to adopt this mantle herself, and she objected to what she called "racist chauvinism" in the Zionist attitude (393). Territorial sovereignty was not the right or sure pathway to Jewish liberty. Halpern attacked her position in the harshest possible terms, even accusing her of "collaboration"![17] Arendt responded that "neither the Arabs nor the British are enemies against whom an all-or-nothing attitude could be justified. With both, we shall have to live in peace" (416). Confrontations like the one with Jaspers took place at several junctures. Both sides tried at times to come to terms with the other, to reconcile, to forgive, but the Jews were constant witnesses to the impossibility of forgiveness.

We see another instance of this kind of intellectual division in the first meeting of European members of PEN (the international association of writers) in the summer of 1947 in Zurich. The professed goal of this meeting was to revive what the war had destroyed and to reestablish PEN Centers in Austria and Germany. The Hebrew and Yiddish members of PEN opposed this move on the grounds that it was too early to reinstate the German branch of PEN.[18] A majority voted in favor of reinstatement, however, while also rejecting a resolution that asked PEN to support the founding of the state of Israel.

The poet Abraham Sutzkever (1913–2010) directed the Yiddish PEN center[19] and was a survivor of the Vilna ghetto, where he fought as a partisan and was directly involved in saving books from various Jewish cultural institutions in Vilna. It is unlikely that Sutzkever ever met Arendt, but their spiritual paths crossed at certain junctures. Like Arendt, Sutzkever was active after the war in the drive to salvage Jewish material from Europe and to bring it to the United States. The Nazi assault on Vilna was especially harsh, since it was one of the great cultural centers of Eastern European Jewish scholarship.[20] Sutzkever was part of a group that succeeded in smuggling as many books and manuscripts out of the ghetto as they possibly could. At around the same time that Arendt and Scholem were working to organize the removal of Jewish cultural treasures from Germany, Sutzkever was doing the same in the Soviet Union. He made sure that much of the material was smuggled to New York, where the Yiddish Scientific Institute, founded in Vilna in 1925, was reestablished in 1941.[21] Sutzkever returned with the Soviet army to liberate Vilna. On February 27, 1946, he became the first Jew to testify at the Nuremberg Trials, where he spoke on behalf of Lithuanian Jewry (95 percent of all Lithuanian Jews – more than 200,000 people – were killed between 1941 and 1945 by the Nazis and their Lithuanian henchmen).

As a Yiddish poet, Sutzkever wanted to testify in Yiddish, the language of his people, but the official languages of the Nuremberg

Tribunal were English, French, Russian, and German, so he testified in Russian about the suffering of the Jews of Vilna, providing a Jewish perspective at the Tribunal in spite of its attempts to exclude personal testimony from the proceedings.[22] Sutzkever also contributed a chapter on the destruction of the Vilna Jews to a documentary on the destruction of Soviet Jewry called *The Black Book: The Nazi Crime against the Jewish People*, one of many works compiled by the World Jewish Congress; it was published in English in 1946.[23] In this chapter, Sutzkever also described the attempts of the Rosenberg office not only to destroy but also to collect Jewish cultural artifacts. He became part of a group that called itself the Paper Brigade, which managed to save thousands of books and documents from the Nazis. As soon as the Vilna ghetto had been liberated, Sutzkever began planning a museum in which the rescued material could be displayed. But the Soviets had no interest in such a museum at that time. What was not smuggled to the United States disappeared into the corners of the Lithuanian National Library (it was discovered only in 1986, was brought to New York in the 1990s, copied, and shipped back to Lithuania). Sutzkever eventually settled in Israel, where he continued to write poetry in Yiddish. At the PEN meeting in Zurich, however, he was reluctant to let the Germans back into the fold of writers' nations. As with Jaspers's book on German guilt, which appealed so much to the Allies, there was an attempt in Zurich to exclude the Jewish experience from the intellectual reconstruction of postwar Europe.

This also became quite clear in a meeting in September 1946 in Geneva that exemplified a universalizing trope that characterized most postwar responses by European intellectuals, and was also affected by a series of conflicting universalisms. The first conference of European intellectuals was organized by Julien Benda under the heading "the European Spirit"; it was held near the site of the former League of Nations, as though the European intellectuals were trying to resurrect the spirit of the League.[24] The participants included Francesco Flora, Jean de Salis, Jean Guehenno, Denis de Rougemont, Stephen Spender, George Bernaros, Karl Jaspers, and Georg Lukács, who would remind the participants of the future division of Europe into western and eastern blocs. The event began with a lecture by Benda opposing nationalism in Europe. He pledged to work for a postnational Europe, a Europe that would serve as a civilizing force in the world. The conflicting versions of universalism were represented by Karl Jaspers and Georg Lukács. Jaspers was the only German intellectual invited to the conference, and his appearance stirred much interest. Jaspers wrote about the meeting to Arendt on September 18, "It was like a dream to be in bodily contact with the intellectual world again. . . . The theme was the European Spirit. And some of the speakers developed something resembling a European nationalism. But all the reasonable people had the world in mind" (Arendt and Jaspers 1992: 56–7). Ironically, Jaspers told Arendt about the new European nationalism at just the time that she was publishing her "Tentative List."

"The European Spirit" was also the title of a lecture by Jaspers. His view of a cosmopolitan Europe was based on the humanistic values he saw as the political antithesis to nationalism and the devastation it had unleashed. For him, Europe should become a cultural project in which the values of the Enlightenment could be preserved. Jaspers's lecture emphasized individualism, liberalism, Christianity, and liberty. The Kantian concept of "autonomy" was central as well to Jaspers's plea for a new cosmopolitan Europe. This cosmopolitan Europe had no geographical boundaries but rather was a locus of values. Its origins were not only in Europe but also in China and Europe, starting around 800 BC when the foundations for world religions were founded. Jaspers called this the "Axial Age," the time when myth ended and history began. It is also the beginning of transcendental thought, which demands a higher law and preserves a tension between this world and the other, transcendental one, a tension, Jaspers argued, that enabled freedom to flourish but had now been abolished by totalitarian societies. The Axial Age, with its world religions – Judaism, Hellenism, Hinduism, Buddhism, Confucianism, and Christianity – guided humankind into modernity. Jaspers meant that Germany could be part of the free world once again, in the sense that European culture was the culture of Homer, Sophocles, Plato, Aristotle, Virgil, Dante, Shakespeare, Goethe, Cervantes, Racine, Molière, Raphael, Michelangelo, Rembrandt, Velázquez, Bach, Mozart, and Beethoven. As at the PEN meeting several months earlier, Jaspers believed that Germany could be integrated into cosmopolitan Europe through its universal heritage and culture.[25] He also tried to distance Europe from the victorious Allies: the United States and the Soviet Union. In his view, Europe needed to steer its own course. If the concept of a cosmopolitan Europe has a father, it is Karl Jaspers. His vision was of a Europe without ethnic groups like the Jews, without the United States, and without the Soviet Union. Jaspers wanted a religious Europe, a Europe of transcendental values.

Hannah Arendt did not attend the conference in Geneva – she was working for the JCR at the time – but she responded to Jaspers's arguments in letters and essays.[26] In her rebuttal to Jaspers's idea of the "Axial Age," she emphasized space and citizenship as the roots of Jaspers's cosmopolitanism. She began her essay "Karl Jaspers: Citizen of the World?" with the statement:

> Nobody can be a citizen of this world as he is a citizen of his country. . . . Political concepts are based on plurality, diversity, and mutual limitations. A citizen is by definition a citizen among citizens of a country among countries. His rights and duties must be defined and limited, not only by those of his fellow citizens, but also by the boundaries of a territory. (Arendt 1968b: 81)

By this time, Arendt had become an American citizen. She agreed with Jaspers that people in the modern era shared a common present, but she needed to remind him that they do not share a common past. Arendt again emphasized "political responsibility" – one's responsibility as a citizen for everything that one's government does in the name of one's country (83). Thus, in Arendt's opinion, "global responsibility" was an unbearable burden.

Although Arendt was not present at the Geneva conference, another opponent of Jaspers, Georg Lukács, was. Lukács was invited as an important Marxist theorist, since Soviet intellectuals refused to attend. He belonged to the Communist Party elite in Hungary. In Geneva, he presented another version of European cosmopolitanism, one that had been attractive to Jews as a way of transcending the ethnic boundaries of identity ever since Marx's essay "On the Jewish Question" appeared in 1844. Like universal citizenship, Lukács observed, socialism provided an escape route from Judaism. Lukács at once attacked Jaspers's existential concept of liberty and dismissed his thinking as bourgeois pessimism, which, Lukács argued, could be held responsible for fascism.[27] Lukács proposed an alliance of progressive and democratic forces in Europe with the Soviet Union, which he saw as the embodiment of European democracy. He favored continuing the alliance of 1941 as a means of advancing the revolutionary spirit. His stance was as cosmopolitan as Jaspers's, but it represented the cosmopolitanism of Marx and Rousseau, of the French and Russian revolutions. The division in Geneva – the fight between Jaspers and Lukács over the soul of an imagined cosmopolitan Europe – reflected the positions of the two sides in the emerging Cold War. The only thing the participants had in common was their mutual neglect of the Jewish experience; Jews were neither remembered nor their extinction mourned. It was as though their disappearance from Europe was a fait accompli that the intellectuals in Geneva would not waste their breath discussing. It was a striking omission.[28]

The same was true of the Soviet postwar attempts to nationalize its brand of socialism. Even before the war, the concept of a separate Jewish identity after the Russian Revolution did not fit neatly into the Soviet system of socialist equality. The danger posed by this view of Jewishness was clearly recognized at the founding meeting of the World Jewish Congress in 1936 and would later be called "totalitarianism." Jews, in this scenario, were the enemy of the Soviet socialist project. The Soviets also started to use the term "cosmopolitanism" as a code word for unwanted Jews,[29] even though two Soviet Jewish writers, Ilya Ehrenburg and Vasilii Grossmann, abhorred this attitude and reflected on World War II not only in patriotic Soviet terms but in a broader European and Jewish context.[30] Both were also active members of the Jewish Anti-Fascist Committee, founded by the Soviets in 1942 to mobilize worldwide support for the Soviet struggle against Nazi Germany. Soviet Jews also met with American Jews to build support for that struggle. The members of this committee also conducted an investigation into the Nazi murder of Jews in the Soviet Union, the *Black Book of Russian Jewry*. The book was suppressed, and most of the committee members were liquidated by the Soviet regime after the war.[31]

The struggle against cosmopolitanism in the Soviet Union was first of all a struggle against Jews. Jews were considered not only cosmopolitan but rootless, which in the late 1940s became a code word for Jews who insisted on their Jewish identity. The attacks against Jewish writers, poets, and actors intensified after the founding of Israel in 1948, which the Soviet Union initially supported. The "anti-cosmopolitan" campaign also encouraged anti-Semitic persecution.[32] Slezkine (2004) argued that Jews were indeed the carriers of transnational modernity. His Jewish gaze did not come from the western parts of Europe, but from the east, where Jews were always considered more traditional and premodern. This was hardly the case, since Eastern European Jews were in fact promoting a Jewish political agenda that translated Western European Jewish aesthetic sensibilities into the realm of action. Jewish political sensibilities also made Jews susceptible to the message of the Russian Revolution, as the promise of equality was as seductive as the promise of equal citizenship in the West. But the revolution betrayed the Jews, becoming increasingly national and defining itself as an ethnic Russian project, a continuation of the czarist regime in which Jews had no asocial or political equality. Clearly, the destruction of Soviet Jewry (more than one million Soviet Jews were killed by the Nazis) could not be ascribed a special place in Soviet memory.

Attempts to universalize the experience of the Nazi genocide were also evident in postwar legal deliberations pertaining to Nazi war criminals, which involved both the Americans and the Soviets. This prompted Jaspers to insist on the legitimacy of the trials. The Nuremberg War Crimes Tribunal introduced a set of legal precedents concerning violations of human rights, which limited the sovereignty of a state vis-à-vis its citizens. What today seems normative was, before and during the trial, highly charged and contested terrain on which various political and legal forces struggled to impose their vision of justice on international relations. At the outset, the American understanding of the destruction of European Jewry, which formed the basis for the Nuremberg Trials, was universalistic: the Nazi war crimes had been committed against sixty million people, among them six million Jews. The crimes against the Jews formed a small percentage of the total indictment handed down at Nuremberg; the Jews themselves remained abstract, absent victims. In spite of, or perhaps because of, what was later called the Holocaust, the fate of the Jews remained a neglected aspect of the Nuremberg Trials and their universalist message. The struggle at Nuremberg was perceived as a struggle between civilization and barbarism, in which civilization was the victim, Nazi barbarism the perpetrator. The Jews thus stood for "humanity as a whole." Justice Jackson opened the trial with the following words:

> The privilege of opening the first trial in history for crimes against the peace of the world imposes a grave responsibility. The wrongs which we seek to condemn and punish have been so calculated, so malignant, and so devastating, that civilization cannot tolerate their being ignored, because it cannot survive their being repeated. That four great nations, flushed with victory and stung with injury, stay the hand of vengeance and voluntarily submit their captive enemies to the judgment of the law is one of the most significant tributes that Power has ever paid to Reason.[33]

Jaspers's hope for a new cosmopolitan Europe appeared to be emerging out of the Nuremberg Trials; as we have seen, Jaspers thought that the Nazis should be treated as common criminals. Nuremberg indeed held out the hope of a new Europe, and recent sociological books on cosmopolitanism interpret the Nuremberg

Trials as a true cosmopolitan moment.[34] In this view, cosmopolitan Europe resisted its own antihumanist tradition by struggling morally, politically, economically, and historically for reconciliation with itself. This would suggest that the Nuremberg Trials were akin to the Geneva conference on the "European Spirit," the goals of which were to reinvent an enlightened Europe without particular interests. Nevertheless, the fundamental idea behind Nuremberg, the legal basis that justified it, was to outlaw war. The shapers of Nuremberg used the term "aggressive war," but, of course, if there are no aggressive wars there cannot be any defensive ones. The Nazi crimes were initially constructed as a "war of aggression" (an existing legal category) rather than as a "crime against humanity" (an emerging legal category). The Nuremberg Trials were aimed at preventing countries from resorting to war as a way to resolve issues. This reasoning in turn was premised on the idea that no country would place itself deliberately outside the legal order; this was a necessary component of the idea – without it, the legal order would be neither valid nor even imaginable. The role of this comprehensive legal order was to engender the civilizing effects of economic cooperation; the term "civilizing" was a minimal reference to the Holocaust and captured the general unease that there was no existing legal language for the barbarous crimes the Nazis had committed. This prompted some leading voices among the Allies to favor summary executions of war criminals rather than the lengthy proceedings of a trial. Ultimately, however, those advocating a legal response prevailed, emphasizing, among other things, the educational significance of such trials for the German populace. From a purely procedural perspective, political show trials tend to appear illegitimate.

Hannah Arendt felt uneasy about the Nuremberg Trials, just as she would about the Eichmann trial fifteen years later. Legal arguments draw their persuasive power from the fact that they are grounded in precedent, as legal positivists at the time took pains to point out.[35] But the argument was not about precedent alone. Hans Kelsen, one of the most prominent legal positivists at Nuremberg, maintained that the punishment of war criminals was likely to turn into an act of revenge, and Nuremberg into a political trial – indeed, a show trial that would hardly differentiate between the politically motivated Stalinist show trials and trials against war criminals who had committed crimes against humanity. Kelsen's argument shows the gap between legality and legitimacy. The trials could not have been conducted without the unconditional surrender of the accused. Their surrender gave the trial its legitimacy but hardly its legality, a contradiction that haunts human rights trials to this day.[36] Thus, the emerging order left two contradictory principles in place: the crime of aggressive war left state sovereignty intact, whereas and yet "crimes against humanity," often conducted by a state against its own citizens, could be punished only by violating state sovereignty. The framers of the postwar order saw the Depression and the years leading up to World War I as a period of heightened tension between economically warring blocs. Not only did they intend to establish a world legal order that would govern the conduct of all nations, they also wanted to create a world economy in which international cooperation would become progressively stronger. They foresaw a world in which cooperation would be the defining trait of international affairs. Since problems could be dealt with legally, there would be no need for a counterproductive arms race. In such a world, they reasoned, tyrannical governments could not last. The people would get rid of them, just as the European system could recover from the historical trauma of world war and genocide.

The Nuremberg Trials thus provided the world with a redemptive moment of hope. Under the Nuremberg approach, no nation was a pariah. This reasoning rested on the notion of universal suffering. Hadn't World War II proved that all countries have a vested interest in cooperating with one another? Had it not shown that the United States and the Soviet Union could cooperate in making the ultimate sacrifices? If these superpowers could do it, then surely any nation could; and if they could do it with so much at stake, then they could do it when the stakes were lower. The longer they cooperated, the more their systems would converge; the more they converged and were governed by law rather than violence, the more they would enshrine the values embedded in the concept of human rights. Thus, even if the Nuremberg Trials were problematic in a legal sense, their legitimacy was based on the fact that they were creating a new world order, such that a cosmopolitan, mutually cooperative Europe would arise from the tribunals of Nuremberg in much the same way that the racial laws of Nuremberg in 1935 ushered in the destruction of enlightened Europe.

The camps the Americans liberated were ethnically and nationally diverse, containing a wide variety of people the Nazis hated, from political prisoners to gypsies. Rather than set off an instant realization that there had been a particular crime against the Jews, the initial experience of opening the camps instead confirmed the Allies in the view that the Jews were one of many groups victimized by the Nazis.[37] During the Nuremberg Trials, the destruction of European

Jewry appeared as a set of facts but not yet as an idea. But, surprisingly perhaps, all the essential facts were there from the beginning, starting with the estimate that 5.7 million Jews had been killed by an intentional plan of the Nazi high command. Still, as noted above, the crimes against the Jews accounted for only a small percentage of the total Nuremberg indictments, and the Jews themselves remained abstract victims.

However, the Nuremberg Trials also served – even if this was not openly acknowledged at the time – as a catalyst for the recognition of specific crimes against Jews per se.[38] The Institute of Jewish Affairs tried to counteract Nuremberg's emphasis on universalization. Jacob Robinson and the Jewish organizations came away from Nuremberg knowing that the crimes committed against the Jewish people would have broader implications for the future. In an address Robinson delivered in London on October 10, 1945, called "The Jewish International Political Agenda," he asked,

> What do we expect from this trial? We expect something much more than can be foreseen at this moment. . . . The Tribunal is not going, by orthodox methods of evidence, to prove that six million Jews were killed. It will accept it as a fact not in need of further evidence. . . . The fact that one day it will be a court decision on the highest level of the four greatest Powers, stating that the beginning of such a crime, the deprivation of human rights, is a crime, may serve us as a substitute for a thing we dream about, the outlawry of anti-Semitism on an international plane.[39]

Robinson and the Institute of Jewish Affairs of the World Jewish Congress wanted to show not only that the Nazi crimes against the Jews were unique but that these crimes set the stage for crimes against humanity, and that the persecution of the Jews was linked to the Nazi state's preparation for an aggressive war.[40]

Jewish organizations did not want to fade into anonymity at Nuremberg; they also did not want to be subordinated to the abstract concept of "humanity." Above all, they wanted to draft a "Jewish indictment" of the Nazi crimes. To this end, in late 1944 Robinson and his staff prepared documentation of the Nazis' crimes against the Jews that tried to demonstrate that the German Nazi Party had devised a deliberate plan to destroy the Jewish people. Robinson wrote on December 28, 1944, "the crimes committed against the Jews were, in essence, one collective crime against a people – a crime in which national differences [among Jews] have no importance"

108

(quoted in Lewis 2008: 192). The institute also provided the prosecution with research data on the number of Jews killed by the Nazis. The institute's review of demographic data and population figures and its tabulation of the survivors yielded an estimate of about 5,700,000 Jews murdered, thus providing the iconic figure of six million for the Nuremberg Tribunal. And yet the institute was unable to obtain a formal "Jewish indictment" at the Nuremberg Trials. Neither the Americans nor the Soviets were interested in acknowledging the particular suffering of the Jews at Nuremberg and preferred general terms like "crimes against humanity"[41] and also Lemkin's neologism "genocide" in the Nuremberg indictment.[42] Thus the efforts of Jewish intellectuals and political leaders after the catastrophe may not have succeeded in pushing a particular agenda on the international order, but they were successful in establishing a Jewish universal agenda that made "crimes against humanity" and "genocide" part of a new cosmopolitan order. "Crimes against humanity" became the Jewish term for dealing with an assault on a stateless people. There was still resistance to recognizing the Jews, who were scattered all over the globe, as a distinct ethnic group, but "crimes against humanity" and "genocide" would have to do. Robinson himself reflected on the concept of "crimes against humanity" later, writing in 1972, "The language of this Article indicated that the Charter has gone a long way from some traditional taboos of international law."[43]

Concerted efforts by the World Jewish Congress, the publication of the *Black Book*, and Lemkin's "Axis Rule" all raised awareness that a catastrophe had taken place for the Jews as a people. The World Jewish Congress supported Lemkin's efforts to push for a genocide convention at the UN for this reason, and it contributed to the ad hoc Committee for the Preparation of a Draft Convention on the Crime of Genocide. Two years earlier, Lemkin had sent a memorandum to the World Jewish Congress requesting that the organization work toward an antigenocide clause at the conclusion of the Nuremberg Tribunal.[44] Jewish politics after the war had moderate success in exposing the details of the destruction of European Jewry, though it formulated the facts in general legal terms. The reformulation of "crimes against humanity" into "crimes against the Jewish people" had to wait until the Eichmann trial in 1961.

Hannah Arendt observed these political developments with keen interest. She corresponded with Jaspers about the Nuremberg Trials and formulated some of her important theories on human rights in response to the trials and the issues they raised. In an early essay on

109

human rights, published in 1949, she made the following observation, which echoed Robinson: "This situation, the emergence of mankind as one political entity, makes the new concept of 'crimes against humanity,' expressed by Justice Jackson at the Nuremberg Trials, the first and most important notion of international law."[45] Arendt knew that these crimes were indeed unprecedented. Concepts such as collective guilt, genocide, and crimes against humanity, which today are universally acknowledged and respected, grew out of Jewish responses to what happened to the Jews during World War II. These were particular concepts couched in universal terms. The stage was thus set for Arendt's next intellectual project: the struggle for human rights and against totalitarianism.

# — 6 —

# FROM NUREMBERG TO NEW YORK
# VIA JERUSALEM

After the Holocaust, Jewish politics followed two parallel tracks. Jews pursued international guarantees on internationally binding agreements like human rights; these rights and agreements, and the struggle against totalitarianism, had to be institutionalized. At the same time, Jews worked to secure an ethnic national state for the Jewish people. Both efforts were considered protective mechanisms. Zionists, in the minority amongst politically thinking Jews before World War II, could now legitimately claim that Jews had been killed simply because they were Jews, and that the Nazi regime had exposed the vulnerability of such concepts as "humanity" and "international responsibility." So-called international protections of minorities had failed the Jews miserably, and only a strong Jewish state could make whole what had been shattered.

Life in the old Jewish centers of Europe had been practically extinguished, and organized Jewry now directed its efforts either toward Israel or toward the United States, where the principles of Jewish sovereignty and pluralism were beginning to have an impact. Human rights became a central issue in this reorientation of Jewish politics and in Arendt's thinking after the war.[1] As we saw in the previous chapter, the World Jewish Congress tried to reformulate its allegiance to minority rights in a new formula of human rights.[2] As in the period between the world wars, cosmopolitan internationalism and Jewish goals were seen as mutually reinforcing. The organization lobbied for passage of the Universal Declaration of Human Rights and the genocide convention in the UN. Motivated by its activists' firsthand knowledge that most of the killings of the Jews were conducted under the cover of war, the World Jewish Congress worked hard to promote the conviction that human rights and fundamental freedoms should not be suspended in times of war and to enshrine this principle as international law.[3] In his survey of the World Jewish Congress's lobbying of the United Nations in 1955, Nehemia Robinson wrote,

> The World Jewish Congress has considered from the very beginning that the new world organization to be established after the holocaust of the Second World War, must deal much more with the rights of the individual than did the League of Nations, because the experience of the Nazi and Fascist regimes have shown the degree to which the negation of the most elementary rights of the person can proceed and the depth of inhumanity to which such negation leads. (N. Robinson 1955: 61)

It was obvious to the World Jewish Congress that the minority rights protections in effect before World War II had failed. The organization thus sought more universal mechanisms of protection in the belief that protection of people "anywhere and everywhere" would be the best protection for the Jews.[4]

At the same time, many Jewish émigrés to the United States, Arendt among them, began writing about "totalitarianism," which had both analytical but primarily moral content.[5] Whitfield (1980) makes it clear that Jewish intellectuals, including Arendt, were not really interested in Italian fascism as the root source of totalitarianism; rather, they saw totalitarianism as an organizing concept of the Cold War.[6] They were concerned with comparing "evil" regimes, their scientific values always contested.[7] But this mission was not about devising scientific tools through which to understand the world, and they were committed to fighting more than just the Cold War. The lumping together of different regimes under the heading "totalitarian" may not satisfy strictly social scientific criteria; it served more important moral and political purposes.

Arendt's *Origins of Totalitarianism*, published in 1951, was not only a scholarly study of totalitarianism but a reflection on the fate of the Jews of Europe in Nazi concentration camps.[8] The book deals as well with German–Jewish émigrés, like Arendt herself, and how they coped with their own past.[9] It traces the development of Arendt's thinking from the late 1930s, when she formulated her first thoughts on anti-Semitism, to the late 1940s, when she extended her ideas to imperialism, minority and human rights, and finally to the destruction of the Jews in the camps. Arendt chose to write about the human condition through the lens of the Jewish condition. In short, she places the destruction of Jewish life in Europe at the core of the decline of western civilization. But, out of the catastrophe, Arendt reinvented and rediscovered the old concept of cosmopolitanism for the global age.

The book begins not with the Third Reich but with the French Third Republic, and draws on Arendt's own experience in France to analyze the French-Jewish emancipation, the Dreyfus Affair, and how the Vichy regime betrayed the Jews during the war.[10] In Arendt's view, modern Jewish history started with the French Revolution and emancipation and ended with the failure of human rights protections to prevent the destruction of European Jews at the hands of the Nazis. Arendt addresses the same questions that the World Jewish Congress tried to operationalize in its attempt to turn the concept of human rights into binding cosmopolitan laws. Her vision is bleak:

> Antisemitism (not merely the hatred of the Jews), imperialism (not merely conquest), totalitarianism (not merely dictatorship) – one after the other, one more brutally than the other, have demonstrated that human dignity needs a new guarantee, which can be found only in a new political principle, in a new law on earth, whose validity this time must comprehend the whole of humanity while the power must remain strictly limited, rooted in and controlled by newly defined territorial entities. (Arendt 1951: ix)

Although *The Origins of Totalitarianism* has found its way into the pantheon of universal political theory, the particular Jewish experience is always center stage. For Arendt and many other Jewish intellectuals, human rights could not be grounded in "nature." How could "nature" protect innocent people from human evil? Human rights must be grounded in a dystopian understanding of a world in which any act and any outcome is possible. Fear that everything might be possible informed the preamble of the Universal Declaration of Human Rights: "Whereas disregard and contempt for human rights have resulted in barbarous acts which have outraged the conscience of mankind, the advent of a world in which human beings shall enjoy freedom of speech and belief and freedom from fear and want has been proclaimed as the highest aspiration of the common people."

Arendt, of course, knew all too well that such a declaration was not enough. The centerpiece of *The Origins of Totalitarianism* is a short section called "The Perplexities of the Rights of Man," in which Arendt picks up where she had left off in her 1949 essay on human rights.[11] Allegedly "emancipated" Jews were forced to bear the consequences of what it meant to be merely "human beings." They had no state of their own, no right to belong to any community. For Jews, the declaration was nothing more than empty, meaningless words. "We can only become aware of the existence of a right to have rights," Arendt had written in 1949, "and the right to belong to some kind of organized community, when there suddenly emerged millions of people who have lost and could not regain their rights because of the new global situation" (Arendt 1949a: 30). She felt great disdain for those who were fighting for human rights on a juridical level. When she wrote in *Origins of Totalitarianism* about "a few international jurists without political experience" (Arendt 1951: 292), she might have had Jacob Robinson or Raphael Lemkin in mind. "No statesman, no political figure of any importance, could possibly take them seriously," she concluded.

This judgment no doubt arose from Arendt's own experience of being thrown into an internment camp in France, and from her knowledge of the fate of the Jews in the camps. Without power to back them up – without cosmopolitanism in action, so to speak – rights were unenforceable; they were no more than words. Arendt shifted between the dream of cosmopolitanism (the guarantee of rights as the substance of social reality) and the need to establish a state that could protect particular identities, even if those identities were only figments of the imagination harnessed to the memories of particularity. This was the context in which the concept of cosmopolitanism emerged. For Arendt, the modern idea of cosmopolitanism arose from the ashes of the Holocaust. The innumerable statements and institutions built on the idea of cosmopolitanism in the second half of the twentieth century eventually produced a new foundation for thought, a new, universalist form of common sense. The experience of the Holocaust also inaugurated a much broader process, in which all social and political theories based on national or ethnic "traits" had to navigate between the universal and the particular. Although this was still more a set of regulatory ideals than a reality, it nevertheless represented a change. Arendt espoused this change in theory, and Jewish organizations tried to put it into practice. In her analysis of the paradoxes inherent in what it means to be "human," Arendt used the destiny of the Jews to characterize the paradox of modern cosmopolitanism – namely, that the international protection of human rights undermines state sovereignty, but at the same time lacks the means to enforce that protection because it lacks sovereignty itself.

Arendt's chapter on human rights thus mirrored the Jewish condition in the twentieth century. In "Total Domination," another section of the book, Arendt analyzed the concentration camps as the fatal outcome of statelessness and the lack of rights.[12] In her attempt to name the unnamable, she called the camps "unprecedented," "images of hell," and manifestations of "radical evil."[13] Arendt felt that the conventional assumptions of the social sciences, based as they were on the Enlightenment concepts of reason and the rational, literally could not comprehend the radical evil of the camps. For example, if one believes that most of our actions are utilitarian and self-regarding, then the camps undermine this belief. The Nazis, Arendt argued, were more interested in exterminating Jews than in winning the war. The camps thus constituted a break with the fundamental values and beliefs of modernity.[14] For Arendt, the Nazis exemplified totalitarianism in their abandonment of the values of pluralism, free speech, critical judgment, and human reason. Nazism did indeed spell the end of what it meant to be human, as philosophers and social scientists had understood the concept.

Arendt did not see Nazism as inherently or intrinsically German but rather as one specific manifestation of totalitarianism.[15] This view arose not only from Arendt's own German cultural heritage and her desire to deflect blame from a German tradition of which she was a part. *The Origins of Totalitarianism* also embodies a conservative vision of the breakdown of modern European society, its public life and civic virtues and values. Totalitarianism signaled above all the reversal of all known political traditions. Part of this reversal involved the privileging of death over life – an overturning of every formulation of the social contract ever conceived. Arendt saw the Holocaust as unique not only in its scope and in the systematic nature of the killings but in its very attempt to deny humanity as such. Conventional categories of crime became irrelevant to her as a result, and this view was indeed incorporated, later, into the legal canon under the aegis of "crimes against humanity." Jewish organizations understood, too, that the social contract needed to be rewritten after World War II. They were not interested in debating the uniqueness of the Holocaust but in fashioning a political framework within which they could come to terms with such an experience.[16] If the camps showed that "everything is possible" (Arendt 1951: 441), then the new cosmopolitan order had to prove that this was not the case, or at least ensure that it would never be possible again.

In *The Origins of Totalitarianism*, Arendt sets forth the three steps to total domination of a person or a people: the killing of the juridical person in man, the murder of the moral person, and the death of individuality. Here Arendt extended her analysis of the Nazi concentration camps to the Soviet system as well. Although she was aware that the Nazi system elevated annihilation as an end in itself, she viewed the camp system as an attack on the human spirit as well. This is precisely the space in which their "radical evil" emerges: "we may say that radical evil has emerged in connection with a system in which all men have become equally superfluous" (459). Arendt also intended *The Origins of Totalitarianism* as an account of the moral and legal meanings of a crime against humanity and an attempt to show a way forward, to suggest ways in which humanity could, theoretically at least, be restored.

The book, as I have argued, was above all an attempt to universalize the Jewish experience, something Arendt continued to do in her work over the next two decades. But she needed to look elsewhere to find universal answers to Jewish questions. Her next books did not deal explicitly with the Jewish condition. They looked for ways to escape totalitarianism.[17] She found the political possibilities she was looking for in the ancient Greek polis and in the founding of the American Republic. We see a piece of her answer to the problem of totalitarianism in a letter she wrote to Jaspers on January 29, 1946. "There is much I could say about America," she told Jaspers. "There really is such a thing as freedom here and a strong feeling among many people that one cannot live without freedom. The republic is not a vapid illusion, and the fact that there is no national state and no truly national tradition creates an atmosphere of freedom or at least one not pervaded by fanaticism" (Arendt and Jaspers 1992: 30). Arendt thought she had found in America the solution to the Jewish problem. She saw there genuine pluralism and the kind of rooted cosmopolitanism she was seeking. In the late 1950s, Arendt started work on a book about the American Revolution, which she compared favorably to the French one. *On Revolution* (Arendt 1963b) is full of admiration for the American revolutionaries and their new republic, a system of government based not on ethnicity, a state that included all its citizens, different in many ways from European ethnic nation-states. These perceptions may have been reinforced by Arendt's own naturalization as an American citizen in 1951.[18]

Arendt saw in America the realization of her European cosmopolitan dreams. Jews could be citizens without ceasing to be Jews. Universalism and particularism could exist side by side. American Jews, though a minority, were at large not a shunned and despised minority as they were in Europe. They could join as Jews the political membership of the United States. Arendt continued to labor over *On Revolution* during her trip to Jerusalem in 1961 to cover the Eichmann trial for the *New Yorker*.[19] In Jerusalem, she returned to some ideas she had developed just after the war. In "Approaches to the 'German Problem,' " an essay published in 1945 in *Partisan Review*,[20] she had suggested taking seriously the European Resistance's call for a non-national Europe. Now she tried to resurrect that idea in the context of the American Revolution as part of a universalist solution to the dangers of nationalism.

In Israel in 1961, Arendt found the reverse of the cosmopolitan tendencies she so admired in the American setting. She saw in Israel an ethnic nation-state based on European principles; her report on the Eichmann trial shows her trying to coming to terms with a European tradition she thought she had buried and left behind.[21] *Eichmann in Jerusalem: A Report on the Banality of Evil* (1963a) became one of the most controversial books of its time and probably the one she is best known for today in the Jewish world.[22] What made this book so famous was not only the phrase "banality of evil," which nurtured an interpretative literature of its own in regard to perpetrators of mass crimes.[23] Arendt's interpretation gave rise to interpretations of the Holocaust as bureaucratic and mechanical, even though this was apparently not her intention at all. What made the book incandescently famous was the enormously heated debate that it set off, among both Jews and non-Jews, about how the Holocaust should be understood.

But *Eichmann in Jerusalem* was not only a book about the Holocaust. Nor was it only a continuation of *The Origins of Totalitarianism* that dealt with the legacy of the Holocaust for human rights. It was a book about the moral evaluation of Nazi crimes as an example of the ever-present possibility of mass murder in modern times. And it was a book about Jewish responsibility and politics during the dark times. Finally, it was a book about Israel and the meaning of Israel for Jews. Not written, of course, in such a vein, the book was read by many of its Jewish detractors as an attack on a Jewish nation still in its infancy. Arendt's interest in the Eichmann trial, however, lay in its status as the first attempt to apply the doctrine of "crimes against humanity" outside the context of occupation authority, and therefore the first attempt to use that doctrine as a real authority for legal action. And yet, as Arendt saw immediately, the concept of a "crime against humanity" was being used by Israel, a Jewish nation-state, on behalf of the Jewish people. It does not get more particular or more self-interested than that.

The trial itself tried to marry two incompatible positions. It sought to establish the uniqueness of the Holocaust, and the unique right of the Jewish people to judge those who committed it, while at the same

117

time it convicted Eichmann of a charge – a crime against humanity
– that by definition had to be devoid of all particular national content
if it was to be legitimate at all. It was in part for this reason that the
prosecution deemed it necessary to supplement the charges against
Eichmann with "crimes against the Jewish people," a category that
fit neither the old framework nor the new. In this sense, Eichmann's
trial was a corrective to the Nuremberg Trials. The background of
the trial, and the debates over it, was the legitimacy of Israel itself,
which the prosecution sought to consolidate both domestically and
internationally, but whose right to its Jewishness would be gravely
undercut if the universalism at the core of crimes against humanity
was taken to its ultimate conclusion.

Arendt explored all of these issues in the book, and more, with
brutal clarity and honesty, and this is what made the book so controversial.[24] To begin with, she wrote about the facts of the Holocaust
and the moral lessons that should be drawn from them, which had
only been done implicitly. Once Arendt shone a searchlight on these
matters, she brought all the contradictions to the fore. She might have
agreed with David Ben-Gurion, the Israeli prime minister, that Jews
are different from other people. But Ben-Gurion wanted to keep this
difference within the boundaries of the ethnic nation-state, whereas
Arendt insisted on another kind of diasporic difference. The question
of what constitutes a crime against humanity and how it differs from
a crime against the Jewish people was crucial in this respect. In
Arendt's book, both universal and particular messages reinforce each
other. We see this clearly when she argues in favor of Israel's legitimacy to conduct the trial at all:

> Israel could have claimed territorial jurisdiction if she had explained
> that "territory," as the law understands it, is a political and a legal
> concept, and not merely a geographical term. It relates not so much,
> and not primarily, to a piece of land as to the space between individuals
> in a group whose members are bound to, and at the same time sepa-
> rated and protected from, each other by all kinds of relationships,
> based on a common language, religion, a common history, customs
> and law. . . . No State of Israel would ever have come into being if
> the Jewish People had not created and maintained its own specific in-
> between-space throughout the long centuries of dispersion, that is,
> prior to the seizure of the old territory. (Arendt 1963a: 241)

In defending Israel's right to conduct the trial, and even to execute
Eichmann, Arendt seemed to have returned to the old days of her
work with Jewish Cultural Reconstruction. This is not a universalist

118

attacking the particularism of the Jewish state; here we have one particularist speaking to another. Arendt's Jewish particularism was bound not to territory but to politics. And it was, in Israeli (and Jewish) eyes, a strange politics, disconnected from sovereignty.

Then there was her attack on Jewish leadership during the Holocaust. This was the point at which most of her critics could not follow her. They interpreted the book as attacking the Jewish leadership for cooperating with the Nazis, while at the same time depicting Eichmann as an average, ordinary man with average, ordinary moral responses. "To a Jew," she wrote, "this role of the Jewish leaders in the destruction of their own people is undoubtedly the darkest chapter of the whole dark story" (104). But in fact Arendt was deliberately returning to her demand for a Jewish army. She wanted Jews to be powerful. She assumed that Jewish leaders were in a position to choose their actions, and she judged them accordingly.[25] For Arendt, the Jewish leaders failed to recognize the true nature of their enemy.

Arendt also had no patience with the witnesses at the trial. She was not of the opinion that public displays of suffering would help the Jewish cause. In a sense, Arendt was still fighting the internal war between Zionists and assimilationists that had raged before the Nazis' rise to power. Many Jews found these arguments out of touch with reality. She was advocating a Jewish cosmopolitanism sandwiched between Israel and the United States. Arendt was writing as a Diaspora nationalist at a time when this stance no longer had legitimacy or supporters among her fellow Jews. She wanted the Eichmann trial to endorse her definition of the Holocaust as unprecedented, and to testify to the enormity of a new type of crime.[26] Arendt did not, of course, deny the uniqueness of the Holocaust: she insisted on its uniqueness, but in her view the court in Jerusalem did not.

Arendt failed to recognize that the victims who testified at the trial were not only displaying Jewish weakness but also articulating their victimization. This may have been the first time that victims had ever become a major voice in what Shosana Felman (2001) calls the "Theater of Justice." Arendt wanted the Jews to be the avant-garde of a new cosmopolitanism. The court in Jerusalem did not, in her view, understand that the Nazi genocide constituted "a crime against humanity, perpetrated upon the body of the Jewish people, and that only the choice of victims, not the nature of crime, could be derived from the long history of Jew-hatred and anti-Semitism" (247). She refused to see that the choice of victims and the nature of the crime could somehow be connected as well.[27] Nevertheless, she was aware of the contradictions in her own account and closed her report with the following words, which pertain to Eichmann's execution: "It was as though in those last minutes, he was summing up the lessons that this long course in human wickedness had taught us – the lesson of the fearsome, word-and-thought-defying banality of evil" (221). It was as though she knew that the "banality of evil" would continue to haunt her for the rest of her intellectual career.

The book left different legacies in different contexts. It became the blueprint for an entire tradition of perpetrator research that downplays evil intentions. It became an inspiration for those who wanted to universalize the Holocaust and see it not as a Jewish tragedy alone but as part of a chain of genocides. In these ways, it became the crucible for debates that continue to this day.

Arendt's responses to her critics are important not only as illustrations of the impact of the book but also for what remains unsaid. In fact, Arendt was at her most explicit when responding to her critics and came closest to providing a formula for the modern concept of cosmopolitanism. The harshest attacks on Arendt came from other Jewish intellectuals in her New York circle, some of whom made things personal and were often vicious.[28] Had she been an outsider, that would have been one thing, but Arendt was writing from within the Jewish community. Her calls for Jewish strength and power, her admiration for the Warsaw ghetto fighters, her disdain for those who cooperated with the Nazis instead of resisting now bore fruit. The Eichmann trial changed the terms of the debate by inaugurating the sanctity of victimhood. Arendt wrote *Eichmann in Jerusalem* in terms of the Jewish self-assertion that had been part of her own political socialization.[29]

Arendt did not respond to most of the criticism, but she did reply to a letter from Gershom Scholem, which revived the debate between these two intellectuals about what it meant to be Jewish after the Holocaust.[30] Most of her critics thought the lesson of the Holocaust was anything but universal, and Arendt shared this view, but this claim provided her with a convenient foil. The broader debate, however, was about the possibility of a cosmopolitan Jewish identity. Many Jewish intellectuals, Scholem among them, thought that the lesson of the Holocaust was that people had to make a choice to be on the side of the Jews or not. The Holocaust taught that Jews had to face the truth of their identity, to accept that being true to oneself also means being true to one's people. It means loyalty and solidarity. Scholem accused Arendt of being disloyal to the Jews; her denunciation of particularism, as her critics saw it, was a form of disloyalty bordering on treason. They interpreted her book as saying that the crimes of Auschwitz could have happened anywhere, to anyone, as though Jews had no special connection to it. Arendt's position appeared to turn the particular sufferings of the Jews into a matter of indifference.

The outrage of Arendt's Jewish critics raises questions about the validity of a cosmopolitan language and the ways in which Jews define themselves in relation to universal values. Scholem and Arendt's exchange concerned not only the Jewish fate after the Holocaust but the theoretical dilemmas of current cosmopolitan theory. In a famous letter of 1964, Scholem accused Arendt of being heartless toward her own people, of lacking sympathy and solidarity with the victims – without which no remedy would ever be possible.[31] "In the Jewish tradition," he told Arendt, "there is a concept, hard to define and yet concrete enough, which we know as 'Ahavat Israel': 'Love of the Jewish people.' In you, dear Hannah, as in so many intellectuals who came from the German Left, I find little trace of it" (Scholem 1976: 302). Scholem's reference to the German left might have pertained to a famous statement by Rosa Luxemburg, another Jewish woman whom Arendt admired greatly. Luxemburg had written in 1916 to her friend Mathilde Wurm,

> Why do you come with your particular Jewish sorrows? I feel equally close to the wretched victims of the rubber plantations in Putumayo, or to the Negroes in Africa with whose bodies the Europeans are playing catch-ball. I have not a separate corner in my heart for the ghetto: I feel at home in the entire world wherever there are cloud and birds and human tears.[32]

Luxemburg wrote this letter long before the Holocaust, in an era when Jews were still either considered citizens of European nation-states or tolerated as subjects of European empires. It was the expression of the Jewish hope of universalism that tempted so many Jews to align their fate with socialism. Arendt admired Luxemburg but was also critical of her European universalism.[33] Thus, foreshadowing some of the debates about cosmopolitanism, Arendt described Luxemburg as belonging to a milieu of European Jews that predestined them to become good Europeans: "While the self-deception of assimilated Jews usually consisted in the mistaken belief that they were just as German as the Germans, just as French as the French, the self-deception of the intellectual Jews consisted in thinking that they had no 'fatherland,' for their fatherland actually was Europe"

121

(Arendt 1968b: 42). She thought that most revolutionaries had no idea of what to do with the kind of European Jewish cosmopolitanism women like Luxemburg had to offer. Arendt made this comment with sadness some years after her exchange with Scholem, but it was clear to her that, in associating her with Luxemburg, Scholem had seriously misread her.

Scholem did not think that after 1945 any Jew could take such blithe universalism seriously, and neither did Arendt. As far as he was concerned, however, Arendt's cosmopolitanism was just another name for universalism, which implied the forsaking of one's ethnic and cultural roots. It meant the principled refusal to acknowledge how one was marked by one's upbringing, and how that upbringing created special obligations. In Scholem's view, one's origins created an obligation of solidarity, in terms of both loyalty and perspective. It was wrong to trample on the feelings of your own people. It was an offense against your own identity. He told Arendt that the "matter of the destruction of one-third of our people" should require more sensitive treatment from "a daughter of our people" (Scholem 1976: 302).

Arendt replied a month later. "I have always regarded my Jewishness as one of the indisputable factual data of my life," she corrected Scholem, "and I have never had the wish to change to disclaim facts of this kind" (Arendt 2007: 466). For Arendt, her Jewishness was a given, a "physei" rather than a "nomos," as she put it. But when it came to Scholem's charge that she felt no love for the Jewish people, she seemed to agree. But it was not just love for the Jewish people that she lacked; she didn't love any people. "You are quite right," she admitted, "I am not moved by any 'love' of this sort, and for two reasons: I have never in my life loved any people or collective – neither the German people, nor the French, nor the American, nor the working class or anything of that sort. I indeed love 'only' my friends and the only love I know of and believe in is the love of persons" (Arendt 2007: 466–7).

At first glance, Arendt seems here to be taking Rosa Luxemburg's ideas several steps further. She acknowledges that Jewishness is a key feature of her identity but leaves unresolved how, or whether, this entails any obligation or solidarity or perspective. It was a bold statement, but it did not ring true, given Arendt's background and politics. Arendt did indeed want to champion individuals as the ultimate reality – after all, her most important book on political theory dealt with the horrors of totalitarianism, and in her most universalistic book, *The Human Condition*, she tried to connect worldliness to the familiar sphere. Against the backdrop of her own life, however, the idea that only friends mattered sounded just a bit ironic. As we have seen, Arendt was not exactly a "cultivator of her garden." She spent all her time wrapped up in national and international and cultural politics. Jewish politics was a big part of her life, and, as *Eichmann in Jerusalem* showed, she was also always passionately involved with Israel. The fate of Israel affected her more personally than that of any other country in the world. She replied to Scholem, "That there can be no patriotism without permanent opposition and criticism is no doubt common ground between us. But I can admit to you that something beyond that, namely, that wrong done by my own people naturally grieves me more than wrong done by other peoples" (Arendt 2007: 467). These obvious disjunctions between deeply held convictions led to the constant argument and agonizing that was the mark of this generation of post-Holocaust Jewish intellectuals. They argued all the time, they wrote all the time, and then the argument would resurface, transformed, with all its little emendations and improvements and answers that had developed in the meantime. These Jewish intellectuals were engaged in a debate about one's capacity to choose one's identity long before it became part of academic and popular discourse. This debate was also about the capacity and willingness to judge. As in her book on totalitarianism, in *Eichmann in Jerusalem* Arendt basically claims that writing is judging. She does not want to free anyone from moral responsibility, particularly not the Jews, and this is why she insisted so adamantly that the victims were responsible for their fate as well. This is never a popular position, neither in the early 1960s nor today.

In the same letter to Scholem, Arendt qualified and clarified her reading of "radical evil" and the "banality of evil," which had become so important in her work. "I changed my mind and no longer speak of 'radical evil,' " she told Scholem. "It is indeed my opinion now that evil is never 'radical,' that it is only extreme, and it possesses neither depth nor any demonic dimension. It can overgrow and lay waste the whole world precisely because it spreads like a fungus on the surface" (Arendt 2007: 470–1).

Both Arendt and Scholem positioned themselves as Jews between the United States and Israel, and both looked at Europe in the same way from their respective Jewish locations. Neither of them was a universalist, and neither of them believed in liberal forms of European assimilation. Both demanded recognition as Jews by their non-Jewish environment. Both were Jewish patriots and cosmopolitans who needed to find a new political home outside Europe. The major question troubling both was how Jews could and should act politically in a world after the Holocaust. Their exchange dealt primarily with the relation of Jewish particularism to universalism, within the larger framework of politics and the mutual desire not to abandon Judaism politically. This shared perspective connected their exchange to Kafka and Benjamin, whose presence lurked between the lines of their correspondence. Part of their exchange examined political strength and weakness, a debate that fuels current discussions about Jewish politics both within and outside Israel. This is a typical problem for cosmopolitan politics. Arendt more often than not criticized the worldlessness of the Jews, their retreat from action and the political world. At the same time, though, she admired this worldlessness, which allowed Jews to be pariahs and to take an ethical standpoint outside politics. The divorce between ethics and politics, weakness and strength, is, of course, not only a Jewish problem, but a more general problem of how to deal with power.

Eighteen months after the exchange with Scholem, Arendt was interviewed on TV by a young German journalist, Günter Gaus, and clarified many of these points.[34] In particular, she affirmed that her politics was Jewish: "If one is attacked as a Jew, one must defend oneself as a Jew. Not as a German, not as a world citizen, not as an upholder of the Rights of Man, or whatever. But, what can I do specifically as a Jew?" (Arendt 1994: 12). When Gaus asked her about her statement to Scholem that she had never loved any people, Arendt responded, "Belonging to a group is a natural condition. You belong to some sort of group when you are born, always" (17). Relating to Jewish worldlessness and Israel she said, "One pays dearly for freedom. The specifically Jewish humanity signified by their worldlessness was something very beautiful, this standing outside of all social connections, the complete open-mindedness and absence of prejudice that I experienced" (17).

These comments remind us that current debates regarding cosmopolitanism must deal with the internal contradiction between human rights and particularistic politics. At times, these two things are at antipodes. The concept of universal human rights belongs to an absolutist framework whose principles admit no compromise. It provides a set of standards against which all governments can be measured and against which all will fall short. Arguably this is appropriate and effective in its proper context, but it is completely inappropriate in the context of power and politics. This is what the Jewish debate regarding loyalty and solidarity was partly about. An even harsher response to *Eichmann in Jerusalem* than Scholem's came from Jacob

Robinson, who had served as a legal consultant to the prosecution in Nuremberg, a consultant to the UN Secretariat in the creation of the Human Rights Commission, and a legal advisor to the Israeli delegation to the United Nations, and had also helped draft the Israeli–German reparations agreement. In 1965, he published a 350-page book with the sole purpose of refuting Arendt's book on Eichmann.[35] His criticism was based on historical facts and legal theory, and his purpose was to show that Eichmann was a zealous idealist and fanatical anti-Semite, something Arendt would not have denied, even though her emphasis was on how people act within totalitarian regimes. Arendt emphasized ruptures with the past, while Robinson stressed continuities. In chapter 2, "War Crime Trials and International Law," Robinson wrote about the legal notions of crimes against humanity and genocide and demonstrated how both notions were connected to the crimes against the Jews, which basically strengthened Arendt's argument while attempting to refute it. Robinson's anger was reserved for the same issue that so troubled Scholem, and he addressed this in chapter 4, "Jewish Behavior in the Face of Disaster." Robinson's debate with Arendt has never been resolved. He accused her of relying on a historiography of the destruction of the Jews that drew exclusively on German sources. Like Scholem, he attacked her for not taking the viewpoint (epistemologically and not only morally) of the victims.[36] Going one step further than Scholem, he implied that Arendt lacked the relevant languages to study the Holocaust (Hebrew, Yiddish, Polish, and Hungarian), and in this way he basically challenged her Jewishness and by extension her grasp of the tragic choices involved in this question. Robinson discussed the hidden tradition of weakness of Jewish life and thought, which refers to survival with dignity and the preservation of even a single life.

Arendt's notion of Jewish politics was different. She was less concerned with human life than with the good life of political virtue. The ghetto fighters of Warsaw, rather than the quiet resistance of ordinary people, were her heroic models. Robinson had been involved in Jewish international politics his entire career. His reading of Jewish history was also Eastern European Jewish, and he attacked Arendt as someone outside the fold. Arendt responded in the pages of the *New York Review of Books* in November 1965.[37] Much of her response was made up of scathing attacks on Robinson's credentials, and she also detailed the organized attacks Jewish organizations had made on her. It appeared to be Arendt's final statement on matters Jewish. In reply to "Jewish behavior in the face of disaster" she wrote,

"It seems that there was not one rabbi who did what Dompropst Bernhard Lichtenberg, a Catholic priest, or Propst Heinrich Grüber, a Protestant minister, had tried to do – to volunteer for deportation" (Arendt 2007: 505). With statements like this, she further enraged her Jewish readers.

But Arendt's relationship with Jewish audiences was reversed at almost the same time, which provided an opportunity to advance the cosmopolitan argument even further. The occasion for this reversal was the publication of the German translation of *Eichmann in Jerusalem* in 1964. Like Scholem, many German intellectuals also construed Arendt's cosmopolitanism as synonymous with universalism. But when it came to the Holocaust, universalism had as much appeal for Germans as it lacked for Jews, and for precisely the same reasons: it deemphasized the particularity of victims and perpetrators.[38] It changed the categories into impersonal ones. It implied retrospectively that the Holocaust could have happened to anyone and made the Nazi crimes simply one instance of a larger class of mass murders, rather than a uniquely evil event perpetrated by uniquely evil people. Arendt was drafted as one of the founders of this functional approach to the study of the Holocaust, which deemphasizes agency (and therefore guilt) and concentrates on bureaucracy and above all universalizes the Holocaust.[39] Although this was an important moment in the history of Holocaust studies (a now burgeoning field that is still marked by this fundamental divide), the decisive debate took place with a young intellectual named Hans Magnus Enzensberger, who was later to become a central figure in the German New Left.[40] In 1964, the same year the translation of *Eichmann* appeared in German, Enzensberger published a collection of essays called *Politics and Crime*, one of the essays of which used Arendt's book as a foundation for its claims. This essay, "Reflections before a Glass Cage," made what Enzensberger thought was the obvious extension of Arendt's argument, which was that all genocides are the same, and we have the same obligation to stop them. He drew people's attention to the prospective nuclear holocaust, which in 1964 weighed heavily on people's minds. It was not only that the two phrases used the same word; it was that the same mechanism that Arendt had described in her book seemed to be at work. Thus, for intellectuals like Enzensberger, everything began with universalism, with the idea that modern warfare would make victims of us all. Hence war as such (and especially nuclear war) became the new universal threat. In the 1950s and 1960s, most people thought that "nuclear holocaust" would mean the end of the world. Enzensberger's generation wanted to universalize the experience because they resented West Germany's alliance with the United States and its membership in NATO.

In Enzensberger's interpretation, evil wasn't inherently banal. It was banalized. The Holocaust and the rise of the Nazis had been explained often enough in terms of Germany's exceptional national development. In Arendt's view, Enzensberger represented a universalism wrongly understood: Enzensberger lifted the Holocaust out of the framework of the German nation and placed it in the context of modernity itself. His was part of a larger criticism of modernity and capitalism.[41] Germany thus ceased to be the exception to the standard path of European national development and instead became the exemplification of a common modernity. World War II was not a disaster suffered by Germany alone; it was a disaster suffered by all of Europe, and one that was prepared by all of Europe in World War I. Germany was simply its epicenter, as it was the epicenter of accelerating industrial development and efficiency and the strain this placed on society. As for the "after period," it was also not simply the aftermath for Germany but a new phase for all of Europe. It was the inception of the European Union, which marked the beginning of a new phase in modernity, where German democracy became the continuation of fascism and its system. But how could Enzensberger and others have inverted all of this and made modernity the focal point? Enzensberger's argument is more implicit than explicit and derives from a reversal of his apparent leftist and universal perspective.

For Enzensberger, the soul of Arendt's book was modernity – not the parts of it that were dedicated to the concrete details of the extermination of European Jewry, but rather the description of the mind of its architect. Enzensberger felt that Arendt had made Eichmann the paradigm of how instrumental-bureaucratic rationality can numb us to millions of dead by reducing them to numbers and sanitized clichés like "collateral damage." This was exactly what put Eichmann on the same level as the future perpetrators of a nuclear holocaust. Enzensberger specifically compared Eichmann to Hermann Kahn, who in 1961–2 had written two books, *On Thermonuclear War* and *Thinking the Unthinkable*. The latter title almost makes his entire argument for him: here was a man who was saying that we should think the unthinkable. It was our moral duty, demanded by rationality. By making the unthinkable thinkable, he was also making it doable. The assumption until then had been that nuclear weapons were too horrible ever to be used. Kahn was trying to convince the establishment that this wasn't true, that thirty million or sixty million dead wouldn't in fact be the end of the world. He advised the world to start preparing for the possibility.

Enzensberger's arguments were very influential. Equating the Holocaust with other mass murders marked a major intellectual milestone. The debate about whether the Holocaust should be considered unique or as simply one instance of genocide is still being fought today. Arendt's response to Enzensberger's book was very interesting. Enzensberger and the German journal *Merkur* asked her to review the book, but she refused. When they asked her why, the result was an exchange of letters between her and Enzensberger that *Merkur* published the following year, in 1965.[42] What is intriguing about these letters, written roughly eighteen months after Arendt's exchange with Scholem, is that she seemed to attack Enzensberger for some of the same things that she had been attacked for, namely, for describing everything in abstract, functionalist terms, which washed away the guilt. Even more striking, she told Enzensberger that he was especially wrong to make such an argument as a German.

Again, more was at stake here. Arendt rejected Enzensberger's claim that "Auschwitz reveals the roots of all politics" (Arendt and Enzensberger 1964: 380). Enzensberger explains that his mistakes are understandable, since he is a Marxist. To say that Auschwitz revealed the roots of all politics was like saying that everyone was guilty, "and where all are guilty, nobody is" (381). One cannot sacrifice the particular for the universal, Arendt argued, adding, "and when a German writes that, it is even more questionable." Her point was that not our fathers but all men were perpetrators, which is simply untrue; and she ended the paragraph by exclaiming, "O Felix Culpa!" – a kind of "blessed fault" attitude she accused Enzensberger of harboring. Arendt defended the American tradition as well: "The non-understanding of the Germans, but not only the Germans of Anglo-Saxon traditions and American reality, is an old story" (Arendt 1994). Europe's relation to America and the meaning of a unified Europe was one of Arendt's preoccupations during the 1950s.[43] She saw America as the locus of liberty through the birth of a new body politic, something that had turned into a dream and a nightmare for Europeans. What she feared most was a new pan-European nationalism that took America as its counter-model. She wrote about anti-American Europeanism, which she saw as the foundation of a unified Europe, reminding her readers that it was Hitler who wanted to destroy Europe's nation-state system and build a united Europe (Arendt 1994: 417). Thus, in her reply to Enzensberger, we see not only Jewish but also American fears about both Germany's and Europe's possible return to totalitarianism.

Enzensberger replied that he was proud to be a Marxist and continued to argue, like Luxemburg, that all suffering had equal worth. He reminded Arendt of the threat of nuclear annihilation. And he deliberately used concepts that many people thought should be reserved for the Holocaust alone, such as "Sonderbehandlung" (special treatment) and "Endlösung" (final solution). "The final solution of yesterday could not be prevented," he told Arendt. "The final solution of tomorrow can be prevented" (382). Enzensberger thus rejected Arendt's argument that his being German made his remarks particularly objectionable. He rejected this argument as entirely illegitimate; worse than *ad hominem*, it was *ad nationem*, and thus violated every canon of universal reason. Enzensberger wanted to be seen as an individual and not as a representative of an ethnic collective (383). He stood by his original point: that we should be against every Holocaust, no matter the perpetrator. "And the worst is that these deeds were committed, and not the fact that they were committed by Germans," he observed. Surely Arendt could not disagree? Clearly Arendt could not, but her main argument lay elsewhere. She tried to tell Enzensberger that he had misunderstood her book. Enzensberger's interpretation of the Holocaust was different from hers. *Eichmann in Jerusalem* was not about universal evil. To the contrary, she stressed that "it did happen in Germany and nowhere else and has turned into an event of German history" (384). She also rejected Enzensberger's comparisons between Auschwitz and war-related deaths in places like Dresden and Hiroshima. For her, Auschwitz had nothing to do with war. Its aim was to exterminate the Jewish people, and it was thus unique and not part of the general practices of warfare.

Once again, this rather brief exchange of letters between a young German leftist and Arendt foreshadowed later European developments. Three years later, in 1967, Arendt engaged in another exchange, this time with a twenty-five-year-old German student.[44] The student was very concerned about Arendt's reading of totalitarianism. He argued that the United States was guilty of crimes during the Vietnam War and expressed concerns about western imperialism in general. Arendt answered that politics always begins at home and that notions of fixing the world are nothing but megalomania. The student's responsibility, she told him, was for Germany. One could not change the world, she said, because one cannot be a citizen of the world, and only those who do not want to be responsible for anything claim responsibility for everything.

Why did Arendt deny that a German could understand the Holocaust without any reference to its particularity? Within Arendt's theory, morality is based on particularity and on identity. It is based on being able to look at ourselves in the mirror and say that we have fulfilled the moral obligations that make us who we are; this means above all the special responsibilities we have to particular others who are linked to us through the accidents of history and birth. To ignore the roots of responsibilities in identity is to misunderstand the basis of morality, and to sweep it all aside is an attempt to forget who you are and to flee personal responsibility. There is a communitarian argument at work here as well, which can also be called rooted cosmopolitanism.[45] This is a point not only about personal identity but also about who you are as a member of a community. Arendt was a Jew and an American, a communitarian and a pluralist. But as a cosmopolitan, membership in a community is the beginning, not the end. Thus, for her, a value-free description of the Holocaust is wrong in itself because the Ought is immanent in the Is. Many Jews were furious with the way Arendt treated facts; they felt she was tampering with sacred taboos. She was not willing to look at victimhood alone. She was trying to make explicit that there is an enormous difference between acting on values and being value neutral.

For Arendt, there is no such thing as value-free description; there is only flight from one's identity. This is the key to understanding *Eichmann in Jerusalem*. In Arendt's view, you can deduce the Ought from the Is. Everything that happens in the world has moral significance. *Eichmann in Jerusalem* is about what it meant to be Jewish after the Holocaust, especially when Israel and Europe were no longer viable options for Arendt. It was Arendt's most personal book and at the same time a book that paved the way for a rooted cosmopolitanism. The notion that the basis of morality lies in identity, and that the basis of personal identity is collective identity – or in overlapping collective identities – was Arendt's answer to the question of how to maintain a tension between the universal and the particular. She was not saying that all morality is based on identity but that some of it is, and that it is an essential part, because it is the part that makes us who we are. This is the part that gives us moral motivation, because it is the basis of our passions and our self. This is the meaning of cosmopolitanism beyond universalism. Arendt saw no problem in speaking with different voices, depending on the circumstances and the audience. This position should not be confused with inconsistency or hypocrisy. She spoke as a Jew when she addressed Jaspers and Enzensberger and when she addressed her German audience in Hamburg in accepting the Lessing Prize. She spoke as an American when she corresponded with Scholem. The audience determined her vantage point, which is part of what cosmopolitanism is all about.

Arendt was also paying homage to her intellectual kinsmen, friends like Benjamin and Kafka. Universal maxims like "we should help the poor" or "we should save the innocent" reflect a kind of allegiance that tries to display ideological consistency – these were the kind of maxims she identified in the young Enzensberger, and in her view they contained no personal element and were therefore merely pious utterances that no one acted on until they were mixed with the passion of identity, the feeling that you just can't look yourself in the eye if you allow a terrible crime or injustice to take place without trying to stop it. Arendt's response to both Scholem and Enzensberger was that they misunderstood her as a universalist, because both of them were unable to go beyond conceiving of the relation between universal and particular as a case of either/or. For her, they were a matter of "both/and." Scholem decried her for being a universalist and betraying her duty to her people, her personal collective identity. Her reply to this was: No. Not everything is particular. The truth is not particular. To Scholem she said, in essence, that identity is not everything. To Enzensberger she said that identity is not nothing. Your identity and my identity matter. The fact that we are individuals does not sever us from our collectivities. Individuals do not emerge out of the void; they are produced socially, and they remain rooted in their emotions and ways of thought in the collectivities that pro-duced them. Even if they reject those collectivities, they reject the terms that have been inculcated in their sense of self, which an out-sider does not feel at all. Similarly, to Scholem she said: Not all morality is particular. We have a duty to mankind. To Enzensberger she said: Not all morality is universal. If all we use is reason, then we could end up with Kantian moral imperatives – or we could end up with the bureaucratic memos justifying torture and nuclear war. Her rooted cosmopolitanism claims that pure reasoning is indifferent to its ends. It is determined by our starting points, which reason does not supply, because real convictions are emotional convictions. The ultimate basis of our emotional convictions is our identity: what we can't imagine ourselves doing to the people to whom we are vitally attached.

For Arendt, this was always the starting point of modern cosmo-politanism. This is what she was trying to make clear in her exchange with other intellectuals. Squaring the circle between the universal and the particular is no easy task, and Arendt by no means finished it. What she showed is that it also requires squaring the circle between thought and feeling, morality and identity, the Ought and the Is. This is not an easy path, but it is the only way not to get stuck in the trap of universalism, where identity doesn't matter and cosmopolitanism does not exist. One can, of course, interpret Arendt's various positions as inconsistent, but that would be too simple. Actually, both Arendt and Enzensberger were right. They were both products of their particular life-worlds, one Jewish, the other German.

# — 7 —

# BETWEEN DROHOBYCH AND NEW YORK: AN END AND A NEW BEGINNING

Arendt wrote these postwar books and letters from New York. She had no intention of returning to Germany or moving to Israel. In 1951, she stopped officially being a refugee and became an American citizen. Like other American Jews, she lived in a world that had no experience of organized state persecution. American Jews did not need to become Marxists to be accepted as universalists, and they did not need to become nationalists to be accepted as equal citizens. America indeed presented Jews after World War II with a new beginning, and their success in embodying the American dream turned them into the political equals of non-Jewish Americans. Needless to say, the sovereignty of the Israeli state challenged this vision of life in the Diaspora. Perhaps Arendt viewed America and the American Revolution through rose-tinted glasses, as opening up a new cosmopolitan space that could offer a model for Europe to emulate. The words of the nineteenth-century Jewish poet Emma Lazarus – "Give me your tired, your poor, your huddled masses yearning to breathe free," engraved on a plaque at the base of the Statue of Liberty – suggested that Jews, among others, could live freely in the new land.

Jews came to America as Jews and became Jewish Americans, just as other immigrants became German Americans, Italian Americans, Polish Americans. There was no need to demand minority rights for these groups, in Arendt's view, because America did not define itself ethnically. It lacked an official, institutionalized majority. The separation between government and people, one of the more significant requirements for a cosmopolitan Europe, was part and parcel of America's self-definition, as was the constitutional right of religious freedom.[1] Of course, these values and characteristics were and still are extremely contested terrain in American history.[2] Americans today still debate the virtues of assimilation and Americanization, on the one hand, and diversity and cultural pluralism, on the other. But these are very different from European issues, since they are conducted within a nonethnic state.[3] What was so attractive to Jews and other immigrants to America was that labels and groups that define the individual can overlap. People are connected to one another horizontally rather than vertically. This also means that each person constitutes a unique combination of connections, which in turn has three ramifications. In the first place, it means that Americans are more individualized than Europeans, since the number of possible combinations increases geometrically. Second, each American individual has more in common with a wider group of people than is the case in other countries. Third, groups of people are less clearly demarcated by boundaries because of all the overlap. These factors might very well constitute a cosmopolitan identity. Unlike the case of Jews in Europe (and in Israel), the weak bonds of association are enough to hold a society of strangers together because they erode, through their very existence, the forces that used to drive people apart, and because they are anchored in individuals' free expression of their desires. Thus Jews could join other groups because they wanted to, not because they were born into those groups. Ethnic identities can become plural. When European Jews arrived on American shores, they arrived like other immigrants, as strangers, and went their separate ways. They could start over in a safe haven.[4]

This more or less idealized vision of American pluralism and liberty was very attractive to Arendt, and her writings on America in the 1950s and 1960s reflected this. It may help to explain why Arendt considered Israel a European ethno-national project, which she criticized from an American pluralistic perspective. This kind of Arendtian criticism is still heard today. The historian Tony Judt looked at Israel from an American perspective in 2003 in an article reminiscent of Arendt's 1944 essay "Zionism Reconsidered." "The problem with Israel," Judt maintained,

> is not – as is sometimes suggested – that it is a European "enclave" in the Arab world, but rather that it arrived too late. It has imported a characteristically late-nineteenth-century separatist project into a world that has moved on, a world of individual rights, open frontiers, and international law. The very idea of a "Jewish state" – a state in which Jews and the Jewish religion have exclusive privileges from which non-Jewish citizens are forever excluded – is rooted in another time and place. Israel, in short, is an anachronism.[5]

Judt suggested a "binationalist" solution for Israel and the Middle East.[6] Juri Slezkine made a similar point in his *Jewish Century*, which tries to preserve the cosmopolitan, nomad Jewish identity over the normalizing tendency of a nation-state. Slezkine describes Israel as "the only postwar European state ('European' in both composition and inspiration) to have preserved the ethos of the great nationalist and socialist revolutions of the interwar period" (Slezkine 2004: 327). Both scholars follow Arendt in criticizing ethnic exclusiveness and the sovereignty of such states as a solution to anything.

Arendt left Israel and Europe behind – not only the ethnic exclusiveness of Israel but also the kind of European universalism she thought it embodied. The Eichmann trial was a test case for her. She attempted to convey to Scholem and other critics that being Jewish is a political choice rather than a matter of destiny and belonging alone. This was not a rejection of Zionism altogether. Arendt never rejected Zionism per se, only certain manifestations of Zionism. It is no coincidence that she ends the section on anti-Semitism in *Origins of Totalitarianism* with the statement: "The only visible result was that it [anti-Semitism] gave birth to the Zionist movement – the only political answer Jews have ever found to anti-Semitism and the only ideology in which they have ever taken seriously a hostility that would place them in the center of world events" (Arendt 1951: 120). Her concern was not love and morality but power and politics.

For Arendt, Zionism was only one face of Jewish identity. Israel defines itself ethnically, and its criteria for citizenship, much like its criteria for collective memory, are exclusivist. Postnationalist European notions of citizenship and memory would seem to require that Israel forfeit the ethnic basis according to which it defines its nationals, and turn instead to the conventional territorial principle, including equality before the law for all citizens living within Israeli territory, without regard to ethnic origin, race, religion, or sex. We have seen how this process was part of the postwar era in Europe and how both the Nuremberg Trials and Jaspers's proposals contributed to it.[7] This process also entails that memory, too, can be universalized, which is exactly what happened in Europe and also in the United States.

Traumatic metaphors address acts of extreme violence as well as innocence; they are exemplified through representations of the Holocaust and have become a key mechanism in addressing the precarious balance between universal and particular modes of identification (and theoretical interpretations of the same). The particular experience of the Holocaust has been dislodged from its historical context and inscribed as a universal code of suffering. By emphasizing the

135

traumatic and subsequent therapeutic dimensions of this process, the dividing line between perpetrators and victims, as well as the distinction between historical specificity and universal applicability, is frequently blurred. In this view, representations of Holocaust memories carry implications for both theories of collective memory and the ongoing search for a common European founding moment. In contrast to early nation-building efforts that relied on mythological inventions of political communities, nascent European identities seem to revolve around a negative foundational moment commemorating the universal lessons of the Holocaust.

We saw the beginning of the process in Enzensberger's attempt to incorporate Arendt's *Eichmann in Jerusalem* into his theory of universalized crime and his criticism of liberal society and the liberal state as potentially fascist. We see the same tendencies today in theories such as those put forward by Giorgio Agamben, who like Enzensberger appeals to Arendt for his universalist claims.[8] Agamben's universalist vision sees totalitarian and liberal states as similar enough in their basic structures to warrant historical distinction. Auschwitz is everywhere, and it is the consequence of bio-politics, bio-politics being the sum total of demography, public health, welfare measures, and the consequences of all three. The concentration camp as structural trauma has become one of the leading metaphors of modernity. But Agamben is not interested in the camp as a historical entity; for him, no historical questions remain to be clarified.[9] He has blurred the distinction between a criminal state and a state that commits crimes, a distinction that was one of the most important aspects of Arendt's reading of the political world and especially of her theory of totalitarianism. The Jews are written out of Agamben's account and dissolved into the universal category of "human beings," a point that Arendt rejected in her debate with Enzensberger.

Agamben, of course, represents the intellectual avant-garde of this universalizing mechanism, which has delegitimized particular memories in the name of a greater good: humanity. The specific Jewish dimension of the Holocaust has not only been dissolved; it has also been delegitimized as part of the Nazi racist project. Murdered by the Nazis only because they were Jewish, after the Holocaust Jews were elevated to the status of "human beings." To emphasize their Judaism, Agamben's argument goes, would be a concession to racist thinking. There is a dynamic at work here in which the Holocaust serves as the background and motivating factor in articulating a newly defined European cosmopolitanism that is reminiscent of a Kantian universalism in which there is no room for the particular.

Situated between the extremes of civilization and barbarism, the Holocaust has become a prism through which modernity can be reassessed. And in that reassessment, modernity is perceived as the realization of progress, firmly embedded in Enlightenment ideals; barbarism is considered the opposite. A central question nevertheless links the two: does barbarism constitute a breakdown of civilization, or is it, as Arendt argued in *Eichmann in Jerusalem*, the result of modern rationalization and bureaucratization? Was the Holocaust an aberration, a deviation from the emancipatory path, or is it the natural – some would say inevitable – outcome of modernity and the Enlightenment thinking on which it rests?

Civilizational rupture[10] encompasses the breakdown of ontological security and coheres with Hannah Arendt's position as she developed it in *The Origins of Totalitarianism*. It can be characterized as a breakdown in the rational understanding of the world, in the basic belief that life is more important than death, a reversal of values by which survival is accidental and destruction becomes the rule. Arendt recognized that civilization needs to be made whole again through the creation of new understandings and taboos. She resisted the moralizing discourse on victimhood without distinction that she had detected in the 1960s and that has become increasingly popular in recent years.

As understandable as these universalizing tendencies may have been in the era of postwar reconstruction in Europe, they could not appeal to Jews in Israel, with its very clear foundation myth.[11] Israel defines itself both as universal-democratic and particular-Jewish, such that its universality is inherently limited. Israel suggests a different reading of European history, undermining the project of reconciliation between former enemies brought on by the collapse of the Eastern European socialist regimes. This alternative reading of European history keeps alive the memory of the destruction for which Nazi Germany and its collaborators were responsible. The Eichmann trial contributed its part to this alternative reading of the past. This narrative is a challenge to European reconciliation, and thus to cosmopolitan Europe's project.

The strongest manifestation of this difference between Jewish and European memory pertains, of course, to the destruction of European Jewry in the Holocaust. The Zionists thought that only territorial sovereignty could repair the damage done by the Nazis, by giving the Jews a state and thus turning a homeless, stateless people into a people with a state and a home. Zionism spelled the end to the experience of the Diaspora, an experience that has often been identified as a kind of Jewish cosmopolitanism. Many Israeli Jews see the Holocaust as a result of their own statelessness, not of extreme German nationalism, as many Europeans have come to see it. The protection of Jews at any price has become one of the pillars of Israel's identity. Israel was founded just as the new Europe was rising from the ruins of World War II. While both Israel and this new Europe took shape against the same backdrop, the former perpetrators and their former victims drew very different conclusions from their respective memories of the Holocaust, interconnected as these memories were. That Israel was designed to negate European and diasporic Jewish life made Israel an inherently European project in its own eyes. At the same time, postwar Europe views the Holocaust as a universal tragedy that happened to befall Jews.

Thus, for many critics of Israel, modern Zionism, despite being a reaction to modern European nationalism and its unwillingness to accept Jews, was essentially a rejection of the cosmopolitan ideal. Yet critics of Israel reject the very notion of a "Jewish state," alleging that it is rooted in the very prewar European nationalism that led to World War II. Israel, in their eyes, is thus an anachronism, in some ways an ironic throwback to the ideal of warrior virtue.[12] In Israel's self-understanding, the Jewish cosmopolitan ideal was destroyed in the Holocaust, and Jewish Israelis have made themselves into warriors in an attempt to prevent another Holocaust. Critics assail Israel for its willingness to fight and its constant preparedness for war.[13] In many ways, Israel considers itself the defender of Jewish cosmopolitanism, providing a home for Jews from all over the world. In this sense, Israel is a product of Diaspora Judaism, gathering in Jews from all over the world with different experiences and backgrounds. We return to our starting point: unlike Christianity, Judaism is an ethnicity as much as a religion, and this feature is written into the very foundation of the state of Israel and its citizenship laws. Israel is therefore not willing at this point to define itself as a neutral state on the French or American model. People active in Jewish minority politics, like Jacob Robinson, decided after 1945 (some even earlier, with the rise of Nazism) to abandon minority politics in favor of territorial sovereignty. The goal was the same – the protection of the Jews – a goal that, for Arendt, did not express the lofty aspirations of what politics should be.

Israel often sees a clear correspondence between nation, territory, society, and culture, but Europe and America may look secular when compared with their medieval and Puritan pasts, respectively. What Arendt may have overlooked was that the fundamental divisions that form the salient and constant features of Euro-American culture – the division between public and private, between civil society and the state – are the profound cultural markers of its secularized Christianity. However, it is possible to have modernity without them. They do not violate the essence of modernity, because that essence is not secularism per se but a moral order based on individuation. Arendt got us close to this point. With typical, unsentimental clarity, she recognized the dangers of the abstract notion of "man," a concept as abstract as the concept of "nature." "Man of the twentieth century has become as emancipated from nature as eighteenth-century man was from history," she wrote in *The Origins of Totalitarianism*. "History and nature have become equally alien to us, namely, in the sense that the essence of man can no longer be comprehended in terms of either category" (Arendt 1951: 298).

At times, Arendt looked at Israel through American eyes and judged ethnic nationalism through the Jewish European eyes of the past. She left European universalism and the Enlightenment behind, just as she saw Israel's ethnic particularism as part of Europe's totalitarian past. To leave behind means also to begin anew. For Arendt, America was a miracle.[14] It enabled a new beginning not only for Jews but for the entire European tradition. Thus American pluralism, the tension between the "no longer" and the "not yet," the chasm between power and morality, universalism and particularity, the political space between miracle and pragmatism, the radical separation between religion and state coupled with strong faith in the power of God, appealed to Arendt as a new variant of a lost European tradition. It was this kind of American exceptionalism that seemed to realize the cosmopolitan dream of the Enlightenment. It was a federal form of cosmopolitanism, transcending the European nation-state. For many Jews, it was a revival of the European empires of old in a new and modern form. What Arendt observed was that never had modern Jews been so integrated into the mainstream of a Diaspora country as they were in America.

Is cosmopolitanism based on Jewish experience at all possible? Can the last Europeans turn into the first cosmopolitans? The Diaspora was never, nor is it now, a closed culture; Jewish culture has always mixed with other cultures. If one understands culture as something heterogeneous, open to the outside, then one can see how the newly emerging cosmopolitan culture is becoming "Jewish." At the beginning of the twentieth century, the Jewish Diaspora experience and its cosmopolitan exponents were at antipodes to the national-territorial forms of memory constitutive of the European nations.

Today, identification with a group (be it ethnic, national, or religious) whose historical roots lie outside the spatial and temporal coordinates of the adopted homeland is often a matter of preference and, not infrequently, of pride. In addition to its social impact, this stance also has political repercussions. In the face of oppression or real disadvantage, maintaining a status that is not based upon fixed geographic boundaries fuels political striving and protest. The Jewish Diaspora can serve as the paradigm for de-territorialization as such. A particular awareness of place and the relationship to being Other are played out on an immediate experiential level. But the Diaspora was never a closed-off sphere. Actual Jewish culture was not only mixed with other cultures; it was itself a mixture of cultures. In a certain sense, its cosmopolitanism lay in Judaizing the mixture of cultures it absorbed – it gave them a unifying cast without negating them.

The experience of Diaspora, of life in exile, is the clearest example modernity offers of a sustained community life that does not need a territorial container in order to preserve its history. In the Jewish experience, life outside the nation-state is nothing new. Prior to the Holocaust and to the founding of the state of Israel, the Jewish experience was determined by a mixture of yearning to be territorially independent and a longing to serve as universal ambassadors of the Diaspora.[15] Nowadays, however, these desires can no longer be considered specifically Jewish but instead constitute the broader arena in which issues of citizenship, civil society, and cultural identity are played out. Jews were simultaneously cosmopolitan and citizens of a particular country. Although they were aware of the need to straddle the poles of universalism and particularism, this state of tension has increasingly become the norm in today's world. Jewish existence before the Holocaust and Israel mixed longing for territorial independence with the appeal of belonging to other cultures. This condition of Diaspora did not grow out of Judaism per se but out of tensions between citizenship, civil society and cultural identity.

But one should not overextend this concept. Not all ex-territorial experiences are diasporic.[16] Does the Diaspora offer a genuine alternative to life in a specific territory and as part of a specific national group? For Jews, these alternatives were never mutually exclusive. Thus, in one of her first columns for *Aufbau*, an essay that scolds Jews who want to replace Moses with George Washington, Arendt writes,

> The history of humanity is no hotel where someone can rent a room
> whenever it suits him, nor is it a vehicle which we board or get out of

140

at random. Our past will be for us a burden beneath which we can only collapse for as long as we refuse to understand the present and fight for a better future. Only then – but from that moment on – will the burden become a blessing, that is, a weapon in the battle for freedom. (Arendt 2007: 150)[17]

In this passage, Arendt addresses not only identity but also citizenship. After 1945, the classic notion of cosmopolitanism had to be rethought. Americans could teach Europeans that universal citizenship comes in many shapes and shades. Jewish cosmopolitanism, because it is based on experience and catastrophe, cannot be arbitrary and it cannot be universal. Particularity is about identity, and identity needs to be exclusive if it is to function as identity: there is our history (Moses) and then there is theirs (Washington). Without boundaries, there can be no identities. Particular worlds are antagonistic; there is struggle, honor, and fame, and there is also, of course, death. Its antithesis is the principle of universalism. Nations, religions, cultures are being transcended, and equality of all has become a major virtue.

Universalism denies cultural difference and dignity along with it. It is a dream of rationality beyond the here and now. But this dream can also turn into a nightmare. Therefore, Jewish cosmopolitanism is not foundationalist but is based on and woven into history and experience. It is based on a dual strategy that recognizes the contingency of foundational assumptions as well as the malleability of ontological principles. It rests on the lives of people, their dignity and their desire to be able to live without pain and suffering. This involves not only the preservation of what we have but the fear of what will happen when home and livelihood are lost. This also means that the cosmopolitanism of fear includes the theory and practice of avoidance. It involves knowing what is possible and what on no account should become possible. It is a matter of a cosmopolitan power of judgment and the ability to distinguish good from evil. This is why the notion of "evil" was one of the pillars of Arendt's political theory.

But cosmopolitanism is not merely a mental attitude; it starts with the body and its vulnerability – its mortality. Cosmopolitans are not heroes in the old sense. Since 1945 no cosmopolitan thought can "innocently" appeal to the old world and its transcendental certainties of reason. A break in civilization also means a break in cosmopolitanism. Hence cosmopolitanism at the beginning of the twenty-first century must be formulated in relation to "eternal fear" and not in the service of universal values. Jewish cosmopolitanism exists in the here and now. It needs taboos in the form of horizons (humanism,

141

individualism, freedom) but also institutionalized taboos such as international law, which buttresses and patrols national law and jurisprudence – even when this law serves no other purpose than to maintain order between states. But in this case, too, Jewish cosmopolitanism is a global civilizing force. It does not wait passively for redemption but provides a politics of redemption. If the concept of transnational human rights can moderate pain and cruelty, then it is holding fast to these fundamental principles of modernity. Even if cosmopolitanism, as its critics have astutely pointed out, merely attempts to conceal its claim to power through an "inflation of norms," it is still acting within its pluralist definition of power, opposing the ever-present threat of totalitarianism. True cosmopolitanism is not about competing claims to victimhood, nor is it about proving that the destruction of European Jewry was unique.[18] It is also not about the universal claim of critical theories. This is also what distinguished Arendt's claims from those of others who wrote about these issues. Arendt was never a universalist, and this is why she can be considered a theorist of Jewish cosmopolitanism.

I started this book with the German writer Feuchtwanger and I want to conclude it with the writer and graphic artist Bruno Schulz. In his life and death, Schulz personifies the concerns of this book. Schulz was born in 1892 in the town of Drohobych, part of the Austrian-Hungarian Empire at the time. Drohobych became part of Poland in 1918, was occupied by the Soviet Union between 1939 and 1941, was occupied by the Nazis during the war, became part of the Soviet Union after the war, and since 1990 has been part of western Ukraine. In the last century or so, Drohobych has changed hands eight times. It now lies beyond the eastern borders of the European Union; it belongs neither to the West nor to the East. Some may argue it is in the center of Europe. Jews (and others) have called this region Galicia since 1772 in an effort to provide some linguistic stability and continuity to an ever-changing borderland.[19] Drohobych is part of a region in which Poles, Ukrainians, and Jews lived side by side, at times with indifference and at times with deadly hostility. This region was one of the cruelest killing fields in history, and it is part of the region that triggered Rafael Lemkin's conceptualization of genocide around the time that Schulz was killed. In Schulz's stories, Drohobych is a Jewish dreamland at times as worldless as the fantasy worlds of Kafka and Benjamin.[20] Schulz wrote in Polish, was fluent in German, and knew some Yiddish and Hebrew. The Drohobych in which he grew up, and the cultural world of which it was a part, no longer exists. Nazism and Bolshevism destroyed it, and today it is part of a homogenized national narrative.[21] In 1939, ten thousand Poles, ten thousand Ukrainians, and fifteen thousand Jews lived in Drohobych. Today the city is inhabited almost exclusively by Ukrainians. Only four hundred Jews remain there.

Schulz and Arendt never met face to face. He was killed by a Gestapo officer when she was already in New York writing about the need for a Jewish army. According to his biographer, Jerzy Ficowski (2003: 133ff.), Schulz was part of a group that catalogued confiscated books for the Nazis. As usual in such cases, the purpose of this cataloguing was to select some books for destruction and others for shipment back to Germany. It might very well be that some of the books Schulz catalogued were later distributed by Arendt and her team at the JCR.[22] In 1942, Schulz was forced to paint the walls of the home of German SS officer Felix Landau with images from German fairy tales.[23] His artistic talent was able to preserve his life for a little bit longer. Landau briefly became his protector. Shortly thereafter he was shot in the street by another German officer, who apparently had accounts to settle with Landau. Several hundred other Jews were killed in the streets of Drohobych that day. As Ficowski reports, Schulz's killer declared triumphantly, "You killed my Jew – I killed yours" (138).

Schulz disappeared in a mass grave – no one knows where – and most of his art and writings disappeared with him. The painted wall was lost for decades behind the Iron Curtain but was rediscovered by a German documentary filmmaker in 2001. Soon thereafter, the wall was moved to the Holocaust Memorial Museum Yad Vashem in Jerusalem, an action that triggered a debate about the legal and moral rights of the Israeli Museum.[24] The specifics of the ensuing debate are at the center of this book because they involve questions of Polish, Ukrainian, Israeli, Jewish, and finally European identity. Israel has claimed Schulz as one of its own on the grounds that he was a victim of the Holocaust. He was killed in the street not as a human being, a Pole, or a Ukrainian, but as a Jew. The Israeli museum argues that his painted images belong to Jerusalem, just as the fledgling Israeli state insisted that Eichmann be tried in Jerusalem forty years earlier. If you define art and culture territorially, then Schulz is a Ukrainian, and if you define them linguistically, then he is a Pole. The Jewish world of East Galicia no longer exists. Thus all of these claims can be considered equally valid from their respective viewpoints. Schulz has become text and image, but he is a symbol, no longer a reality. It would be noble to argue that art belongs to everyone – a positive statement of the concept of "crimes against humanity." The murals have been on display since 2009 in the museum in Jerusalem.[25]

Schulz is, of course, not the sole example of how Jewish cultural property is being debated. Negotiations over cultural property ownership have become part of the new globalized world.[26] Many of the debates about cultural property involve the return of artworks to their respective homes.[27] The case of Bruno Schulz's murals is not about repatriation, however, since his "patria" no longer exists. Schulz's so-called cultural heritage no longer exists in Galicia, or in Israel. In modern nation-states, the distinction between the memories of perpetrators and the memories of victims was an important element of mutual non-understanding; and this was a piece of the conflict over Schulz's murals as well. A truly cosmopolitan modern order should allow for compromises that, although fragile, are made possible by the mutual recognition of the Other's history. This linking of perspectives makes the act of reconciliation a key experience of memory. It is no longer the original crimes that are on the agenda – many victims and perpetrators having died in the meantime – rather, it is the question of how their descendants deal with these histories and memories. In other words, the inclusion of the Other erodes the barrier between the memories of perpetrators and those of victims. What remains is the memory of a common history that nevertheless cannot be shared and, of course, mutual resentment. Thus Ukrainians commemorate the atrocities committed against them by Poles in the region (Snyder 2004) but seem to have forgotten their cooperation with the Nazis.

A cosmopolitan memory of the past emerges from the conscious and deliberate inclusion of the Other's suffering – not from the idea of some community of fate, inspired by mythical delusions and serving to construct some false historical continuity. New moral and political fields of action and responsibility emerge from communication and interdependence. Ukrainians, Poles, and Jews might have shared the same space, they might have shared the tragedy of inter-ethnic conflict, but they never shared history. That Schulz's murals were moved to Jerusalem does not mean that ethnic and religious pluralism ceased to exist in Eastern Europe, as some have argued. "The work of Bruno Schulz," a group of art historians averred, "reminds us that this region was long one of unique cultural richness and diversity; an effort by any single group to monopolize his memory erases this history of pluralism."[28] But that pluralism did cease to exist when Schulz was murdered on the streets of Drohobych. Does the effort of the Yad Vashem museum have the same result? A group of Israeli and Jewish scholars offers one reply: "As anyone who has studied the Holocaust knows, one of the keys to understanding this terrible period in history is to recognize not only its universal, but its specific and particular characteristics. The contexts in which to understand Bruno Schulz's works are the Holocaust and the state of commemoration in Drohobych over the last fifty-seven years."[29]

These scholars also refer to Hannah Arendt, though not by name, when they explain why the murals needed to be taken to Jerusalem: Schulz's paintings reflect the "power of radical evil in a totalitarian society to crush pluralism and diversity." This statement echoes the debate over the Eichmann trial, this time in cultural rather than legal and political terms, as does the response of the young German film-maker who discovered the murals in Drohobych. "For me," he said, "it is very tragic to see Bruno Schulz only as a Jewish victim or only as a Polish writer. He is simply Bruno Schulz, and this [the removal of his murals from Drohobych to Jerusalem] is a violent post-mortem attack against him."[30] This humanization (or de-ethnification) of Schulz recalls Enzensberger's response to Arendt after the Eichmann trial. This kind of retroactive universalization of the Jewish experience of the Holocaust informs contemporary discourse on European cosmopolitanism, but stripped of its historical context. Bruno Schulz was turned into a European vision, his art made part of European modernism, transcending national boundaries and ethnic membership. In this (German) vision, Schulz embodies the nobility of cosmopolitanism, because as a rootless Jew he came from a place subjected to multiple changes of geopolitical identity. But we must not forget that he was murdered because he was a Jew, not because he was "simply Bruno Schulz." The removal of the mural partly acknowledged his existence (and his death), although it cannot do him complete justice.

This is exactly where the tension between cosmos and polis is located, between citizenship in the world, European vision, and Jewish experience. Cosmopolitanism is not just folklore; it is a political space that cannot exist without pluralism. Moreover, when cosmopolitanism is rooted in historical experience, it is practically the equivalent of pluralism, something Arendt developed in her analysis of the United States. The European cosmopolitan vision became reality for Arendt and many other Jews when they left Europe for America. This involved acknowledging that Israel was not the only alternative for homeless Jews. Israel is the Jewish polis, America the cosmos. But, as in Drohobych, the Jewish-European space remains empty. Jews still live in Europe, but Jewish culture and politics have been relocated to the United States and Israel. The books the JCR saved from the depots in Europe are texts that everyone can read. They belong to all and are indeed cosmopolitan texts, whose origins are sometimes difficult to recognize. They may perhaps be able to live without this recognition, but this is also the problem for cosmopolitan Europe. A cosmopolitan theory has to confront its own past and reformulate its own traditions. It cannot rest on the Enlightenment and its concepts of rational progress and universal equality. This negates Jewish existence and the perspectives from which a realistic cosmopolitanism can be developed. Arendt, Scholem, Feuchtwanger, Baron, Schulz, and Kafka all suggested ways out of this quandary.

Israel now confronts this cosmopolitan Europe, which in many ways rests on a hidden tradition of Jewish intellectuals without at times being aware of it. A Jewish perspective on Europe thus also attempts to "deprovincialize" Europe. In an ironic reversal of fortune, this Jewish perspective may also have the critical potential to "deprovincialize" Israel. There is, of course, a lively memory culture in Europe regarding the Holocaust, but it is a memory without Jewish languages, Jewish cultures, or Jewish politics. Europeans still insist on "humankind" and universal citizenship; they like difference as long as it expresses itself culturally. Arendt reminded her European readers that the pluralism and federalism of North America could serve as a counterweight to the homogenizing pressures Europe had exerted on Jews. Clearly, Tony Judt is right when he writes in his conclusion to *Postwar*, "the recovered memory of Europe's dead Jews has become the very definition and guarantee of the continent's restored humanity. It wasn't always so" (804).

Europe remembers and it memorializes; most European capitals have monuments commemorating the Holocaust. Judt closes his book with this short remark: "European Union may be a response to history, but it can never be a substitute" (831). This statement has implications for Israel as well. Historical memories do not run the same way there as they do in Europe. Israel's normalizing structures and institutions make it use force, often excessively. But, more than anything else, Israel sees itself as responsible for the safety of Jews. It also does not see why it should give up the ethnic character of its state. This in turn leads to strong and violent conflicts, not commodifiable conflicts, but fundamental conflicts that do not accept compromise and that run counter to any form of Jewish cosmopolitanism. Israel has always been conceived as a Jewish state, even by Jews who consider themselves secular. But it is also seen as a modern democratic state, even by Jews who consider themselves religious.

Clearly, Zionism is not the same thing as Judaism. Zionism equals Judaism plus Liberalism, Liberalism with a capital "L," Liberalism as the founding creed of a modern nation-state. Thus Europe would have reluctantly to accept that the Jewishness that lurked in the subconscious of the "secular" founding fathers was Judaism as a modern nationality, in the way Arendt understood it. Judaism is no longer a "spaceless" religion but a people with a land and a history. Today Jewish cosmopolitanism is in danger of disappearing.[31] Theories of cosmopolitanism rarely relate to Jewish experiences anymore; at the same time, much of current Jewish experience ignores the Jews' own cosmopolitan heritage. Jewish cosmopolitanism is being swallowed up by an increasingly aggressive Jewish ethnic nationalism, on the one hand, and a universalism that denies the expression of any kind of particularity at all, on the other. The urgency of Arendt's project is still relevant, not only for the Jews but for humankind.

# NOTES

1   Arendt's "Organized Guilt and Universal Responsibility" first appeared in *Jewish Frontier* in 1945 and is reprinted in Arendt 1994, pp. 121–32.

2   Many inspiring books have been written on Arendt's political theory. The most important for this study include Benhabib 1996; Canovan 1992; Hansen 1993; Kateb 1983; and Villa 1999.

3   A groundbreaking work on Arendt and Jewish identity is Bernstein 1996. See also "Hannah Arendt: Hannah and Rahel, Fugitives from Palestine," in Birnbaum 2008, pp. 203–41. Arendt's writings on Jewish matters were recently published in a volume edited by Jerome Kohn and Ron Feldman, *The Jewish Writings* (Arendt 2007). Many of the essays published there – especially those of the 1940s – were scattered throughout small Jewish journals and magazines, and some (like her columns in the German émigré magazine *Aufbau*) were available only in German. With the publication of this volume, her writings on matters Jewish can now be incorporated into her political canon.

4   For an attempt to locate Arendt within the Jewish theological tradition, see, for instance, Celermeyer 2010.

5   For a good biography, see Young-Bruehl 2004.

6   For a recent overview of Arendt's life and theoretical concerns, see Villa 2009.

7   Arendt knew that this was a crucial question after she published *Eichmann in Jerusalem*, first as a series of articles and then as a

book in 1963. The debate was also about the modes of "speaking" about the Holocaust. See chapter 6.

8 See www.un.org/en/documents/udhr/ for the wording of the Universal Declaration of Human Rights. For historical contextualization, see Levy and Sznaider 2010.

9 On the connections between the events of World War II and the text of the Universal Declaration of Human Rights, see Morsink 2000.

10 For the full declaration, see the website of the Israeli government, at www.mfa.gov.il/MFA/Peace+Process/Guide+to+the+Peace+Process/Declaration+of+Establishment+of+State+of+Israel.htm.

11 Many history departments in Israel are still divided between general (or universal) history and Jewish history.

12 On this point, see Beck and Sznaider 2006, 2010.

13 For contemporary debates on these issues, see Benhabib 2006. There the issue is the tension between cosmopolitan norms and democratic politics. Benhabib advocates mediation between moral universalism and ethnic particularism. These issues are usually discussed in more general terms and are part of a universal philosophical debate about human groups and state power. This book is one way to show how it was theorized and practiced by Jewish intellectuals and politicians.

14 See especially Appiah 1998. See also another closely related concept in Werbner 2006. An early formulation of "rooted cosmopolitanism" in its Jewish context is Cohen 1992.

15 See also Cheah 1997.

16 Durkheim 2001, originally published in France in 1912.

17 Craig Calhoun makes this point in Calhoun 2002.

18 The conceptualization of Europe in schoolbooks is by now a sociological enterprise in itself. See especially Soysal 2002.

19 Gerard Delanty proposed a civilizational approach to postnational Europe. He writes about three civilizations that make up Europe: Occidental Christian Europe, Byzantine–Slavic Eurasian Europe, and Ottoman Islamic Europe. See Delanty 2003.

20 See Tony Judt 2005.

21 Hans Kohn first made this distinction in *The Idea of Nationalism* (Kohn 1944). Kohn was a contemporary of Kafka from the Prague era, and in his youth was a proponent of a Jewish ethical Zionism that considered Jews a nation without the need for sovereignty. On Kohn's background, see Craig Calhoun's introduction to the 1995 Transaction edition of the book.

22 On Jewish civilization as a central component of Europe, see Eisenstadt 1992.

23 Gilroy 1993, p. 1.

24 Lionel Feuchtwanger (1884–1958) is typical of the well-educated Jewish group of intellectuals who were also creating German culture. He escaped from Germany to France, was held prisoner in a French internment camp, but escaped to the United States in 1941.

25 Feuchtwanger's characters move between Jewish tradition and secularism and constantly try to transcend the boundaries of their communities. Feuchtwanger also explores the limits of our actions and judgments.

26 Hannah Arendt, "On Humanity in Dark Times," in Arendt 1968b, p. 11.

27 On this conundrum, see Birnbaum and Katznelson 1995.

28 Sachs 2002, p. 50.

29 For more on this point, see Boyarin 1997.

30 A telling example of this can be seen in the work of Isaiah Berlin, whose ideas on pluralism were formulated before theories of cosmopolitanism became popular. Much of Berlin's "anti-universalist" intellectual taste was informed by his Jewish background. Like many other Jewish thinkers, Berlin was highly suspicious of the hyperrational thought of the Enlightenment, which was also hostile to Jews. See Arie Dubnov 2007. Like Arendt, Berlin was mostly preoccupied with the search for the origins of totalitarianism.

31 Lessing 1860, p. 340.

32 The new edition of Arendt's *Jewish Writings* (2007) collects her writings on matters Jewish from the 1930s to the 1960s. The essay "The Enlightenment and the Jewish Question" opens this volume. Much of the voluminous secondary literature on Arendt treats her as a German Jew, with the emphasis on German.

33 See the correspondence between the two (which has not been translated into English) in Arendt and Blumenfeld 1995. This volume is a good source for Arendt's thinking on Jewish and Zionist issues. On the friendship between Arendt and Blumenfeld, see the concluding essay by Ingeborg Normann, "Eine Freundschaft auf Messers Schneide," pp. 349–73. Arendt met Blumenfeld in 1926. Apparently he convinced her of the impossibility of assimilation.

34 A professorial thesis written in German universities after the completion of the PhD.

35 She completed the book in Paris in 1938 after she escaped, but it was not published until 1958, several years after her reputation was well established. One year later, in 1959, the book was published in Germany. See Arendt 1997. For Arendt's reading of Rahel Varnhagen, see Benhabib 1995. For the story of the book manuscript's migration from Paris to Palestine and the United States, see Leibovici 2007.

36 Arendt's appreciation of Herder is reminiscent of the stance taken by Isaiah Berlin. Berlin considered Herder a thinker who criticized the Enlightenment for its monism of reason. Like Arendt (whom Berlin disliked for many reasons), Berlin appreciated Herder for his politics of pluralism (a concept not far from current understandings of cosmopolitanism). See especially Berlin 1976. Berlin's and Arendt's readings of Herder may be highly idiosyncratic and probably served their own intellectual interests. Herder was as much a figure of the Enlightenment as Arendt and Berlin were. Like Arendt, Berlin was interested in what the "Counter-Enlightenment," as he called it, had to offer to humankind in general and the Jews in particular. And like Arendt, he had to navigate between his pluralist and Zionist tendencies, between humanity and community. For Arendt's reading of Herder, see also Heuer 1992.

37 Multilingualism has turned into one of the defining problems of Europe's unification process. The European commission has a multilingualism section; see http://ec.europa.eu/education/languages/index_en.htm.

38 As mentioned above, Arendt is far from the only Jewish thinker for whom the Holocaust transformed the Enlightenment into a problem. For a good survey, see Traverso 2004. Like many others, Traverso emphasizes the contribution of German Jews; the Eastern European experience is neglected.

39 Ulrich Beck calls this having roots and wings at the same time. See especially Beck 2005, pp. 282ff.

40 Arendt used this term in a 1944 essay called "The Jew as Pariah: A Hidden Tradition," reprinted in Arendt 2007, pp. 275–302.

41 On Arendt's Jewish political thought, see Barley 1988 and Pilling 1994. Both contributions concentrate on Arendt's writings prior to 1950.

42 For a suggestive reading on this point, see Disch 1995.

43 Quoted in Hunt 1996, pp. 86–8.
44 For a sociologically and politically informed account of these events, see Birnbaum and Katznelson 1995.
45 See also Sutcliffe 2006.
46 On this point, see Hertzberg 1968. Hertzberg accused those thinkers trying to emancipate the Jews of anti-Semitism.
47 The concepts of "exit visas" and "entry tickets" are taken from an insightful essay by Zygmunt Bauman (1988).
48 See Arendt 1942. This essay was the starting point for a lengthy Arendtian project of criticizing the French concept of universal nationhood and almost ten years later became the first part of her *Origins of Totalitarianism*.
49 For the links between the European-Jewish question and contemporary concerns about postcolonialism, see Mufti 2007, especially ch. 2, "Jewishness as Minority," in which Mufti casts the European-Jewish question as a challenge to universal homogeneity. This is also how Mufti reads Marx's 1843 essay on the "Jewish question."
50 Karl Marx, "On the Jewish Question" (1843) in Marx 1976.
51 See the insightful study by the German–Jewish literary critic Mayer (1975), linking the fate of the Jews with those of homosexuals and women.
52 This "nation within a nation" principle often prompted Arendt to argue for a Jewish army (as though the Jews were indeed a nation), before the foundation of the state of Israel, to combat enemies of the Jews. As she stated many times, "If one is attacked as a Jew, one must defend oneself as a Jew."

CHAPTER 2  PARIS, GENEVA, AND PORT BOU: THE LAST EUROPEANS

1 "Juden sterben in Europa und man verscharrt sie wie Hunde." See Arendt and Scholem 2010. This letter is also reprinted in a volume exploring the relationship between Hannah Arendt and Walter Benjamin (Arendt and Benjamin 2006, p. 145).
2 See Hannah Arendt, "Walter Benjamin, 1892–1940," in Arendt 1968b, p. 170. This essay was written as an introduction to an English collection of essays by Benjamin called *Illuminations*, edited by Arendt.
3 The essay was reprinted in English in Arendt 2007, pp. 258–63 (quotation on p. 258). This essay is only the beginning of her

analysis of the French revolutionary tradition, which culminated in her *On Revolution*, published in 1963.

4  On this point, see Diner 2007.

5  Benjamin 1999 (edited with an introduction by Hannah Arendt). In this book, his essay "The Concept of History" is titled "Theses on the Philosophy of History" (pp. 245–55). Two essays on Kafka are on pp. 108–43.

6  Besides the readings of Arendt and Benjamin on Kafka, see the contemporary essay in Preece 2002, pp. 1–8.

7  She not only wrote several essays about him, but also edited his diaries for the Schocken Publishing House in New York in the late 1940s. A large portrait of Kafka hung in the entrance hall of her apartment in New York (pers. comm., Jerome Kohn).

8  See Hannah Arendt, "Walter Benjamin, 1892–1940," in Arendt 1968b, p. 185.

9  For an insightful discussion of Kafka's Jewish languages, see Suchoff 2007. Suchoff emphasizes the Jewish aspects of Kafka's work. See this essay also for its richness of sources and footnotes.

10  Amichai 1994.

11  See also Suchoff 1997. In 1948, Arendt reviewed Scholem's book on Jewish mysticism for a Jewish journal. Reprinted in *The Jewish Writings* as "Jewish History, Revised," pp. 303–11, where she thought that "Jewish mysticism alone was able to bring about a great political movement and to translate itself directly into real popular action" (p. 311).

12  For an inspired reading of Rosenzweig and his relationship to Heidegger, see Gordon 2003. The locus classicus of Rosenzweig's thinking in this regard is *Star of Redemption*, published in 1921.

13  See the analysis by Karl Lowith (Lowith 1942), especially p. 72.

14  For a rather unsympathetic reading of the relation between Heidegger's Jewish students – one that also connects Lowith to Arendt – see Wolin 2003.

15  Zygmunt Bauman has recently taken the "We Refugees" essay as an opportunity to argue that European Jews wrestling with assimilation were the pioneers of the postmodern condition. See Bauman 2008.

16  Without any references to Arendt but as part of a critique of territoriality in Jewish thinking, see Gurevitch 1997, pp. 203–16.

17  Hannah Arendt, "Stefan Zweig: Jews in the World of Yesterday," in Arendt 2007, pp. 317–28. For an Arendtian reading of Zweig's dilemmas, see Botstein 1982.

18 One year later, in an article in the "Aufbau" (April 21, 1944) commemorating the anniversary of the Warsaw ghetto uprising, she entitled her essay "For the Honor and Glory of the Jewish people" and remarked that honor and glory are new words in the political vocabulary of the Jews (Arendt 2007: 199).

19 On the so-called Goldstein affair, see Aschheim 2001a, pp. 64–72; Albanis 2002, pp. 43–145; Flohr 1999, pp. 45–65.

20 Like Arendt, Moritz Goldstein left Germany in 1933 and went to New York via England. This letter, dated December 15, 1968, can be found in the Hannah Arendt Papers at the Library of Congress, Correspondence Collection. For Goldstein's essay, see Goldstein 1912.

21 I address this issue in more detail in chapter 3.

22 This is especially clear in her *Eichmann in Jerusalem*, which created a controversy as heated as the Goldstein affair fifty years earlier. It is no coincidence that Arendt returned to the subject in her 1968 essay on Benjamin. *Eichmann in Jerusalem* is a typical example of a message in a bottle, as I will show.

23 On Walter Benjamin's early dealings with his Jewish identity, see Anson Rabinbach 1985, especially pp. 91–9, and Smith 1991.

24 See Benjamin 1972, pp. 836–44.

25 Goldstein 1957.

26 Goldstein 1914.

27 Hannah Arendt, "Rosa Luxemburg: 1871–1919," in Arendt 1968b, pp. 33–56.

28 One essay on Kafka is part of her 1944 essay "The Jew as Pariah: A Hidden Tradition," in Arendt 2007, pp. 275–97 (especially 288ff. called "Franz Kafka: The Man of Goodwill"). The other essay was also published in 1944 in *Partisan Review* 11: 412–22, called "Frank Kafka: A Revaluation," reprinted in Arendt 1994, pp. 69–80.

29 On Kafka's prophetic readings of the Holocaust, see Traverso 1997.

30 Ulrich Beck discusses this connection in Beck 2009.

31 See Kushner 1994. In a rather late essay by Arendt, "The Destruction of Six Million," originally published in 1964 in the "Jewish World," she argues that the failure to recognize the Jewish particularity of the victims was not a failure of European humanism, but a failure of European liberalism and socialism. This essay is reprinted in *The Jewish Writings*, pp. 490–5.

32  For a theory of Arendt's storytelling, see Benhabib 1990 and Disch 1994, pp. 1–19. On Benjamin's influence on Arendt's mode of storytelling, see Herzog 2000.

33  Walter Benjamin, "Theses on the Philosophy of History," in Benjamin 1999, pp. 245–55 (quotation from p. 247).

34  For an English translation, see Bialik 1923.

35  This essay by Benjamin was first published in the German Zionist newspaper "Die Jüdische Rundschau" in 1934. The editorial board wrote a short introduction to the essay, stating that the question of whether Kafka is a Jewish writer is moot. The essay was included in the reader Hannah Arendt prepared on Benjamin for an English-speaking audience and is called "Franz Kafka: On the Tenth Anniversary of his Death," in *Illuminations*, London: Pimlico, 1970, pp. 108–35 (quotation from p. 118) without the English translations of the Aggadah or Halacha.

36  Two of her former students who attended that seminar remember it vividly and describe it in Young-Bruehl and Kohn 2007. Kohn (p. 1049) mentions that she taught that seminar in 1955 and 1965 and that 1968 was the third and last time.

37  For a similar reading, see Diner 1997.

38  See Janowsky 1933; for a recent analysis, see Fink 2004.

39  For the protocols of the founding of the World Jewish Congress, see Institute for Jewish Affairs 1948. 280 delegates represented Jews from 32 countries.

40  For research on Nahum Goldmann's life and work (a contemporary of Arendt's), see Raider 2009.

41  The little that is known comes from her correspondence with her future husband, Heinrich Blücher. See Arendt and Blücher 2000.

CHAPTER 3  FRANKFURT, JERUSALEM, OFFENBACH, AND NEW YORK:
JEWS AND EUROPE

1  For a comprehensive essay on this topic, see Whitfield 2002. For an expanded concept attempting to define a term for "killing" books and libraries, see Knuth 2003. In this book, Knuth compares the destruction of written culture by Nazi Germany, Serbia, Iraq, and China.

2  For a philosophical reading of the centrality of the book in Jewish singularity, see Trigano 2009.

NOTES TO PAGES 40–46

3 See Friedman 1957/8. Friedman was not only a scholar, but also part of the restitution efforts.

4 Genocidal events often include moments of communal transgression which can explain the somewhat religious ritual of burning books. For genocide as transgression, see Stone 2004.

5 For an overview of this so-called *Judenforschung*, see Dirk Rupnow 2008. For an older (1946) but still valid study, see Weinreich 1999. A more recent and updated study is Steinweis 2006. For Rosenberg in particular, see Collins and Rothfelder 1983. See also Hill 2001.

6 For a detailed history of the Institut and the opening ceremonies, see Piper 2005, pp. 481ff.; and Poliakov and Wulf, pp. 131ff. (The program of the opening can be found on pp. 140–1.)

7 An English translation of this speech can be found in Stackelberg and Winkle 2002, pp. 337–9.

8 For plundering in the Soviet Union, see Kennedy Grimsted 2005 and Kennedy Grimsted 2006. For Poland, see Borin 1992.

9 Arendt 1946 (quotation from p. 294).

10 Roth 1944 (quotation from p. 254).

11 See Diner 2008.

12 Moses 1944; Robinson 1944. Robinson was the brother of Jacob Robinson, legal advisor to many Jewish organizations for minority rights and reparations.

13 See for example Adorno and Horkheimer 1999 [1944].

14 Thus one of the postwar activists of *Jewish Cultural Reconstruction*, the historian Joshua Starr (who committed suicide in 1949) related exactly to that problem of Nazi so-called book saving. See Starr 1950.

15 For the history of some of these successor organizations, see Zweig 2001. See also Waite 2002.

16 Scholem was already an eminent scholar of Jewish mysticism, Yaari was the Head of the Hebrew Department of the Jewish National and University Library (JNUL) at the time, Bergmann was a philosopher and former rector of the university, and Shunami, a librarian, was the head of the special section of the JNUL in charge of collecting and housing the materials brought to the JNUL.

17 The archival collection of the Jewish Cultural Reconstruction has been lost. Some of what remains can be found in the Salo Baron Papers at Stanford University. Some of these records suggest that the relationship between the Jerusalemites and the New Yorkers was often rather tense. In addition, key issues of

Zionism and diaspora existence were played out in this relationship. See the very extensive exchange of letters between Gershom Scholem and Hannah Arendt on this matter (Arendt and Scholem 2010). For the larger context, see Sznaider 2008, pp. 45–65, and Sznaider 2009.

18 The issue of the international recognition of the Jewish people as a collective body in law had been addressed earlier, especially by the so-called "Balfour Declaration" issued by the British government to the Zionist organization, which recognized Jewish collective claims to a national home in 1917. For the legal ramifications, see Feinberg 1948.

19 For a study of how Jewish organizations started to conceptualize this transition to collective status via victimhood, see Karbach 1962. See also the essay by Takei 2002.

20 For a biography of Baron, see Liberles 1995.

21 Baron 1928, reprinted in Baron 1964.

22 For an insightful reading of Baron, see Engel 2006. Engel does not, however, draw the connection between Baron and Arendt. He explains Baron's attraction to the international order through his biography of Galician Jews living in Austria without legal documents.

23 The subject of Baron's dissertation was Jewish diplomatic activity at the Congress of Vienna in 1815.

24 Baron 1935.

25 On this point, see especially Baehr 2002. Baehr connects Arendt's thought mostly to other sociologists writing about the camps.

26 Baron recalls this visit in his obituary of Hannah Arendt: see Baron 1976. See also the biography of Arendt: Young-Bruehl 2004, pp. 165ff.

27 Arendt 1942. This essay would later be incorporated into the first part of her "Origins of Totalitarianism" book.

28 Baron was present the evening Arendt died in her apartment in New York. Their close relationship awaits study.

29 Janowsky and Fagen 1937.

30 In a book review published in *Commentary* in 1946, Arendt argued that the Nazi death factories constituted "a crime against humanity committed on the bodies of the Jewish people," a formula she would use seventeen years later in her controversial *Eichmann in Jerusalem*, Arendt 1946: 292.

31 The remaining papers of the JCR are scattered throughout archives in the United States, Israel, and Germany, among them the important Salo W. Baron Papers, which are at Stanford

University, Manuscript Division, M0580, and the Hannah Arendt Papers, Manuscript Division, Library of Congress, Washington, DC. Some other important papers are housed in the Center for Jewish History, New York. In Israel, there are additional papers in the Central Archives for the History of the Jewish People, the Jehuda Magnes Papers, and the Gershom Scholem Collection.

32 Baron 1945.
33 Many of these essays are now collected in Arendt 2007. There, the reader can find informed introductions by Jerome Kohn and Ron Feldman. Her essays from the 1940s make up the largest part of this book (pp. 125–419).
34 The English translation of the *Aufbau* columns can be found in Arendt 2007. The original German essays are collected in Arendt 2000.
35 See Diner 2008. See also Young-Bruehl 2004, pp. 170ff. Arendt was not the only one, of course, calling for a Jewish army. The call came as well from right-wing Zionist circles, from Jews who had founded the Committee for a Jewish Army. In many ways, their reading of the situation in Europe and Arendt's were not very far apart, but Arendt wanted nothing to do with right-wing Jews and delivered a stinging attack on this Committee in the *Aufbau* on March 6, 1942 (Arendt 2007, pp. 146–8; see also Young-Bruehl 2004, pp. 175ff.). See also Eddon 2006.
36 She founded this group with a colleague of hers from the *Aufbau*, Josef Maier (1911–2002). Maier was born in Leipzig and emigrated to the USA in 1933. There he studied philosophy at Columbia University in New York. Maier was also connected with the Frankfurt School circles in New York. Maier became a member of the Sociology department at Rutgers University. About Maier's life and work, see Markus 1999.
37 The protocols of the group can be found in the "Hannah Arendt Papers," Library of Congress, Washington, DC, Speeches and Writings file. There are protocols of five meetings of the group which took place between March and June 1942, the same time, when in Poland the Belzec, Sobibor and Majdanek extermination camps became operational, and the first transport of Jews from France reached Auschwitz for extermination. If Arendt had not escaped from France and the Gurs internment camp, she might have shared that fate. This might explain the urgency of the language.

38  An English translation of his letter can be found in Scholem 2002, pp. 330–3.
39  The current literature on this issue, which is mostly unrelated to Jewish matters, tends to use the term "long-distance nationalism" for Diaspora nationalism. See Benedict Anderson 1998 for the Southeast Asian context. Most studies of long-distance nationalism start with a state and people far away from it. Jewish Diaspora Nationalism does not need a state.
40  The same idea is being debated in the context of the Middle East conflict today. For the ideas of this organization and binationalism, see Aschheim 2004a, pp. 6–41; Weiss 2004.
41  Arendt's response is reprinted in the Scholem volume cited above, p. 333.
42  Arendt 1994, p. 143.
43  This essay was also reprinted in the *Jewish Writings* (2007), pp. 423–52.
44  See also Beiner 2000.
45  For a thorough analysis of Scholem's post-Enlightenment Judaism, his friendship with Benjamin and his correspondence, see Aschheim 2004b.
46  The inventory was first published as a supplement to the journal *Jewish Social Studies* VIII (1), 1946, Supplement: 1–103. In the following years, four more lists were published: "Tentative List of Jewish Educational Institutions in Axis-Occupied Countries, *Jewish Social Studies* VIII (3), Supplement: 5–95; "Tentative List of Jewish Periodicals in Axis-Occupied Countries", *Jewish Social Studies*, IX(5) (1947): 7–44; "Addenda and Corrigenda to Tentative List of Jewish Cultural Treasures in Axis-Occupied Countries," *Jewish Social Studies* 10(1) (1948): 3–16; and "Tentative List of Jewish Publishers of Judaica and Hebraica in Axis Occupied Countries," *Jewish Social Studies* X(2) (1948): 5–50. Arendt was actively involved in supervising the first three lists. For the questionnaires Arendt worked with, see the Salo Baron Papers, M0580, Stanford University.
47  Baron 1974 (quotation from p. 8).
48  One entry on the list read:

221. Zidu Historius Etnografius Draugija namo Simon Dubnow (Historical and ethnographical Society named in honor of Simon Dubnow) Founded in 1926, the Museum housed the coll. of Rabbi Isaac Elhahan; coll. of Torah-curtains and – mantles; menorot, lamps, etc. Coll. of portraits of Jewish personalities; photographs of

towns and synagogue. Archives : Coll. of old books, including old Talmud editions; the pinkassim of the towns of Kejdanie, Wilkowiszki; mss. of rabbis, scholars and writers, including some of Abraham Mapu; coll. of letters; the archives of former Jewish National Council of Lithuania; archives of Jewish Communities which had been dissolved by the authorities. The private documentary collections of Dr. Simon Chorazyeki, Dr. Abba Lapin, and others. Source: *Yor ein-yor ois. Jarbuch Kalendar* (Report and Inventory) (Kaunas 1939) (Tentative List 1946, p. 44).

49  On the Offenbach depot, see, among others, Gallas 2006; Kurtz 2006 (especially ch. 8); Waite 2002.

50  Arendt 1945. Some of her thoughts on statelessness were included in her later book on totalitarianism, but this was a much more urgently written essay relating to burning issues of the times. For context, see Cohen 2006.

51  The letter can be seen on the website of the United States Holocaust Memorial Museum, www.ushmm.org/museum/ exhibit/online/oad/documents/restitution.pdf and can also to be found in the Salo Baron Papers, Stanford University, Special Collection.

52  On the negotiations conducted by Jerome Michael with the American State Department and military government in Germany, see Kurtz 2006.

53  The metaphor "making whole what has been smashed" is from Walter Benjamin's essay "Theses on History" where Benjamin describes a painting by Paul Klee depicting the angel of history who wants to make whole what has been smashed. John Torpey uses this metaphor as the title for his study on reparations (Torpey 2006).

54  The documents regarding these negotiations are in the Salo Baron Papers, Stanford University, Manuscript Division.

55  The documents of the Jerusalem Committee are located in the Central Archives for the History of the Jewish People in Jerusalem. *Jehuda Magnes Papers P3-2056-2060.* The bulk of the materials are in Hebrew.

56  For the decades-long relation between Hannah Arendt and Gershom Scholem including work on *Jewish Cultural Reconstruction*, see the exchange of letters between them, Arendt and Scholem 2010 (interestingly enough, most of the correspondence between Arendt and Scholem with regard to their joint work is written in English; however, letters of a more personal nature were written in their native tongue – German.)

57 Scholem wrote a lengthy report about his trip to Europe. This report (written in English), "Report of Prof. G. Scholem on his Mission to Europe concerning the Libraries of the Diaspora," can be found in the archive of the *Jewish Cultural Reconstruction* in the Salo Baron Papers at Stanford. See also Schidorsky 2006. One can also find a rather adventurous story about Scholem's visit to Offenbach in Friedman 2001, pp. 106–12.

58 This letter is part of the correspondence between Arendt and Scholem in regard to *Jewish Cultural Reconstruction*. The original letters are in the Gershom Scholem Archive of the Hebrew University in Jerusalem (4-793-288). The letter is also part of the published correspondence between the two.

59 See the various field reports she sent to New York in which she wrote about her dealings with the Germans. These reports were published for the first time in 2010 as part of the Arendt–Scholem correspondence.

60 See the papers of the Synagogue Council of America, which are part of the American Jewish Historical Society at the Center for Jewish History in New York City. See also Diner 2009.

61 The correspondence between Hannah Arendt and Heinrich Blücher is published in English translation (Arendt and Blücher 2000); the correspondence dealing with her trip to Germany can be found on pp. 99ff.

62 Theodor Heuss was the first elected president of the Federal Republic of Germany after World War II. He had been in office since September 13, 1949, two and half months before Arendt wrote this letter.

63 See in particular the exemplary studies by Barnouw 1990 and Aschheim 2001b.

64 World Jewish Congress: "Germany," in *Resolutions Adopted by the Second Plenary Assembly of the World Jewish Congress, Montreux, Switzerland, June 27th–July 6th, 1948*, p. 7. The World Jewish Congress Archives, Series A, Box 46, file 5.

65 On the rivalry between transnational Jewish organizations and the new emerging Jewish communities in Germany, see Takei 2002.

66 The field reports are numbered and are part of the Salo Baron Papers, Stanford University, Manuscript Division. Arendt's field reports start with Nr. 12 on December 1949. There is a report (Nr. 15) written February 10, 1950; Nr. 16 dated February 18, 1950; Nr. 18, February 15–March 10, 1950 and an unnumbered report dated April 12, 1950.

67 The appeal was published in *Nachrichten für wissenschaftliche Bibliotheken*, 3. Jg., Heft 4, April 1950, p. 62.

68 Hannah Arendt to Salo Baron, Basel, December 30, 1949, Salo Baron Papers, Stanford University.

69 This letter between Scholem and Arendt, like many others dealing with their common work, can be found in the archives of the Jewish National and University Library in Jerusalem. Gershom Scholem Papers, Arc. 4 o 793 JCR.

70 Hannah Arendt, "The Jew as Pariah" (1944), in Arendt 2007, p. 295.

71 After Arendt's return to New York, Meir Ben-Horin, one of the field officers filed a report (Nr. 21) on September 1950 that the German government wanted basically to terminate its cooperation with the American-Jewish organizations and to start negotiating with the newly established Jewish communities. For a short description of her work with the organization, see Arendt 1949b.

72 See also Suchoff 1997. Suchoff discusses the exchange between Scholem and Arendt regarding Scholem's book on Jewish mysticism and its hidden tradition, which took place around the same time as their joint work for Jewish Cultural Reconstruction.

73 For Scholem's views on Germans and how to talk to Germans as a Jew, see his "Jews and Germans," in Scholem 1976, pp. 71–92.

74 Hannah Arendt, "The Aftermath of Nazi Rule: Report from Germany" (1950), in Arendt 1994, pp. 248–69.

75 They are often paired in readers dealing with the concept of genocide. See Hinton 2001. Like many other readers, they include excerpts from both Arendt and Lemkin. For a recent attempt to read them jointly but through different theoretical prisms, see Benhabib 2009a and 2009b. Benhabib tries to draw a contrast between the two based on their respective thinking about groups. Arendt is portrayed as someone who believes in groups as formed and constituted through creative acts while Lemkin is portrayed as someone who believes in group ontology.

CHAPTER 4 THE VIEW FROM EASTERN EUROPE: FROM WARSAW TO NEW YORK

1 The academic journal of the US Holocaust Memorial Museum in Washington, DC is called *Holocaust and Genocide Studies*, indicating how these two concepts are joined at the hip today.

2   On Lemkin and the Holocaust, see Stone 2005. Stone reports on several texts by Lemkin in which he refers to the killing of the Jews. He refers in particular to the research done by the New York-based Institute for Jewish Affairs, about which more below.

3   She already used this formula in a 1945 essay called "The Image of Hell" (*Commentary* 1945), and it reappeared in her study on Eichmann.

4   See Cooper 2008, p. 35. For Lemkin's role in the formation of the concept of genocide and the process of the Genocide Convention, see among others Samantha Power 2002, chs 2–4; special issue "Lemkin Redux: In Quest of a Word" in the *Journal of Genocide Research* 7(5), 2005, which contains several essays on different aspects of Lemkin's biography and theory. See also the conceptually important essay by Curthoys and Docker (2008).

5   For an important element in this debate, see, among many others, Bloxham 2009. The title of the book, *The Final Solution: A Genocide*, is both an epistemological and a moral statement. Even thinkers who are ideologically against construing the Holocaust as unique are now constrained by language to designate it as such every time they use the term.

6   After the Holocaust, when hardly any Polish Jews were left alive, Polish and Jewish memories of the past were divided. On this subject, see especially Gross 2006. In Polish collective memory, the body politic is the ultimate victim, almost a political Christ figure. Poland's history is the history of endless partitions and occupations, ending with the two worst occupations conceivable, first by the Nazis and then the Stalinists, the two archetypal totalitarian regimes. Gross's argument is that surviving Jews reminded Poles of the fact that they had witnessed the Holocaust. It reminded them of their moral breakdown during the occupation. Moreover, since Poles legitimized and witnessed the killings on their doorstep, they were forced to renounce their own claims to victimhood. This is why Jews were persecuted by Poles after the war – and why their memories clashed.

7   Lemkin's autobiography was finally published in 2002 by Steven Jacobs and Samuel Totten (Jacobs and Totten 2002). The story is also reported by Amson Rabinbach (2005), which also provides an excellent background to the politics of the Genocide Convention of 1948 and how it was informed by the Cold War externally and racial issues internally. See also Claudia Kraft 2005.

8   For Dubnow's formulation of Diaspora nationalism in English, see Dubnow 1958 (edited with an introductory essay by Koppel S. Pinson). Dubnow's ideas on Jewish autonomism jibed with ideas of cultural autonomy within circles of Austrian Marxism of the time. For this context, see, among others, Nimni 2005. See also Dohrn 2004. Also Rabinovich 2005.

9   See the comprehensive essay, Weitz 2008.

10  See Pinson 1958. See also the excellent German study on Dubnow's view of nationalism: Hilbrenner 2007.

11  See Löwy 1992.

12  This attempt at reconciliation can be seen at its clearest in her reading of minority and human rights in *Origins of Totalitarianism* (1951) and in *Eichmann in Jerusalem* (1963a).

13  For a historical account of Jewish minority politics after World War I that provides the context for Arendt's and Lemkin's thoughts on these matters, see Fink 2004; for an older but still valid study, see Janowsky 1933. For a study linking Arendt's thought to the minority politics between the two world wars, see Motzkin 2000.

14  For the collection of documents, see Chasanowitsch and Motzkin 1919. On Motzkin's activities, see Nesemann 2007.

15  For a theory of Eastern European nationalism, see Brubaker 1996.

16  This point was emphasized by Janowsky 1933, pp. 260ff., whose study was written with a view backwards and not with what would happen to the Jews of this region following the publication of his book. This distinction is also important because the delegations of British and French Jews were, of course, satisfied with their civil and political equality. It was the coalition of the Eastern European and American Jews that pushed for national minority rights. As was very often the case, Arendt was torn between these two poles.

17  See on this point, Levene 1993.

18  For the internal debates, see Janowsky 1933, pp. 282ff., a book Arendt was familiar with.

19  For this, see Hedetoft and Hjort 2002.

20  In the late 1950s, in her study on the human condition, she analyzed worldlessness as the condition of the modern world. At that point, she looked at these issues in more abstract terms.

21  Thus the Hebrew concept of "Olam" can mean eternity and it can mean world. The Jews often call themselves "Am Olam,"

which can mean the "Eternal People" but also the "People of the World." It is my contention that the minority politics of that time was an attempt to navigate between these poles. Arendt also had conceptualizations about the world and worldlessness, which came from a more philosophical direction, but were very much in tune with these Jewish tendencies.

22 On these efforts within contemporary European politics of the Baltic States, see Smith and Kordell 2007. This article demonstrates the relevance of the period between the World Wars for current minority politics in Europe.

23 The European Congress of Minorities is practically a forgotten episode in European history. For further references, see: Bamberger-Stemman 2000; Glass 2004; Hiden and Smith 2006 (this essay deals with the Baltic side of the issue); Nesemann 2007. See also Graf 2008. Arendt had nothing positive to say about the Congress.

24 Norbert Gürke, "Der Nationalsozialismus, das Grenz-und Auslanddeutschtum und das Nationalitätenrecht," *Nation und Staat* VI, 1932: 7–30.

25 Her reading of the Congress can be found in *Origins of Totalitarianism*, 1951, pp. 273–90.

26 See on this point Bernstein 1996, especially chapter 3, "Statelessness and the Right to Have Rights" (pp. 71–87).

27 The letter is translated and reprinted in Arendt 2007 as "The Minority Question," pp. 125–33. See also Heuer 2007.

28 Note that four years before she wrote this letter, Arendt herself took part in the inaugural event of the World Jewish Congress, which emerged out of these "rootless" organizations (see chapter 2).

29 Jonathan Frankel clearly shows how Arendt's reading of Jewish politics in the nineteenth century ignored some very important issues. See, for example, Frankel 1997 for an analysis of Jewish attempts in the mid-nineteenth century to counter accusations of ritual murder. On Eastern European Jewish politics, see Frankel 1984.

30 Arendt's reading of the minority treaties precedes her much more famous accounts of the "Perplexities of the Rights of Man," in *Origins of Totalitarianism* (Arendt 1951, pp. 269–90).

31 Without actually using the term "parvenus," Arendt continued to criticize the Jewish leadership in the Holocaust era in *Eichmann in Jerusalem*, which in the end would prompt many Jews to distance themselves from Arendt.

32   Arendt edited a collection of texts by Lazare for Schocken Books in New York in 1948 (see Lazare 1948).

33   For a view which treats minority rights as compensation for the historical "losers," see Lieblich 2008. Lieblich claims this is why neither those who grant nor those who are awarded minority rights feel satisfied by these arrangements.

34   For a portrait of German–Jewish exiles and their attempts to come to terms with the destruction of European Jewry, see Traverso 2004.

35   On "groupism," see Brubaker 2004. The theoretical literature on "cultural autonomy" has now become extremely rich. For a good survey, see Nimni 2005.

36   For this vocabulary, see the current postcolonial literature. A good introduction is Childs and Williams 1997 (especially the chapter on Spivak, pp. 157–84).

37   For a superb summary of this literature, see Brubaker 2009.

38   For a reading connecting Lemkin to colonialism, see Moses 2008. Jon Docker in particular in Docker 2008 provides many references to Lemkin's published and unpublished sources on genocide. For an attempt to read Arendt's *Origins of Totalitarianism* outside the European context, see King and Stone 2007.

39   See Shaw 2007, pp. 23ff., linking minority rights and the laws of war in Lemkin's thought. For the international legal context behind this connection, see Schabas 2000, pp. 14–50.

40   For a view of genocide and the Holocaust as a locus of Eastern European interethnic relations, see among others Bartov 2008 and Snyder 2009.

41   See also Schabas 2000, pp. 112ff. Schabas also mentions that Lemkin had the destruction of the Jews in mind even though Schabas also claims (p. 113) that the Jews cannot be termed a national group. However, Lemkin's perspective was that of an Eastern European Jew who (along with Dubnow) considered the Jews to be a national group like many others in Eastern Europe. On the distinction between the assimilated western Jew and the national Eastern European Jew, see Diner 2003. For a criticism of Lemkin's thinking about groups, see especially Holmes 2002.

42   For an analysis of Lemkin's concept of culture, see Moses 2010 and the literature cited therein. Moses links Lemkin's concept of culture to another fellow Polish national, Bronislaw Malinowski, and his anthropological view of culture as "serving precultural needs of a biological life" (p. 25). Moses also links Lemkin's

views on culture to his socialization in Eastern Europe between the wars. Moses is right to relate Lemkin's views to what the sociologist Rogers Brubaker calls "groupism" – the tendency to treat ethnic groups as real entities.

43  For the details of this process see Schabas 2000, pp. 179–89; Morsink 1999; for an earlier statement, see Robinson 1960. Robinson, who was himself active in the minority politics of the Jews between the wars, was very much aware of the connection between minority rights and cultural genocide legislation.

44  For these connections, see Ahonen 2003.

45  For the continuities and especially the discontinuities between minority rights and human rights, see Mazower 2004; see also Levy and Sznaider 2010.

46  For the historical context of Jewish diplomacy after World War I, see Fink 2004.

47  For the debates in the UN, see again Schabas 2000.

48  About the Madrid conference and Lemkin's paper, see among others: Power 2002, ch. 2.

49  The paper can be found at www.preventgenocide.org/lemkin/madrid1933-english.htm, a website dedicated to the work of Lemkin.

50  For the history of the term Holocaust and the distinction from the notion of genocide, see Levy and Sznaider 2005. For a critical essay on the conflation of the terms or the superiority of Holocaust over genocide, see Moses 2004.

51  Lemkin 1946a. For the connections between Lemkin's reading of genocide and the Holocaust, see Stone 2005.

52  For the full text of the convention, see www.hrweb.org/legal/genocide.html.

53  For Dubnow's appeal to collect materials, see Fishman 2005a, pp. 139ff.

54  The concept of "enlarged mentality" originates in Kant's theory of aesthetic judgment. Kant was referring to taste when he argued that we are able to disregard the subjective private conditions of our own judgment, and be able to reflect upon it from a *universal standpoint*. Arendt's last work deals with these Kantian notions and how they can be translated into political thought. See Arendt 1992. See also Fine 2008.

55  A comprehensive biography of Robinson is still waiting to be written. In English, there is a short note in the Encyclopedia Judaica, 2nd edn, vol. 17, "Jacob Robinson," pp. 355–6. For more comprehensive information, see Feuereisen 2004. Another

source is the archives of the World Jewish Congress at the American Jewish Archives, Cincinnati, USA, especially Series C, "The Institute of Jewish Affairs. Robinson is the author of one of most bitterly critical books on Arendt: Robinson 1965.

56 Robinson 1928. Robinson also published several articles in the aforementioned *Nation und Staat*.

57 For the relevant documents, see "The World Jewish Congress Collection," Series A: Central Files, Subseries 2: Executive Files, Box A9, File 6: Proposals for Institute to Study Jewish Situation, American Jewish Archives, Cincinnati, USA.

58 On the origins of the institute, see Institute of Jewish Affairs 1948.


CHAPTER 5   ZURICH, VILNA, AND NUREMBERG: GENERALIZED GUILT

1 For an English translation of their correspondence, which began in 1926 and lasted until 1969, see Arendt and Jaspers 1992. For a cosmopolitan reading of the correspondence, see Curthoys 2005, no pagination. See also Disch 1995.

2 Altogether Arendt published six essays in *Die Wandlung*, all of which appeared in English as well. This made her part of the immediate German discourse about the past. Her *Wandlung* essays were about guilt, imperialism, Kafka, concentration camps, parties and movements and human rights. Most of them were integrated in her *Origins of Totalitarianism* book.

3 Gershom Scholem, "Jews and Germans" (1966), in Scholem 1976, p. 71.

4 For more on this subject, see Habermas 2000.

5 See also Schaap 2001.

6 Jaspers 1946b. The book was translated a year later as *The Question of German Guilt*, New York: Dial Press.

7 Diner 2000c. Diner's claim is that Jaspers's text has become a founding text for the new (West) German collective identity. I think that this can be broadened from Germany to Western Europe.

8 Rabinbach 1997. He calls the text the founding narrative of the European German (p. 133).

9 Clark 2002. See also Olick 2005 and 2007.

10 Fine 2000a.

11 Beck and Grande 2007 (especially 3.6, "European Society as Memory", pp. 131–6).

12 Arendt began to grapple with these issues at the end of the war, while she was working for *Jewish Cultural Reconstruction*. The first essay she published was "Organized Guilt and Universal Responsibility" which appeared in *Jewish Frontier* in 1945 (reprinted as Arendt 1994, pp. 121–32). A German version of this essay was published after the war in *Die Wandlung*. These issues would preoccupy Arendt throughout her intellectual life. Many of her later essays on responsibility are collected in Arendt 2002.

13 This remark and the concept of "banality" would come back to haunt Arendt 15 years later when she subtitled her Eichmann book "A Report on the Banality of Evil."

14 The editors of the correspondence explain that "our problem" refers to a letter Gertrud wrote to Arendt on April 17, 1946, in which she complained bitterly that she could not talk to Germans about the Jews.

15 Halpern 1948. *Jewish Frontier* was the magazine of the American Labor Zionist Movement. Arendt also published there on occasion; amongst her publications there is the original 1945 version of "Organized Guilt and Universal Responsibility" (Arendt 1994, pp. 121–32) and a review of Scholem's book where she relates to the so-called hidden tradition of Judaism.

16 On this disagreement, see Young-Bruehl 2004, pp. 230–1. Arendt published an article in *Commentary* in 1948 called "Saving the Jewish Homeland" (Arendt 2007, pp. 388–401), which Halpern criticized in *Jewish Frontier*. Arendt reacted to this criticism with a response, "About 'Collaboration,' " also in *Jewish Frontier* (Arendt 2007, pp. 414–16). The response in *Commentary* is another round in Arendt's struggle with American Jewry. Jacob Robinson also reacted to this article in a letter to the editor in *Commentary*, June 1948. The letter tried to tackle Arendt's political arguments in legal terms. Arendt answered in the same issue that political situations should be explained politically and not legally.

17 The response to Arendt's *Eichmann in Jerusalem* in 1963 in effect continued Arendt's long-standing debate with Jewish intellectuals like Halpern. Jacob Robinson, for example, wrote a critical book about Arendt in 1965. For more on this subject, see the following chapter.

18  On the PEN meeting, see Wilford 1979.
19  On Abraham Sutzkever, see Hirsch 1986; Roskies 1984 (especially chapter 9, "The Burden of Memory," pp. 225–57); Wisse 1983.
20  Arendt's "Tentative List" has several libraries in Vilna listed under its Poland entry including the Straszun Library and the library of the Yiddish Scientific Institute (Tentative List of Jewish Cultural Treasures in Axis Occupied Countries, Supplement to *Jewish Social Studies*, viii, 1, 1946: 45); in addition there is a listing of several Jewish important cultural institutions in Vilna (Tentative List of Jewish Cultural Treasures in Axis Occupied Countries, Supplement to *Jewish Social Studies*, viii, 1, 1946: 53–4).
21  On the reestablishment of the Yiddish Scientific Institute in New York, see Lucy Davidowicz 1989. Davidowicz was at the Offenbach Depot at roughly the same time as Scholem and was able to transport much of the Jewish cultural goods from there to New York. She also reports on Sutzkever's work. For more specifics on the Nazi destruction of Jewish cultural treasures in Vilna and the rescue of what remained, see Fishman 2005a (ch. 10: "Embers Plucked from the Fire. The Rescue of Jewish Cultural Treasures in Vilna," pp. 139–54).
22  On Sutzkever's testimony in Nuremberg, see Schwarz 2005.
23  Arendt reviewed this book unfavorably in *Commentary* 1946 as "The Image of Hell" (Arendt 1994: 197–205). There she criticized the book because of its mass of details. As in her Eichmann Trial commentary 15 years later, she did not think that detailed testimony could contribute to understanding.
24  The contributions of this first postwar intellectual meeting are collected in French in Benda 1947.
25  Jaspers developed his ideas about the "Axial Age" not only in his "European Spirit" lecture but also in a programmatic statement in 1949, translated into English as *The Origin and Goal of History* (Jaspers 1953). Jaspers's philosophical statement about the Axial Age was translated into a sociological program of modernity by S. N Eisenstadt (see Eisenstadt 1986). This is the origin of the concept of "multiple modernities."
26  Arendt published two essays on Jaspers (1957 and 1958) called "Karl Jaspers: A Laudatio" and "Karl Jaspers: Citizen of the World?" both published in *Men in Dark Time*s (Arendt 1968b), pp. 71–80 and 81–94.
27  In 1954, Lukács published *The Destruction of Reason* (Lukács 1980), in which he attacked what he called the irrational tradition

in German thought, basically lumping together all individual and existential thought as bourgeois and holding it responsible for European fascism. He treated Heidegger and Jaspers together without much distinction.

28  There was one small exception, not in one of the speeches but in the discussion that followed them. Twenty-six-year-old Jean Starobinksi, who would become a literary specialist, observed at one point that the silence of the dead Jews was louder than all the speeches. But his comment fell on deaf ears.

29  See Azadovskii and Egorov 2002; Figes 2007, pp. 493ff.

30  See the article by Clark (2009).

31  For the Committee, see Redlich 1995; for the liquidation of its members, see Rubenstein 2005.

32  For the connections between Jews and modernity in the Soviet Union, see Slezkine 2004.

33  In Trial of the Major War Criminals before the International Military Tribunal. Volume II. Proceedings: 11/14/1945-11/30/1945. Nuremberg: IMT, 1947, p. 98.

34  For example, Beck 2006; Fine 2007; Levy and Sznaider 2005.

35  Kelsen 1947.

36  See also Luban 1987.

37  Alexander 2002.

38  See especially Marrus 1998 and 2005.

39  World Jewish Congress Collection, American Jewish Archives, Cincinnati, WJC/C176/9.

40  Lewis 2008; Aronson 1988; for an early statement of the World Jewish Congress itself, see World Jewish Congress 1948.

41  The distinction at Nuremberg between the different crimes was apparently suggested by Hersh Lauterpacht, a British legal expert and a Jew from Eastern Europe. On Lauterpacht, see Koskenniemi 2001. Lauterpacht worked closely with the British Chief Prosecutor Hartley Shawcross. Lauterpacht would also be influential in the formulation of an international bill of rights.

42  Crimes against humanity were defined as such in the indictment: "murder, extermination, enslavement, deportation, and other inhumane acts committed against any civilian population, before or during the war, or persecutions on political, racial, or religious grounds . . . whether or not in violation of domestic law of the country where perpetrated." This definition is indeed universal, and includes Lemkin's notion of genocide.

43 Robinson 1972: 4.
44 Lemkin 1946b.
45 Arendt 1949a: 37. A German version of this text was published the same year in *Die Wandlung* as "Es gibt nur ein einziges Menschenrecht." This article appeared with very few revisions in her *Origins of Totalitarianism*, in a chapter called "The Perplexities of the Rights of Man."

CHAPTER 6   FROM NUREMBERG TO NEW YORK VIA JERUSALEM

1 For a reading of Arendt's human rights thinking in reference to the Jewish question, see Bernstein 1996 (see chapter 3: "Statelessness and the Rights to Have Rights," pp. 71–87). There are now many works which analyze Arendt's work on human rights. Two of the most important are: Benhabib 2006 and Birmingham 2006. Birmingham provides a philosophical reading of Arendt's theory of rights. For less philosophical and more politically inclined readings of Arendt's theory of rights, see Isaac 1996 and 2002; and Parekh 2004.
2 Galchinsky 2008.
3 On the lobbying work of the World Jewish Congress for the Universal Declaration of Human Rights, see the first-person account of one its major activists: Riegner 2006 (especially chapter 3: "The Struggle for Human Rights," pp. 164–233). Riegner, who served during the war as the representative of the World Jewish Congress in Geneva, informed the Allies in a telegram (the so-called Riegner Telegram) in August 1942 of the Nazi attempt to carry out the final solution in Europe. Riegner obtained this information from a German industrialist, but his memo was met with much suspicion. See also Robinson 1955.
4 The World Jewish Congress was not the only Jewish lobby trying to propose international guarantees at human rights conventions; other lobbies included the American Jewish Congress and the Board of Deputies of British Jews. See Nehemiah Robinson's brother Jacob Robinson (Robinson 1946).
5 For an in-depth reading connecting Jewish intellectuals to the concept of totalitarianism, see Whitfield 1980. There is a huge literature debating the heuristic value of the concept of "totalitarianism," but this is not our concern here. For a review

of the vicissitudes of the concept and its historical twists and turns, see Rabinbach 2006. Rabinbach shows convincingly how the concept was developed by people who had firsthand experience of it.

6　On this point, see Gleason 1995.

7　For current evaluations of the concept, see Geyer and Fitzpatrick 2009, pp. 1–37.

8　See Benhabib and Eddon 2008; Diner 2007.

9　This is argued for instance by Söllner 2004. Söllner places Arendt's theories within the context of other theorists like Ernst Fraenkel, Franz L. Neumann, Sigmund Neumann, Carl Joachim Friedrich, and Zbigniew Brezinski. At the same time, he paints a fascinating picture of American intellectual life in the early 1950s.

10　There is an interesting parallel with Theodor Herzl, the founder of political Zionism, who as a correspondent followed the Dreyfus trial in Paris in real time. Herzl also considered the Dreyfus affair as a symbol of the breakdown of Jewish assimilation and emancipation. Arendt's Jewish Nationalism was, however, true to a cosmopolitan concept of the Jewish Nation as a Diaspora Nation. For Durkheim, on the other hand, the Dreyfus affair was an opportunity to strengthen the claims of moral individualism.

11　For a comparison of these two renderings of human rights in Arendt's thought, see Menke 2007.

12　Arendt was consistently preoccupied with the camps as a defining feature of totalitarianism. She published an article in *Jewish Social Studies* in 1950 called "Social Science Techniques and the Study of the Concentration Camps," reprinted in *Essays in Understanding* (Arendt 1994, pp. 232–43). Earlier, she published a paper called "The Concentration Camps (Arendt 1948). This essay also appeared in German in *Die Wandlung* the same year. Even earlier (Arendt 1946), she published a review of the *Black Book* entitled "The Image of Hell."

13　For a sociological interpretation of Arendt's anti-sociological approach to these matters, see Baehr 2002; Fine 2000b. For the context of her thinking on the camps, see also Young-Bruehl 2004, pp. 204ff. See also Bernstein 1996, ch. 3, "The Descent into Hell," pp. 88–100. She wanted to found a research institute, claiming that there was a lack of Jewish intelligentsia and research institutions (Young-Bruehl 2004, pp. 204–5).

14 In this respect, Arendt's reading of the concentration camps and the destruction of the Jews parts ways with later analyses trying to link this event with more familiar patterns of modernity. Examples of this approach include Bauman 1989. Bauman's intervention is in many ways a continuation of Lukács's approach mentioned earlier only under postmodern assumptions. Arendt insisted on the anti-utilitarian character of the camps and saw this as a break with modernity. For a recent attempt to show the utilitarian (modern) character of the Holocaust, see Aly 2008. This book caused quite a stir in Germany after its publication in 2005.

15 On this point, see especially the analysis of Canovan 1992, pp. 17–62.

16 Morsink 2000. He argues that the drafters of the Universal Declaration had very much the destruction of European Jews on their mind when composing the Declaration. On these connections, see also Levy and Sznaider 2010.

17 Arendt 1958 and Arendt 1963b. Both books deal with politics and political action on the most abstract level. Whereas *Origins of Totalitarianism* looked at the destruction of political action, these books try theoretically to restore it.

18 On Arendt's relationship to America at this time, see Botstein 1983.

19 The Israeli Secret Service captured Adolf Eichmann in May 1960 in Argentina and brought him to trial in Israel. Eichmann's responsibilities included the organization of the transportations of the Jews to the camps. For a historical study of Eichmann that takes issue with Arendt's reading of Eichmann, see Cesarani 2005. For another perspective aligning itself with Arendt's views, see Zertal 2005. This is a book which assumes that Arendt took an anti-Zionist stance and identifies with it. For a reversal of fortunes that defines Arendt as an anti-Zionist and resents her for it, see Yakira 2006. It is interesting to note that both Zionist accusers and anti-Zionist defenders ignore the Jewish side of Arendt's story.

20 This essay is reprinted in Arendt 1994, pp. 106–20.

21 In an interview published in the *New York Times* on December 18, 1960, the prime minister of Israel claimed that "only a Jewish state can try him from a moral point of view" ("The Eichmann Case as Seen by Ben-Gurion", NYT, December 18, 1960). In the same interview, Ben-Gurion insisted on Israel's legitimacy to conduct the trial and stressed sovereignty: "Israel

does not need the protection of an international court." By doing so, Ben-Gurion laid to rest Jewish appeals during the interwar period to international courts for protection. Ben-Gurion wanted to reestablish Jewish power and normalcy by judging Eichmann.

22  Benhabib calls this book Arendt's "most intensely Jewish work" in Benhabib 2000. For a summary of the controversy the book stirred up amongst Jewish intellectuals in the USA, see Rabinbach 2004. For the meaning of the Eichmann Trial for interpretations of the Holocaust in the USA, see Novick 1999. For the reactions of German Jews who saw their legacy threatened by Arendt's account, see Cohen 1993.

23  For the twists and turns of Arendt's definitions of evil, see Bernstein 1996 and Diner 1997. The book even inspired the famous Milgram experiments in the 1970s on obedience, even though the book does not really deal with obedience at all.

24  For the trial from an Israeli perspective, see Steven Aschheim, "Hannah Arendt in Jerusalem," in Aschheim 2001a, pp. 73–85; Bilsky 2004; and Yablonka 2004.

25  Arendt basically continued her criticism of post-emancipatory Jewish leadership she already wrote about in the 1940s. Her dichotomy between Jewish Parvenus trying to accommodate non-Jews and Jewish Pariahs is part of her understanding of Jewish history. See also Muller 1981.

26  On this point, see Felman 2001.

27  For this line of criticism, see Postone 2000.

28  For a short summary of these attacks, see Elon 2006/7; also Rabinbach 2004.

29  Miller 2002.

30  On the exchange and on the Arendt–Scholem relationship from different perspectives, see Eddon 2003; Kaposi 2008, Kaposi 2009; Suchoff 1997.

31  The exchange was first published in English as "Eichmann in Jerusalem: An Exchange of Letters" (Scholem and Arendt 1964). Scholem's letter dated June 23, 1963 can also be found Scholem 1976, pp. 300–6. Arendt's answer dated July 24, 1963 can also be found in Arendt 2007, pp. 465–71.

32  The original letter is in Luxemburg 1958, p. 13; an English translation can be found in Luxemburg 1995.

33  See Arendt 1968b, pp. 33–56.

34  The interview was reprinted in English as "'What Remains? The Language Remains': A Conversation with Günter Gaus," in Arendt 1994: 1–23.

35   Robinson 1965.
36   For the victims' point of view as epistemological, see Diner 2000b.
37   Her reply is reprinted in Arendt 2007 as "The Formidable Dr Robinson. A Reply by Hannah Arendt," pp. 496–511. It is actually a reply to Walter Laqueur's review in the same journal.
38   See on this point Aschheim 2001a, pp. 105–43.
39   Clearly, this is not an ethnically predetermined view, but a research agenda in its own right. See Bauman 1989. See especially Hans Mommsen's Introduction to the German translation of Arendt's book on Eichmann.
40   On broader connections analyzing how German intellectuals debated the Nazi past, see Moses 2007. Moses looks at Enzensberger's entire generation (born 1929) that came politically of age in the 1960s. Enzensberger's book was published in 1964. An English version was published in 1974 (Enzensberger 1974).
41   On this development, see Herf 1980 and Postone 1980. Both essays start with an analysis of the TV series *Holocaust* and its reception in West Germany but continue with a critical reading of how the German Left universalizes the Holocaust. For a more recent analysis in general terms, see Berg 2003. Berg concentrates on historiography but has a chapter on fascism and its theory in German Leftist thinking (see pp. 444ff.).
42   Arendt and Enzensberger 1964. There is no English translation of the exchange. The translation is mine.
43   In 1954, Arendt published three essays in the progressive Catholic journal *Commonweal* dealing with the trans-Atlantic relationship ("Dream and Nightmare," "Europe and the Atom Bomb," "The Threat of Communism") – these essays are reprinted in Arendt 1994, pp. 409–27. For an analysis of these essays in a different context, see Rensmann 2006.
44   This correspondence with the student was only published in 2008 in the German journal *Mittelweg 36* with a commentary by Wolfgang Kraushaar. See Kraushaar 2008.
45   For a communitarian argument along these lines, see MacIntyre 1981.

CHAPTER 7   BETWEEN DROHOBYCH AND NEW YORK:
AN END AND A NEW BEGINNING

1   For the twists and turns of the distinction between Europe and the USA in terms of Jewish minority politics, see Baron 1984.

Baron mentions the autonomous communal structures Jews developed in the USA without having the need for formally recognized minority rights.

2 Around the same time that struggles for national minority rights were taking place in Europe, American Jews were part of a debate about what it meant to be American. This debate about the meaning of cosmopolitan America was not called this at the time (the terms in use at the time included "melting-pot" and "cultural pluralism"), but it meant something very similar. Thus Randolph Bourne published an article in 1916 in the Jewish magazine *Menorah Journal* called "The Jew and Trans-national America," defending hyphenated American identities and arguing that immigrants should not give up their cultural allegiance and disappear into the so-called melting pot; instead, Bourne argued, anticipating the "identity politics" of the late twentieth and twenty-first centuries, they should resist assimilation and "Americanization."

3 For a useful analysis of the historical debates in present-day America, see Streich 2009.

4 For a history of Jewish immigration to the USA, see Herzberg 1998b.

5 Judt 2003.

6 For a historical analysis of binationalism, which does not necessarily correspond to cosmopolitanism, see Weiss 2004.

7 For the larger context, see Judt 2005. Clearly Judt's *New York Review of Books* essay and his claim that Israel is an anachronism is part of looking at the world from postwar Europe.

8 See especially Agamben 1998 and 1999.

9 For a historical critique of Agamben's theories, see Mazower 2008.

10 This term (*Zivilisationsbruch* in German) is not only identified with Arendt but also with the work of Dan Diner. See Diner 2000a.

11 This is, of course, a contested area in Israeli intellectual discourse. Israeli critics calling themselves "Post-Zionists" want to de-ethnicize the state. Some of them explicitly draw on Arendt. See for instance the reader based on a conference in Jerusalem, Aschheim 2001c. Here especially the essays by Amnon Raz-Krakotzkin, "Binationalism and the Question of Palestine," pp. 165–80, and Moshe Zimmermann, "Hannah Arendt, the Early Post-Zionist," pp. 181–93, both written by Israeli critics of Israel's concept of sovereignty. For a good summary and various statements of their positions, see Silberstein 2008.

12 Another typical example of this amongst many others, also relying specifically on Arendt, is Rose 2005, which considers Arendt as part of a group displaying "a melancholic counter-narrative to the birth of a nation-state" (p. 70); also Zertal 2005. Zertal also aligns herself with Arendt to criticize the ethnic nature of Israel. She calls one of her chapters "Between Love of the World and Love of Israel," setting Arendt up as a universalist against the nationalist particularist and Zionist Scholem. Both these critics (as many others) miss, of course, Arendt's admiration for Jewish warriors and the dignity of defending oneself by force. Arendt was not a critic of Jewish political action but one of Jewish sovereignty.

13 This is also the background for Israel's insistence on its sovereignty as opposed to international legal rules and regulations, as the controversy over the Goldstone Report in 2009 amply demonstrates. The report accuses Israel of violating international humanitarian law during the Gaza operation 2008/9 while Israel insists on its right to defend itself as a sovereign nation. In the background looms the international system of protection which failed the Jews in Europe during World War II. For the report, see http://www2.ohchr.org/english/bodies/hrcouncil/docs/12session/A-HRC-12-48.pdf (last accessed January 2010).

14 Arendt wrote on miracles in connection to politics. In particular, her theory of "new beginnings" is part of her reading of miracles. See, for instance, Hannah Arendt 1968a (esp. pp. 169–71). Or as she writes in her book *On Revolution* with regard to the American Revolution: "The revolution . . . was precisely the legendary hiatus between end and beginning, between a no-longer and a not-yet" (Arendt 1963b: 205). It is interesting to note that *On Revolution* and *Eichmann in Jerusalem* came out the same year. The Zionist Revolution was not a real miracle in her opinion, even though it considers itself as between a no-longer and a not-yet. On the other hand, in her eyes, the American Revolution was.

15 See also Eisen 1986.

16 For criticism of the overextension of the concept of Diaspora in the social and cultural sciences, see Brubaker 2005. For an elaboration and even celebration of the concept, see Clifford 1994. Clifford argues for broadening the concept of Diaspora out of the limiting context of Jewish history and to open it up to general concerns.

17 Arendt, "Moses or Washington," *Aufbau*, March 27, 1942. This attitude might explain why Arendt supported school segregation between blacks and whites in the American South in an article she wrote in 1959. The principle that people have the freedom and the right to associate with whomever they wish was sacred for her. See Arendt 2003.

18 This debate is a core element of French political discourse, where features of Catholic universalism emphasizing universal suffering coupled with political concepts of universal citizenship clash with Jewish attempts to emphasize their unique experiences. For an English summary of these debates, see Dean 2006. For an attempt to look at European debates on anti-Semitism and to cut through the dichotomy between so-called alarmists and deniers, see Fine 2009.

19 For a personal journey to contemporary Galicia and its connection to the once-Jewish Galicia, see Bartov 2007.

20 For these wondrous stories, see Schulz 2008. For a biography of Schulz, see Ficowski 2003. Schulz was an inspiration for many writers like Philip Roth, Cynthia Ozick, David Grossman and others who fictionalized him in their own stories. For a literary homage to Schulz, see Grossman 2009.

21 See Snyder 2004.

22 In the "Tentative List of Jewish Cultural Treasures in Axis-Occupied Europe," there is a small entry for Drohobych. It lists the Library of the Jewish Community and the Archives of the Jewish Community (pp. 48–9).

23 On Felix Landau and his role in the mass killings of Jews in this region, see Bartov 2000, which also includes excerpts from Landau's diary.

24 For the story and the subsequent debate, see Powers 2003. In the last chapter of his 2003 biography, "The Last Fairy Tale of Bruno Schulz," Ficowski expresses his anger about the removal of the murals. Ficowski died in 2006, before the story came to its conclusion. Ficowski personified some of the virtues of cosmopolitanism. A Christian, his poetry memorializes the suffering of Jews and Roma in Poland. For Ficowski, however, Schulz was and remains a Polish artist and a representative of Polish modernism. Schulz received a prize in 1938 from the Polish Academy of Literature.

25 A compromise was reached between the Israeli and Ukrainian governments. The murals belong officially to the Ukraine and are on long-term loan to the museum.

26 This issue has become an academic field in itself. See the journal *International Journal of Cultural Property* founded in 1992 which regularly debates issues of cultural heritage and property.

27 See also Appiah 2006, who discusses issues of cultural property in the African context.

28 "Bruno Schultz's Frescoes," letter to the editors from a group of American scholars of the art and history of Eastern Europe, *New York Review of Books*, November 23, 2002, www.nybooks.com/articles/14876 (accessed January 2010).

29 "Bruno Schulz's Wall Paintings: Response to Bruno Schultz's Frescoes," *New York Review of Books*, May 23, 2002, www.nybooks.com/articles/15424 (accessed January 2010).

30 Benjamin Geisler, interview by Celestine Bohlen, "Artwork by Holocaust Victim is Focus of Dispute," *New York Times*, June 20, 2001.

31 For an intriguing analysis of Jewish cosmopolitanism as a challenge to Jewishness, see Miller and Ury 2010.

# REFERENCES

Adorno, T. and Horkheimer, M. (1999 [1944]) *Dialectic of Enlightenment*, Herder and Herder: New York.

Agamben, G. (1998) *Homo Sacer: Sovereign Power and Bare Life*, Stanford: Stanford University Press.

Agamben, G. (1999) *Remnants of Auschwitz: The Witness and the Archive*. New York: Zone Books.

Ahonen, P. (2003) *After the Expulsion: West Germany and Eastern Europe 1945–1990*, Oxford: Oxford University Press.

Albanis, E. (2002) *German-Jewish Cultural Identity from 1900 to the Aftermath of the First World War: A Comparative Study of Moritz Goldstein, Julius Bab and Ernst Lissauer*, Tuebingen: Max Niemeyer Verlag.

Alexander, J. (2002) On the Social Construction of Moral Universals: The Holocaust from War Crime to Trauma Drama. *European Journal of Social Theory* 5(1): 5–85.

Aly, G. (2008) *Hitler's Beneficiaries: Plunder, Racial War and Hitler's Welfare State*, New York: Holt.

Amichai, Y. (1994) Temporary Poem of my Time, in *Yehouda Amichai: A Life of Poetry*, New York: Harper Collins, p. 465.

Anderson, B. (1998) *The Spectre of Comparisons: Nationalism, Southeast Asia, and the World*, London: Verso.

Appiah, K. A. (1998) Cosmopolitan Patriots, in P. Cheah and B. Robbins (eds), *Cosmopolitics: Thinking and Feeling beyond the Nation*, Minneapolis: University of Minnesota Press, pp. 91–114.

Appiah, K. A. (2006) *Cosmopolitanism: Ethics in a World of Strangers*, New York: Norton.

Arendt, H. (1942) From the Dreyfus Affair to France Today, *Jewish Social Studies* 4: 195–240.

Arendt, H. (1945) The Stateless People, *Contemporary Jewish Record* 8 (April): 137–53.

181

Arendt, H. (1946) The Image of Hell, *Commentary* 2: 291–4.

Arendt, H. (1948) The Concentration Camps, *Partisan Review* 15(7): 743–63.

Arendt, H. (1949a) The Rights of Man: What Are They? *Modern Review* 3(1): 24–37.

Arendt, H. (1949b) New Homes for Jewish Books, *American Hebrew*, 159 (Nov. 18) pp. 2, 18.

Arendt, H. (1951) *Origins of Totalitarianism*, New York: Harcourt.

Arendt, H. (1958) *The Human Condition*, Chicago: University of Chicago Press.

Arendt, H. (1963a) *Eichmann in Jerusalem: A Report on the Banality of Evil*, New York: Viking.

Arendt, H. (1963b) *On Revolution*, New York: Penguin Press.

Arendt, H. (1968a) What is Freedom?, in *Between Past and Present*. New York: Viking, pp. 143–71.

Arendt, H. (1968b) *Men in Dark Times*, New York: Harvest Books.

Arendt, H. (1992) *Lectures on Kant's Political Philosophy*, Chicago: University of Chicago Press.

Arendt, H. (1994) *Essays in Understanding*, New York: Harcourt Brace.

Arendt, H. (1997) *Rahel Varnhagen: The Life of a Jewess* (ed. by Liliane Weissberg). Baltimore: Johns Hopkins University Press.

Arendt, H. (2000) *Vor dem Antisemitismus ist man nur auf dem Monde sicher. Beiträge für die deutsch-jüdische Zeitschrift Aufbau*, ed. M. L. Knott, Piper: München.

Arendt, H. (2002) *Responsibility and Judgment*, New York: Schocken.

Arendt, H. (2003) Reflections on Little Rock, *Responsibility and Judgment*, New York: Schocken Books, pp. 193–214.

Arendt, H. (2007) *The Jewish Writings*, ed. Jerome Kohn and Ron Feldman, New York: Schocken.

Arendt, H. and Benjamin, W. (2006) *Arendt und Benjamin: Texte, Briefe, Dokumente*, ed. Detlev Schöttker and Erdmut Wizisla, Frankfurt: Suhrkamp.

Arendt, H. and Blücher, H. (2000) *Within Four Walls: The Correspondence between Hannah Arendt and Heinrich Blücher 1936–1968*, ed. L. Kohler, Southpark: Harcourt Press.

Arendt, H. and Blumenfeld, K. (1995) . . . *In Keinem Besitz Verwurzelt*, Berlin: Rotbuch.

Arendt, H. and Enzensberger, M. (1964) Politik und Verbrechen: Ein Briefwechsel, *Merkur* 19(4): 380–5.

Arendt, H. and Jaspers, K. (1992) *Correspondence 1926–1969*, ed. Lotte Kohler and Hans Saner, New York: Harcourt Brace Jovanovich.

Arendt, H. and Scholem, G. (2010) *Der Briefwechsel: 1939–1964*, Hsg. von Marie Luise Knott, Frankfurt: Suhrkamp.

Aronson, S. (1988) Preparation for the Nuremberg Trial: The O.S.S., Charles Dwork, and the Holocaust, *Holocaust and Genocide Studies* 12(2): 257–81.

REFERENCES

Aschheim, S. (2001a) *In Times of Crisis: Essays on European Cultures, Germans, and Jews*, Madison, WI: University of Wisconsin Press.
Aschheim, S. (2001b) *Scholem, Arendt, Klemperer: Intimate Chronicles in Turbulent Times*, Bloomington, IN: Indiana University Press.
Aschheim, S. (ed.) (2001c) *Hannah Arendt in Jerusalem*. Berkeley: University of California Press.
Aschheim, S. (2004a) *The German-Jewish Legacy Abroad*, Princeton: Princeton University Press.
Aschheim, S. (2004b) The Metaphysical Psychologist: On the Life and Letters of Gershom Scholem, *Journal of Modern History* 76: 903–33.
Azadovskii, K. and Egorov, B. (2002) From Anti-Westernism to Anti-Semitism: Stalin and the Impact of the "Anti-Cosmopolitan" Campaigns on Soviet Culture, *Journal of Cold War Studies* 4(1): 157–76.
Baehr, P. (2002) Identifying the Unprecedented: Hannah Arendt, Totalitarianism and the Critique of Sociology, *American Sociological Review* 67(6): 804–31.
Bamberger-Stemman, S. (2000) *Der Europäische Nationalitätenkongress 1925 bis 1938: Nationale Minderheiten zwischen Lobbyisten und Grossmachtinteressen*, Marburg: Herder Institut.
Barley, D. (1988) Hannah Arendt: Die Judenfrage. Schriften in der Zeit zwischen 1929–1950, *Zeitschrift für Politik* 35(2): 113–29.
Barnouw, D. (1990) *Visible Spaces: Hannah Arendt and the German-Jewish Experience*, Baltimore: Johns Hopkins University Press.
Baron, S. (1935) Germany's Ghetto, Past and Present. A Perspective on Nazi Laws against the Jews, *International Journal of Columbia University* 3: 1–4.
Baron, S. (1945) The Spiritual Reconstruction of European Jewry, *Commentary* 1: 4–12.
Baron, S. (1964 [1928]) Ghetto and Emancipation. Shall We Revise the Traditional View? in L. W. Schwarz (ed.), *The Menorah Treasury*, Philadelphia: Jewish Publication Society of America, pp. 50–63.
Baron, S. (1974) The Journal and the Conference of Jewish Social Studies, in A. G. Duker and M. Ben-Horin (eds), *Emancipation and Counter-Emancipation*, New York: KTAV Publishing House, pp. 1–9.
Baron, S. (1976) Hannah Arendt 1906–1975, *Jewish Social Studies* 38(2): 187–9.
Baron, S. (1984) Is America Ready for Ethnic Minority Rights? *Jewish Social Studies* 46(3/4): 189–214.
Bartov, O. (ed.) (2000) *The Holocaust: Origins, Implementation, Aftermath*, London: Routledge, pp. 185–204.
Bartov, O. (2007) *Erased: Vanishing Traces of Jewish Galicia in Present-Day Ukraine*, Princeton: Princeton University Press.
Bartov, O. (2008) Eastern Europe as the Site of Genocide, *Journal of Modern History* 80(September): 557–93.
Bauman, Z. (1988) Exit Visas and Entry Tickets: Paradoxes of Jewish Assimilation, *Telos* 77: 45–77.

Bauman, Z. (1989) *Modernity and the Holocaust*, Ithaca, NY: Cornell University Press.

Bauman, Z. (2008) Jews and Other Europeans, Old and New, *JPR: Institute for Jewish Policy Research* (June): 1–8.

Beck, U. (2005) *Power in the Global Age*, Cambridge: Polity.

Beck, U. (2006) *The Cosmopolitan Vision*, Cambridge: Polity.

Beck, U. (2009) *The God of One's Own*, Cambridge: Polity.

Beck, U. and Grande, E. (2007) *Cosmopolitan Europe*, Cambridge: Polity.

Beck, U. and Sznaider, N. (2006) Unpacking Cosmopolitanism for the Social Sciences: A Research Agenda, *British Journal of Sociology* 57(1):1–23.

Beck, U. and Sznaider, N. (2010) The New Cosmopolitanism in the Social Sciences, in B. Turner (ed.), *The Routledge Handbook of Globalization Studies*, Abingdon: Routledge, pp. 635–52.

Beiner, N. (2000) "Arendt and Nationalism," in D. Villa (ed.), *The Cambridge Companion to Hannah Arendt,* Cambridge: Cambridge University Press, pp. 44–62.

Benda, J. (ed.) (1947) *L'Esprit européen*, Neuchâtel: Les Éditions de la Baconnière.

Benhabib, S. (1990) Hannah Arendt and the Redemptive Power of Narrative, *Social Research* 57(1): 167–96.

Benhabib, S. (1995) The Pariah and her Shadow: Hannah Arendt's Biography of Rahel Varnhagen. *Political Theory* 23(1): 5–24.

Benhabib, S. (1996) *The Reluctant Modernism of Hannah Arendt*, Thousand Oaks, CA: Sage.

Benhabib, S. (2000) Arendt's Eichmann in Jerusalem, in D. Villa (ed.), *The Cambridge Companion to Hannah Arendt*, Cambridge: Cambridge University Press, pp. 65–85.

Benhabib, S. (2006) *Another Cosmopolitanism*, New York: Oxford University Press.

Benhabib, S. (2009a) International Law and Human Plurality in the Shadow of Totalitarianism: Hannah Arendt and Raphael Lemkin, *Constellations* 16(2): 331–50.

Benhabib, S. (2009b) From the "Dialectics of Enlightenment" to the "Origins of Totalitarianism" and the Genocide Convention: Adorno and Horkheimer in the Company of Arendt and Lemkin, in W. Breckman, P. Gordon, D. Moses, S. Moyn, and E. Neuman (eds), *The Modernist Imagination: Intellectual History and Critical Theory*, New York: Berghahn Books, pp. 299–330.

Benhabib, S. and Eddon, R. (2008) From Antisemitism to the "Rights to Have Rights": The Jewish Roots of Hannah Arendt's Cosmopolitanism, in P. Lassner and L. Trubowitz (eds), *Antisemitism and Philosemitism in the Twentieth and Twenty-first Centuries. Representing Jews, Jewishness and Modern Culture*, Newark, DE: University of Delaware Press, pp. 63–80.

Benjamin, W. (1972) *Gesammelte Schriften*, II, 3, Frankfurt: Suhrkamp.
Benjamin, W. (1999) *Illuminations: Essays and Reflections*, London: Pimlico.
Berg, N. (2003) *Der Holocaust und Westdeutsche Historiker*, Göttingen: Wallstein Verlag.
Berlin, I. (1976) *Vico and Herder: Two Studies in the History of Ideas*, London: Chatto and Windus.
Bernstein, R. (1996) *Hannah Arendt and the Jewish Question*, Cambridge: MIT Press.
Bialik, H. (1923) *Law and Legend or Halakah and Aggadah*, New York: Bloch.
Bilsky, L. (2004) *Transformative Justice: Israeli Identity on Trial*, Ann Arbor: University of Michigan Press.
Birmingham, P. (2006) *Hannah Arendt and Human Rights*, Bloomington, IN: Indiana University Press.
Birnbaum, P. (2008) *Geography of Hope: Exile, the Enlightenment, Disassimilation*, Stanford: Stanford University Press.
Birnbaum, P. and Katznelson, I. (1995) Emancipation and the Liberal Offer, in P. Birnbaum and I. Katznelson (eds), *Paths of Emancipation*, Princeton: Princeton University Press, pp. 3–36.
Bloxham, D. (2009) *The Final Solution: A Genocide*, Oxford: Oxford University Press.
Bohlen, C. (2001) Artwork by Holocaust Victim is Focus of Dispute, *New York Times*, June 20th.
Bohman, J. and Lutz-Bachmann, M. (eds) (1997) *Perpetual Peace: Essays on Kant's Cosmopolitan Ideal*, Cambridge, MA: MIT Press.
Borin, J. (1992) Embers of the Soul: The Destruction of Jewish Books and Libraries in Poland during World War II, *Libraries & Culture* 28(4): 445–60.
Botstein, L. (1982) Stefan Zweig and the Illusion of the Jewish European. *Jewish Social Studies* 44(1): 63–84.
Botstein, L. (1983) The Jew as Pariah: Hannah Arendt's Political Philosophy, *Critical Anthropology* 8: 31–46.
Boyarin, D. (1997) *A Radical Jew: Paul and the Politics of Identity*, Berkeley: University of California Press.
Brubaker, R. (1996) *Nationalism Reframed. Nationhood and the National Question in the New Europe*, Cambridge: Cambridge University Press.
Brubaker, R. (2004) *Ethnicity without Groups*, Cambridge, MA: Harvard University Press.
Brubaker, R. (2005) The "Diaspora" Diaspora, *Ethnic and Racial Studies* 28(1): 1–19.
Brubaker, R. (2009) Ethnicity, Race and Nationalism, *Annual Review of Sociology* 35: 21–41.
Calhoun, C. (2002) Imagining Solidarity: Cosmopolitanism, Constitutional Patriotism, and the Public Sphere, *Public Culture* 14(1): 147–71.
Canovan, M. (1992) *Hannah Arendt: A Reinterpretation of her Political Thought*, Cambridge: Cambridge University Press.

Celermeyer, D. (2010) "Hannah Arendt: Athens or Perhaps Jerusalem?" *Thesis Eleven* 102(1): 24–38.

Cesarani, D. (2005) *Eichmann: His Life and Crimes*, Vintage: New York.

Chasanowitsch, L. and Motzkin, L. (1919) *Zur Judenfrage der Gegenwart: Dokumentensammlung*, Stockholm: Bokvorlaget.

Cheah, P. (1997) Rethinking Cosmopolitan Freedom in Transnationalism, *boundary 2* 24: 157–97.

Childs, P. and Williams, P. (1997) *An Introduction to Post-Colonial Literature*, Prentice Hall: Harvester Wheatsheaf.

Clark, K. (2009) Ehrenburg and Grossmann. Two Cosmopolitan Jewish Writers reflect on Nazi Germany at War, *Kritika: Explorations in Russian and Eurasian History* 10(3): 607–28.

Clark, M. W. (2002) A Prophet Without Honor: Karl Jaspers in Germany, 1945–1958, *Journal of Contemporary History* 37(2): 197–222.

Clifford, J. (1994) Diasporas, *Cultural Anthropology* 9(3): 302–38.

Cohen, G. D. (2006) The Politics of Recognition: Jewish Refugees in Relief Policies and Human Rights Debates, 1945–1950, *Immigrants & Minorities* 24(4): 125–43.

Cohen, M. (1992) Rooted Cosmopolitanism, *Dissent* 39: 478–83.

Cohen, R. I. (1993) Breaking the Code: Hannah Arendt's Eichmann in Jerusalem and the Public Polemic, in *Michael: On the History of the Jews in the Diaspora*, Tel-Aviv: The Diaspora Research Institute, pp 30–85.

Collins, D. and Rothfelder, H. (1983) The Einsatzstab Reichsleiter Rosenberg and the Looting of Jewish and Masonic Libraries during World War II, *Journal of Library History* 18(1): 21–36.

Cooper, J. (2008) *Raphael Lemkin and the Struggle for the Genocide Convention*, Houndmills: Palgrave Macmillan.

Curthoys, N. (2005) The Emigre Sensibility of "World-Literature": Historicizing Hannah Arendt and Karl Jaspers' Cosmopolitan Intent, *Theory & Event* 8(3).

Curthoys, A. and Docker, J. (2008) Defining Genocide, in D. Stone (ed.), *The Historiography of Genocide*, Houndmills: Palgrave Macmillan, pp. 9–41.

Davidowicz, L. (1989) *From that Place and Time: A Memoir 1938–1947*, New York: Bentam.

Dean, C. J. (2006) Recent French Discourses on Stalinism, Nazism, and "Exorbitant" Jewish Memory, *History and Memory* 18(1): 43–85.

Delanty, D. (2003) The Making of a Post-Western Europe: A Civilizational Analysis, *Thesis Eleven* 72: 8–25.

Diner, D. (1997) Hannah Arendt Reconsidered: On the Banal and the Evil in her Holocaust Narrative, *New German Critique* 71: 177–90.

Diner, D. (2000a) *Beyond the Conceivable: Studies on Germany, Nazism, and the Holocaust*, Berkeley: University of California Press.

Diner, D. (2000b) Historical Understanding and Counterrationality, in his *Beyond the Conceivable. Studies on Germany, Nazism, and the Holocaust*, Berkeley: University of California Press, pp. 130–7.

Diner, D. (2000c) On Guilt Discourse and Other Narrations. German Questions and Universal Answers, in his *Beyond the Conceivable: Studies on Germany, Nazism, and the Holocaust*, Berkeley: University of California Press, pp. 218–30.

Diner, D. (2003) *Gedächtniszeiten. Über Jüdische und andere Geschichten*, München: C. H. Beck.

Diner, D. (2007) Marranische Einschreibungen. Erwägungen zu verborgenen Traditionen bei Hannah Arendt, *Babylon* 22: 62–71.

Diner, D. (2008) Ambiguous Semantics: Reflections on Jewish Political Concepts, *Jewish Quarterly Review* 98(1): 89–102.

Diner, H. (2009) *We Remember with Reverence and Love: American Jews and the Myth of Silence after the Holocaust, 1945–1962*, New York: New York University Press.

Disch, L. J. (1994) *Hannah Arendt and the Limits of Philosophy*, Ithaca: Cornell University Press.

Disch, L. J. (1995) On Friendship in Dark Times, in B. Honig (ed.), *Feminist Interpretations of Hannah Arendt*, University Park, PA: Penn State University Press, pp. 285–312.

Docker, J. (2008) Are Settler-Colonies Inherently Genocidal? Re-reading Lemkin in A. D. Moses (ed.), *Empire, Colony, Genocide. Conquest, Occupation and Subaltern Resistance in World History*, New York: Berghahn Books, pp. 81–101.

Dohrn, V. (2004) State and Minorities: The First Lithuanian Republic and S. M. Dubnov's Concept of Cultural Autonomy, in A. Nikzentaitis, S. Schreiner and D. Staliunas (eds.), *The Vanished World of Lithuanian Jews*, Amsterdam: Rodopi, pp. 155–73.

Dubnov, A. (2007) Between Liberalism and Jewish Nationalism: Young Isaiah Berlin on the Road Towards Diaspora Zionism, *Modern Intellectual History* 4(2): 303–26.

Dubnow, S. (1958) *Nationalism and History: Essays on Old and New Judaism*, Cleveland: Meridian Books.

Durkheim, E. (2001 [1912]) *The Elementary Forms of Religious Life*, Oxford: Oxford University Press.

Eddon, R. M. (2003) Gershom Scholem, Hannah Arendt and the Paradox of "Non-Nationalist" Nationalism, *The Journal of Jewish Thought and Philosophy* 12(1): 55–68.

Eddon, R. (2006) Arendt, Scholem, Benjamin: Between Revolution and Messianism, *European Journal of Political Theory* 5(3): 261–79.

Eisen, A. M. (1986) *Galut: Modern Jewish Reflection on Homelessness and Homecoming*, Bloomington, IN: University of Indiana Press.

Eisenstadt, S. N. (1986) *The Origins and Diversity of Axial Age Civilizations*, Albany: SUNY Press.

Eisenstadt, S. N. (1992) *Jewish Civilization*, New York: Oxford University Press.

Elon, A. (2006/7) The Excommunication of Hannah Arendt, *World Policy Journal* 23(4): 93–102.

Engel, D. (2006) Crisis and Lachrymosity: On Salo Baron, Neobaronianism, and the Study of Modern European Jewish History, *Jewish History* 20: 243–64.

Enzensberger, H. M. (1974) *Politics and Crime*, New York: Seabury Press.

Feinberg, N (1948) The Recognition of the Jewish People in International Law, *Jewish Journal of International Law* 1: 1–26.

Felman, S. (2001) Theaters of Justice: Arendt in Jerusalem, the Eichmann Trial, and the Redefinition of Legal Meaning in the Wake of the Holocaust, *Critical Inquiry* 27(2): 201–38.

Feuchtwanger, L. (1955) *Die Jüdin von Toledo*, Berlin: Aufbau.

Feuereisen, O. K. (2004) Geschichtserfahrung und Völkerreicht. Jacob Robinson und die Gründung des Institute of Jewish Affairs, *Leipziger Beiträge zur Jüdischen Geschichte und Kultur* 10: 307–27.

Ficowski, J. (2003) *Regions of Great Heresy. Bruno Schulz: A Biographical Portrait*, New York: Norton.

Figes, O. (2007) *The Whisperers: Private Life in Stalin's Russia*, New York: Picador.

Fine, R. (2000a) Crimes against Humanity: Hannah Arendt and the Nuremberg Debates, *European Journal of Social Theory* 3(3): 293–311.

Fine, R. (2000b) Hannah Arendt: Politics and Understanding after the Holocaust, in R. Fine and C. Turner (eds.), *Social Theory after the Holocaust*, Liverpool: Liverpool University Press, pp. 19–45.

Fine, R. (2007) *Cosmopolitanism*, Milton Park: Routledge.

Fine, R. (2008) Judgment and the Reification of the Faculties. A Reconstructive Reading of Arendt's Life of the Mind, *Philosophy & Social Criticism* 34(1–2): 157–86.

Fine, R. (2009) Fighting with Phantoms: A Contribution to the Debate on Anti-Semitism in Europe, *Patterns of Prejudice* 43(5): 459–79.

Fink, C. (2004) *Defending the Rights of Others: The Great Powers, the Jews, and International Minority Protection 1878–1938*, Cambridge: Cambridge University Press.

Fishman, D. (2005) Embers Plucked from the Fire: The Rescue of Jewish Cultural Treasures in Vilna, in his *The Rise of Modern Yiddish Culture*, Pittsburgh: Pittsburgh University Press, pp. 139–54.

Flohr, P. M. (1999) The German-Jewish Parnassus, in his *German Jews: A Dual Identity*, New Haven: Yale University Press.

Frankel, J. (1984) *Prophecy and Politics: Socialism, Nationalism and the Russian Jews, 1862–1917*, New York: Cambridge University Press.

Frankel, J. (1997) *The Damascus Affair: Ritual Murder, Politics and the Jews in 1840*, New York: Cambridge University Press.

Friedman, H. (2001) *Roots of the Future*, New York: Gefen Publishing House.

Friedman, P. (1957/8) The Fate of the Jewish Book During the Nazi Era, *Jewish Book Annual* 15, pp. 3–13.

Galchinsky, M. (2008) *Jews and Human Rights: Dancing at Three Weddings*, Lanham: Rowman and Littlefield.

Gallas, E. (2006) Gedächtnisspuren. Restitution jüdischer Kulturgüter nach 1945 und ihre Wirkungsgeschichte am Beispiel des Offenbach Archival Depot, *Bulletin des Simon-Dubnow-Instituts* 8: 74–85.

Gellner, E. (1983) *Nations and Nationalism*, Ithaca: Cornell University Press.

Geyer, M. and Fitzpatrick, S. (2009) *Beyond Totalitarianism: Stalinism and Nazism Compared*, Cambridge: Cambridge University Press.

Gilroy, P. (1993) *The Black Atlantic: Modernity and Double-Consciousness*, Cambridge, MA: Harvard University Press.

Glass, H. (2004) Ende der Gemeinsamkeit. Zur deutsch-jüdischen Kontroverse auf dem Europäischen Nationalitätenkongress 1933, *Leipziger Beiträge zur jüdischen Geschichte und Kultur* 2: 259–82.

Gleason, A. (1995) *Totalitarianism: The Inner History of the Cold War*, New York: Oxford University Press.

Goldstein, M. (1912) Deutsch-Jüdischer Parnass, *Der Kunstwart* 25: 281–94.

Goldstein, M. (1914) Wir und Europa, in *Vom Judentum: Ein Sammelbuch*, Leipzig: Kurt Wolf Verlag, pp. 194–208.

Goldstein, M. (1957) German Jewry's Dilemma: The Story of a Provocative Essay, *Leo Baeck Institute Yearbook*, 2, pp. 236–54.

Gordon, P. E. (2003) *Rosenzweig and Heidegger: Between Judaism and German Philosophy*, Berkeley: University of California Press.

Gosh, A. (1992) *In an Antique Land*, New York: Vintage Press.

Graf, P. (2008) *Die Bernheim-Petition 1933. Jüdische Politik in der Zwischenkriegszeit*, Göttingen: Vandenhoeck and Ruprecht.

Gross, J. (2006) *Fear: Anti-Semitism in Poland after Auschwitz. An Essay in Historical Interpretation*, Princeton: Princeton University Press.

Grossman, D. (2009) The Age of Genius. The Legend of Bruno Schulz, *New Yorker*, June 8.

Gurevitch, Z. (1997) The Double Site of Israel, in his *Grasping Space: Space and Place in Israeli Discourse and Experience*, Albany, NY: SUNY University Press, pp. 203–16.

Gürke, N. (1932) Der Nationalsozialismus, das Grenz-und Auslanddeutschtum und das Nationalitätenrecht, *Nation und Staat* VI: 7–30.

Habermas, J. (2000) *The Inclusion of the Other: Studies in Political Theory*, Cambridge: MIT Press, pp. 203–16.

Hacohen, M. (1999) Dilemmas of Cosmopolitanism: Karl Popper, Jewish Identity and Central European Culture, *The Journal of Modern History* 71: 105–49.

Halpern, B. (1948) Guilty, but not Answerable, *Jewish Frontier* (April): 41–60.

Hansen, P. (1993) *Politics, History and Citizenship*, Stanford: Stanford University Press.

Hedetoft, U. and Hjort, M. (eds) (2002) *The Postnational Self: Identity and Belonging*, Minneapolis: University of Minnesota Press.

Herf, J. (1980) The *Holocaust* Reception in West Germany: Right, Center, and Left, *New German Critique* 19(1): 30–52.

Hertzberg, A. (1968) *The French Enlightenment and the Jews*, New York: Columbia University Press.

Hertzberg, A. (1998a) *Jews: The Essence and the Character of a People*, San Francisco: Harper.

Herzberg, A. (1998b) *The Jews in America: Four Centuries of an Uneasy Encounter*, New York: Simon and Schuster.

Herzog, A. (2000) Illuminating Inheritance. Benjamin's Influence on Arendt's Political Storytelling, *Philosophy and Social Criticism* 26(5): 1–27.

Heuer, W. (1992) *Citizen: Persönliche Integrität und poltisches Handeln. Eine Rekonstruktion des politischen Humanismus Hannah Arendts.* Berlin: Akademie Verlag.

Heuer, W. (2007) "Europe and its Refugees: Arendt on the Politicization of Minorities," *Social Research* 74(4): 1159–72.

Hiden, J. and Smith, D. (2006) Looking Beyond the Nation State: A Baltic Vision for National Minorities between the Wars, *Journal of Contemporary History* 41(3): 387–99.

Hilbrenner, A. (2007) *Diaspora-Nationalismus: zur Geschichtskonstruktion Simon Dubnows*, Göttingen: Vandenhoeck & Ruprecht.

Hill, L. E. (2001) The Nazi Attack on "Un-German" Literature, 1933–1945, in J. Rose (ed.), *The Holocaust and the Book: Destruction and Preservation*, Amherst: University of Massachusetts Press, pp. 9–46.

Hinton, A. (2001) *Genocide: An Anthropological Reader*, Hoboken, NJ: Wiley.

Hirsch, D. (1986) Avraham Sutzkever's Vilna Poems, *Modern Language Studies* 16: 37–50.

Holmes, S. (2002) Looking Away, *London Review of Books* 24(22).

Hunt, L. (ed. and trans.) (1996) *The French Revolution and Human Rights: A Brief Documentary History*, Bedford: St Martin's Press.

Institute for Jewish Affairs (1948) *Unity in Dispersion: A History of the World Jewish Congress*, New York: World Jewish Congress, pp. 45–74.

International Military Tribunal (1995) *Trial of the Major War Criminals Before the International Military Tribunal, Nuremberg, 14 November 1945–1 October 1946*, Buffalo: William S. Hein.

Isaac, J. (1996) A New Guarantee on Earth: Hannah Arendt on Human Dignity and the Politics of Human Rights, *American Political Science Review* 90(1): 61–73.

Isaac, J. (2002) Hannah Arendt on Human Rights and the Limits of Exposure, or Why Noam Chomsky Is Wrong About the Meaning of Kosovo, *Social Research* 69(2): 505–37.

Jacobs, S. and Totten, S. (2002) Totally Unofficial Man, in S. Jacobs and S. Totten (eds.), *Pioneers of Genocide Studies*, New Brunswick: Transaction Books, pp. 365–99.

Janowsky, O. (1933) *The Jews and Minority Rights, 1898–1919*, New York: Columbia University Press.

Janowsky, O. I. and Fagen, M. M. (1937) *International Aspects of German Racial Policies*, New York: Oxford University Press.

Jaspers, K. (1946a) *The Question of German Guilt*, New York: Dial Press.

Jaspers, K. (1946b) *Über die Schuldfrage*, München: Piper.

Jaspers, K. (1953) *The Origin and Goal of History*, New Haven: Yale University Press.

Judt, T. (2003) Israel: An Alternative Future, *New York Review of Books* (Oct. 23).

Judt, T. (2005) *Postwar: A History of Europe since 1945*, New York: Penguin.

Kaposi, D. (2008) To Judge or Not to Judge: The Clash of Perspectives in the Scholem–Arendt Exchange, *Holocaust Studies* 14(1): 93–116.

Kaposi, D. (2009) The Unbearable Lightness of Identity: Membership, Tradition and the Anti-Semite in Gershom's Letter to Hannah Arendt, *Critical Discourse Studies* 6(4): 269–81.

Karbach, O. (1962) The Evolution of Jewish Political Thought, in *Institute of Jewish Affairs – The Institute Anniversary Volume (1941–1961)*, New York: World Jewish Congress, pp. 23–48.

Kateb, G. (1983) *Hannah Arendt: Politics, Conscience, Evil*, Totowa, NJ: Rowman & Littelfield.

Kelsen, H. (1947) Will the Judgment in the Nuremberg Trial Constitute a Precedent in International Law? *The International Law Quarterly* 1(2): 153–71.

Kennedy Grimsted, P. (2005) Roads to Ratibor: Library and Archival Plunder by the Einsatzstab Reichsleiter Rosenberg, *Holocaust and Genocide Studies* 19(3): 390–485.

Kennedy Grimsted, P. (2006) The Postwar Fate of the Einsatzstab Reichsleiter Rosenberg Archival and Library Plunder, and the Dispersal of ERR Records, *Holocaust and Genocide Studies* 20(4): 278–308.

King, R. H. and Stone, D. (eds) (2007) *Hannah Arendt and the Uses of History. Imperialism, Nation, Race, and Genocide*, New York: Berghahn Books.

Knuth, R. (2003) *Libricide: The Regime-Sponsored Destruction of Books and Libraries in the Twentieth Century*, Westport, CT: Praeger.

Kohn, H. (1994 [1944]) *The Idea of Nationalism*, New York: Macmillan.

Koskenniemi, M. (2001) *The Gentle Civilizer of Nations: The Rise and Fall of International Law, 1870–1960*, Cambridge: Cambridge University Press, pp. 353–412.

Kraft, C. (2005) Völkermord als delictum iuris gentium: Raphael Lemkins Vorarbeiten für eine Genozidkonvention, *Jahrbuch des Simon-Dubnow-Instituts/Simon Dubnow Institute Yearbook* 4: 79–98.

Kraushaar, W. (2008) Hannah Arendt und die Studentenbewegung, *Mittelweg* 36(1): 9–13.

Kurtz, M. J. (2006) *America and the Return of Nazi Contraband: The Recovery of Europe's Cultural Treasures*, Cambridge: Cambridge University Press, pp. 155–62.

Kushner, T. (1994) *The Holocaust and the Liberal Imagination: A Social and Cultural History*, Cambridge, MA: Blackwell.

Lazare, B. (1948) *Job's Dungheap: Essays on Jewish Nationalism and Social Revolution*, ed. Hannah Arendt, New York: Schocken Books.

Leibovici, M. (2007) Arendt's Rahel Varnhagen: A New Kind of Narration in the Impasses of German-Jewish Assimilation and Existenzphilosophie. *Social Research* 74(3): 903–22.

Lemkin, R. (1944) *Axis Rule in Occupied Europe: Laws of Occupation, Analysis of Government, Proposals for Redress*. Washington, DC: Carnegie Foundation.

Lemkin, R. (1946a) Genocide, *American Scholar* 15: 227–30.

Lemkin, R. (1946b) *Memorandum on the Necessity to include Anti-Genocide Clauses*, World Jewish Congress Collection, American Jewish Archives, Cincinnati, WJC/C14-21.

Lessing, G. E. (1860) *Nathan the Wise: A Dramatic Poem in Five Acts*, trans. by A. Reich, London: A. W. Bennett.

Levene, M. (1993) Nationalism and its Alternatives in the International Arena: The Jewish Question at Paris, 1919, *Journal of Contemporary History* 28: 511–31.

Levinas, I. (2007) Sociality and Money, *Business Ethics: A European Review* 16(3): 203–7.

Levy, D. and Sznaider, N. (2005) *The Holocaust and Memory in the Global Age*, Philadelphia: Temple University Press.

Levy, D. and Sznaider, N. (2010) *Human Rights and Memory*, Philadelphia: Penn State University Press.

Lewis, M. A. (2008) The World Jewish Congress and Institute of Jewish Affairs at Nuremberg: Ideas, Strategies, and Political Goals, 1942–1956, *Yad Washem Studies* 36(1): 181–210.

Liberles, R. (1995) *Salo Wittmayer Baron, Architect of Jewish History*, New York: New York University Press.

Lieblich, A. (2008) Minority as Inferiority: Minority Rights in Historical Perspective, *Review of International Studies* 34: 243–63.

Lowith, K. (1942) M. Heidegger and F. Rosenzweig or Temporality and Eternity, *Philosophy and Phenomenological Research* 3(1): 53–77.

Löwy, M. (1992) *Redemption and Utopia: Jewish Libertarian Thought in Central Europe*, London: The Athlone Press.

Luban, D. (1987) The Legacy of Nuremberg, *Social Research* 54(4): 779–827.

Lukács, G. (1980 [1954]) *The Destruction of Reason*, London: Merlin Press.

Luxemburg, R. (1958) *Das Menschliche Entscheidet: Briefe an Freunde*, München: List Verlag.

Luxemburg, R. (1995) No Room in my Heart for Jewish Suffering, in P. Mendes-Flohr and J. Reinharz, (eds), *The Jew in the Modern World*, New York: Oxford University Press, pp. 261–2.

MacIntyre, A. (1981) *After Virtue*, London: Duckworth.

REFERENCES

Markus, J. (ed.) (1999) *Surviving the 20th Century: Social Philosophy from the Frankfurt School to the Columbia Faculty Seminars*, New Brunswick, NJ: Transaction Publishers.

Marrus, M. (1998) The Holocaust at Nuremberg, *Yad Vashem Studies* 26: 4–45.

Marrus, M. (2005) A Jewish Lobby at Nuremberg: Jacob Robinson and the Institute of Jewish Affairs, 1945–1946, *Cardozo Law Review* 27: 1651–65.

Marx, K. (1976 [1843]) On the Jewish Question, in his *Collected Works, Vol. 3*, Moscow: Progress Publishers, pp. 146–74.

Mayer, H. (1975) *Aussenseiter*, Frankfurt: Suhrkamp.

Mazower, M. (2004) The Strange Triumph of Human Rights, 1933–1950, *The Historical Journal* 47(2): 379–98.

Mazower, M. (2008) Foucault, Agamben: Theory and the Nazis, *boundary 2* 35(1): 23–34.

Menke, C. (2007) The "Aporias of Human Rights" and the "One Human Right": Regarding the Coherence of Hannah Arendt's Argument, *Social Research* 74(3): 739–62.

Miller, M. and Ury, S. (2010) Cosmopolitanism: The End of Jewishness. *European Review of History* 17(3): 337–59.

Miller, Y. (2002) Creating Unity through History: The Eichmann Trial as Transition, *Journal of Modern Jewish Studies* 1(2): 131–49.

Morsink, J. (1999) Cultural Genocide, the Universal Declaration, and Minority Rights, *Human Rights Quarterly* 21(4): 1009–60.

Morsink, J. (2000) *The Universal Declaration of Human Rights: Origins, Drafting, and Intent*, Philadelphia: University of Pennsylvania Press.

Moses, A. D. (2004) The Holocaust and Genocide, in D. Stone (ed.), *The Historiography of the Holocaust*, Houndmills: Palgrave Macmillan, pp. 533–55.

Moses, A. D. (2007) *German Intellectuals and the Nazi Past*, Cambridge: Cambridge University Press.

Moses, A. D. (ed.) (2008) *Empire, Colony, Genocide. Conquest, Occupation and Subaltern Resistance in World History*, New York: Berghahn Books.

Moses, A. D. (2010) Raphael Lemkin, Culture, and the Concept of Genocide, in D. Bloxham and A. D. Moses (eds), *Oxford Handbook on Genocide Studies*, New York: Oxford University Press, pp. 19–41.

Moses, S. (1944) *Die Jüdischen Nachkriegsforderungen*, Tel Aviv: Irgun Olej Merkaz Europa.

Motzkin, G. (2000) Hannah Arendt: Von ethnischer Minderheit zu universeller Humanität, in G. Smith (ed.), *Hannah Arendt Revisited: Eichmann und die Folgen*, Frankfurt: Suhrkamp, pp. 177–201.

Mufti, A. R. (2007) *Enlightenment in the Colony: The Jewish Question and the Crisis of Postcolonial Culture*, Princeton: Princeton University Press.

Muller, S. (1981) The Origins of Eichmann in Jerusalem: Hannah Arendt's Interpretation of Jewish History, *Jewish Social Studies* 43(3/4): 237–54.

Nesemann, F. (2007) Leo Motzkin: Zionist Engagement and Minority Diplomacy, *Central and Eastern European Review* 1: 1–24.

Nimni, E. (2005) The National Cultural Autonomy Model Revisited, in E. Nimni (ed.), *National Cultural Autonomy and Its Contemporary Critics*, New York: Routledge, pp. 1–14.

Novick, P. (1999) *The Holocaust in American Life*, Boston: Houghton Mifflin.

Olick, J. K. (2005) *In the House of the Hangman: The Agonies of German Defeat, 1943–1949*, Chicago: University of Chicago Press.

Olick, J. K. (2007) *The Politics of Regret: On Collective Memory and Historical Responsibility*, London: Routledge.

Parekh, S. (2004) A Meaningful Place in the World: Hannah Arendt on the Nature of Human Rights, *Journal of Human Rights* 3(1): 41–53.

Pilling, I. (1994) *Denken und Handeln als Jüdin, Hannah Arendts politische Theorie vor 1950*. Frankfurt: Peter Lang.

Pinson, K. (1958) Historian and Political Philosopher, in K. Pinson (ed.), *Simon Dubnow: Nationalism and History. Essays on Old and New Judaism*, Philadelphia: The Jewish Publication Society of America, pp. 3–65.

Piper, E. (2005) *Alfred Rosenberg. Hitlers Chefideologe*. München: Karl Blessing.

Poliakov, L. and Wulf, J. (1983) *Das Dritte Reich und seine Denker*, Wiesbaden: Fourier Verlag.

Postone, M. (1980) Anti-Semitism and National Socialism: Notes on the German Reaction to *Holocaust*, *New German Critique* 19(1): 97–115.

Postone, M. (2000) Hannah Arendts "Eichmann in Jerusalem": Die unaufgelöste Antinomie von Universalität und Besonderem, in Gary Smith (ed.), *Hannah Arendt Revisited: "Eichmann in Jerusalem und die Folgen,"* Frankfurt: Suhrkamp, pp. 269–90.

Power, S. (2002) *A Problem from Hell: America and the Age of Genocide*, New York: Harper.

Powers, D. (2003) Fresco Fiasco: Narratives of National Identity and the Bruno Schulz Murals of Drohobych, *East European Politics and Societies* 17: 622–53.

Preece, J. (2002) Introduction: Kafka's Europe, in J. Preece (ed.), *The Cambridge Companion to Kafka*, Cambridge: Cambridge University Press.

Rabinbach, A. (1985) Between Enlightenment and Apocalypse: Benjamin, Bloch and Modern German Jewish Messianism, *New German Critique* 34: 78–124.

Rabinbach, A. (1997) The German as Pariah: Karl Jaspers's The Question of German Guilt, in his *The Shadow of Catastrophe: German Intellectuals between Apocalypse and Enlightenment*, Berkeley: University of California Press, pp. 129–65.

Rabinbach, A. (2004) Eichmann in New York: The New York Intellectuals and the Hannah Arendt Controversy, *October* 108(1): 97–111.

Rabinbach, A. (2005) The Challenge of the Unprecedented: Raphael Lemkin and the Concept of Genocide, *Jahrbuch des Simon-Dubnow-Instituts/ Simon Dubnow Institute Yearbook* 4: 397–420.

Rabinbach, A. (2006) Moments of Totalitarianism, *History and Theory* 45: 72–100.

Rabinovich, S. (2005) The Dawn of a New Diaspora: Simon Dubnov's Autonomism, from St Petersburg to Berlin, *The Leo Baeck Institute Year Book* 50(1): 267–88.

Raider, M. A. (ed.) (2009) *Nahum Goldmann: Statesman without a State*, Buffalo: SUNY Press.

Redlich, S. (1995) *War, Holocaust and Stalinism: A Documentary History of the Jewish Anti-Fascist Committee in the USSR*, Luxemburg: Harwood Academic.

Rensmann, L. (2006) Europeanism and Americanism in the Age of Globalization. Hannah Arendt's Reflections on Europe and America and Implications for a Post-National Identity of the EU Polity, *European Journal of Political Theory* 5(2): 139–170.

Riegner, M. (2006) *Never Despair: Sixty Years in the Service of the Jewish People and the Cause of Human Rights*, Chicago: Ivan Dee.

Robin, R. (2004) *Fear: The History of an Idea*, New York: Oxford University Press.

Robinson, J. (1928) *Das Minoritätenproblem und seine Literatur*, Berlin: Walter de Gruyter.

Robinson, J. (1946) *Human Rights and Fundamental Freedoms in the Charter of the United Nations: A Commentary*, New York: Institute of Jewish Affairs.

Robinson, J. (1965) *And the Crooked Shall be Made Straight. The Eichmann Trial, the Jewish Catastrophe, and Hannah Arendt's Narrative*, New York: Macmillan.

Robinson, J. (1972) The International Military Tribunal and the Holocaust, *Israel Law Review* 7(1): 1–13.

Robinson, N. (1944) *Indemnification and Reparations: Jewish Aspects*, 4 vols, New York: Institute of Jewish Affairs.

Robinson, N. (1955) *The United Nations and the World Jewish Congress*, New York: Institute of Jewish Affairs.

Robinson, N. (1960) *The Genocide Convention: A Commentary*, New York: Institute of Jewish Affairs – World Jewish Congress.

Rose, J. (2005) *The Question of Zion*, Princeton: Princeton University Press.

Roskies, D. (1984) *Against the Apocalypse: Jewish Responses to Catastrophe in Modern Jewish Culture*, Cambridge, MA: Harvard University Press.

Roth, C. (1944) The Restoration of Jewish Libraries, Archives and Museums, *Contemporary Jewish Record* 7: 253–7.

Rubenstein, J. (2005) *Stalin's Secret Pogrom: The Post-War Inquisition of the Jewish Anti-Fascist Committee*, New Haven: Yale University Press.

Rupnow, D. (2008) Racializing Historiography: Anti-Jewish Scholarship in the Third Reich, *Patterns of Prejudice* 42(1): 27–59.

Sachs, J. (2002) *The Dignity of Difference*, London: Continuum.

Schaap, A. (2001) Guilty Subjects and Political Responsibility: Arendt, Jaspers and the Resonance of the "German Question" in Politics of Reconciliation, *Political Studies* 49(4): 749–66.

Schabas, W. (2000) *Genocide in International Law: The Crimes of Crimes*, Cambridge: Cambridge University Press.

Schidorsky, D. (2006) The Salvaging of Jewish Books in Europe after the Holocaust, in *Jüdischer Buchbesitz als Raubgut*, Frankfurt: Zweites Hannoversches Symposium, pp. 197–212.

Scholem, G. (1976) *On Jews and Judaism in Crisis: Selected Essays*, ed. W. Dannhauser, New York: Schocken Books.

Scholem, G. (2002) *A Life in Letters, 1914–1982*, Cambridge: Cambridge University Press.

Scholem, G. and Arendt, H. (1964) Eichmann in Jerusalem: An Exchange of Letters, *Encounter* 22(1): 51–6.

Schöttker, D. and Wizisla, E. (eds) (2006) *Arendt und Benjamin: Texte, Briefe, Dokumente*, Frankfurt: Suhrkamp.

Schulz, B. (2008) *The Street of Crocodiles and Other Stories*, New York: Penguin.

Schwarz, J. (2005) After the Destruction of Vilna: Abraham Sutzkever's Poetry, Testimony and Cultural Rescue Work, 1944–1946, *East European Jewish Affairs* 35(2): 209–24.

Shaw, M. (2007) *Genocide*, Cambridge: Polity.

Silberstein, L. J. (2008) *Post-Zionism: A Reader*, Rutgers: Rutgers University Press.

Slezkine, Y. (2004) *The Jewish Century*, Princeton: Princeton University Press.

Smith, D. and Kordell, K. (2007) The Theory and Practice of Cultural Autonomy in Eastern and Central Europe, *Ethnopolitics* 6(3): 337–43.

Smith, G. (1991) Benjamins frühe Auseinandersetzung mit dem Judentum, *Deutsche Vierteljahrsschrift für Literaturwissenschaft und Geistesgeschichte* 65(2): 318–34.

Snyder, T. (2004) *The Reconstruction of Nations: Poland, Ukraine, Lithuania, Belarus 1569–1999*, New Haven: Yale University Press.

Snyder, T. (2009) Holocaust: The Ignored Reality, *The New York Review of Books* 56(12).

Söllner, A. (2004) Hannah Arendt's "The Origins of Totalitarianism" in its Original Context, *European Journal of Political Theory* 3(2): 219–38.

Soysal, Y. (2002) Locating Europe, *European Societies* 4(3): 265–84.

Stackelberg, R. and Winkle, S. (eds) (2002) *The Nazi Germany Sourcebook: An Anthology of Texts*, London: Routledge.

Starr, J. (1950) Jewish Cultural Property under Nazi Control, *Jewish Social Studies* 12: 27–48.

Steinweis, A. (2006) *Studying the Jew: Scholarly Antisemitism in Nazi Germany*, Cambridge: Cambridge University Press.

Stone, D. (2004) Genocide as Transgression, *European Journal of Social Theory* 7(1): 45–65.

Stone, D. (2005) Raphael Lemkin on the Holocaust, *Journal of Genocide Research* 7(4): 539–50.

Streich, G. W. (2009) Discourses of National American Identity: Echoes and Lessons from the 1910s–1920s, *Citizenship Studies* 13(2): 267–87.

Suchoff, D. (1997) Gershom Scholem, Hannah Arendt, and the Scandal of Jewish Particularity, *The Germanic Review* 72(1): 57–76.

Suchoff, D. (2007) Kafka's Jewish Languages: The Hidden Openness of Tradition, *Journal of Jewish Thought and Philosophy* 15(2): 65–132.

Sutcliffe, A. (2006) Judaism and the Politics of the Enlightenment, *American Behavioral Scientist* 49(5): 702–15.

Sznaider, N. (2008) *Gedächtnisraum Europa. Die Visionen des europäischen Kosmopolitismus. Eine Jüdische Perspektive*, Bielefeld: transcript.

Sznaider, N. (2009) Hannah Arendt in München (1949–1950), *Mittelweg* 36(2): 61–76.

Takei, A. (2002) The "Gemeinde Problem": The Jewish Restitution Successor Organization and the Postwar Jewish Communities in Germany, 1947–1954, *Holocaust and Genocide Studies* 16(2): 266–88.

Taylor, C. (1992) *The Politics of Recognition*, Princeton: Princeton University Press.

Torpey, J. (2006) *Making Whole What Has Been Smashed*, Cambridge, MA: Harvard University Press.

Traverso, E. (1997) *L'Histoire déchirée: essai sur Auschwitz et les intellectuels*, Paris: Cerf.

Traverso, E. (2004) To Brush against the Grain: The Holocaust and German-Jewish Culture in Exile, *Totalitarian Movements and Political Religions* 5(2): 243–70.

Trigano, S. (2009) *The Democratic Ideal and the Shoah: The Unthought in Political Modernity*, Albany: State University of New York Press.

Villa, D. (1999) *Politics, Philosophy, Terror: Essays on the Thought of Hannah Arendt*, Princeton. Princeton University Press.

Villa, D. (2009) Hannah Arendt, 1906–1975, *Review of Politics* 71: 20–36.

Waite, R. G. (2002) Returning Jewish Cultural Property: The Handling of Books Looted by the Nazis in the American Zone of Occupation, 1945–1952, *Libraries & Culture* 37(3): 213–28.

Weinreich, M. (1999 [1946]) *Hitler's Professors: The Part of Scholarship in Germany's Crimes against the Jewish People*, New Haven: Yale University Press.

Weiss, Y. (2004) Central European Ethnonationalism and Zionist Binationalism, *Jewish Social Studies* 11(1): 93–117.

Weitz, E. (2008) From the Vienna to the Paris System: International Politics and the Entangled Histories of Human Rights, Forced Deportations, and Civilizing Missions, *American Historical Review* (Dec.): 1313–43.

Werbner, P. (2006) Vernacular Cosmopolitanism. *Theory, Culture & Society* 23(2–3): 496–8.

Whitfield, S. (1980) The Imagination of Disaster: The Response of American Jewish Intellectuals to Totalitarianism, *Jewish Social Studies* 42(1): 1–20.

Whitfield, S. J. (2002) Where They Burn Books . . . , *Modern Judaism* 22: 213–33.

Wilford, R. A. (1979) The PEN Club, 1930–1950, *Journal of Contemporary History* 14: 99–116.

Wisse, R. (1983) The Last Great Yiddish Poet? *Commentary* (November): 41–8.

Wolin, R. (2003) *Heidegger's Children: Hannah Arendt, Karl Lowith, Hans Jonas, and Herbert Marcuse*, Princeton: Princeton University Press.

World Jewish Congress (1948) *Unity in Dispersion: A History of the World Jewish Congress*, New York: World Jewish Congress, pp. 261–7.

Yablonka, H. (2004) *The State of Israel vs. Adolf Eichmann*, New York: Schocken Books.

Yakira, E. (2006) Hannah Arendt, the Holocaust and Zionism: A Story of a Failure, *Israel Studies* 11(3): 31–61.

Young-Bruehl, E. (2004) *Hannah Arendt: For Love of the World*, New Haven: Yale University Press.

Young-Bruehl, E. and Kohn, J. (2007) Truth, Lies, and Politics: A Conversation, *Social Research* 74(4): 1045–70.

Zertal, I. (2005) *Israel's Holocaust and the Politics of Nationhood*, Cambridge: Cambridge University Press.

Zweig, R. (2001) *German Reparations and the Jewish World: A History of the Claims Conference*, London: Frank Cass.

# INDEX